Library of
Davidson College

NIKOLAJ GUMILEV

1886–1986

PAPERS FROM

THE GUMILEV CENTENARY SYMPOSIUM

HELD AT ROSS PRIORY

UNIVERSITY OF STRATHCLYDE

1986

Edited, with an introduction,
by
Sheelagh Duffin Graham

BERKELEY SLAVIC SPECIALTIES
1987

Natalija Gončarova, *Portrait of Gumilev,* 1917.
Coll. Mr. John Stuart, London.

NIKOLAJ GUMILEV
1886–1986

PAPERS FROM

THE GUMILEV CENTENARY SYMPOSIUM

HELD AT ROSS PRIORY

UNIVERSITY OF STRATHCLYDE

1986

Edited, with an introduction,

by

Sheelagh Duffin Graham

BERKELEY SLAVIC SPECIALTIES
1987

Copyright © 1987 Berkeley Slavic Specialties
All Rights Reserved

Additional copyright notices may be found in the colophon (p. 333).

PRINTED IN U.S.A.

Published by Berkeley Slavic Specialties, Oakland, California

ISBN 0-933884-60-5

CONTENTS

Introduction ... 1

Louis Allain
La recherche de la forme longue dans la
poésie de N.S. Gumilev ... 7

Michael Basker
"Stixi iz snov": art, magic and dream in
Gumilev's *Romantičeskie cvety* ... 27

Jean Bonamour
Remarques sur Gumilev, critique de la
poésie française ... 69

Инна Чечельницкая
Скрытое присутствие Гумилева в
Поэме без героя Ахматовой ... 77

Raoul Eshelman
"Duša i telo" as a paradigm of Gumilev's
mystical poetry ... 102

Ben Hellman
An aggressive imperialist? The controversy
over Nikolaj Gumilev's war poetry (Appendix:
an unpublished poem by Vadim Gardner) ... 133

Denis Mickiewicz
Functioning poetics and poetic functions.
Gumilev's poem "Pered noč'ju severnoj,
korotkoj..." ... 155

Эулялия Папля
Homo peregrinans в лирике Николая Гумилева ... 215

Anthony Parton
"Gončarova i Larionov" - Gumilev's pantum
to art ... 225

Elaine Rusinko
The "Two Adams": Gumilev's creative
personality   243

Earl D. Sampson
The prose fiction of Nikolaj Gumilev   268

Самуил Шварцбанд
Колчан: "Четвертая книга" стихотворений
Н. Гумилева   293

Ewa M. Thompson
N.S. Gumilev and the Russian ideology   311

Notes on the contributors   330

PAPERS FROM

THE GUMILEV CENTENARY SYMPOSIUM

HELD AT ROSS PRIORY

UNIVERSITY OF STRATHCLYDE

1986

INTRODUCTION

When the idea arose of celebrating the Gumilev centennial with a symposium at the University of Strathclyde, Mixail Gorbačev was scarcely known outside the Soviet Union, *glasnost'* had not yet become an international word and Soviet colleagues I spoke to as late as the spring of 1984 saw little likelihood of the centenary of the poet's birth being marked in his own country.

Shortly before the participants in our symposium gathered at Ross Priory, however, we were surprised and pleased to see that the Gorbačev "openness" extended to the history of Russian literature: in April 1986 a few Gumilev poems were published in *Literaturnaja Rossija* (11 April 1986) to mark the poet's centenary (he was born on 15 April [New Style] 1886), and a few days later *Ogonek* followed suit (No. 17, 1986). Then on 14 May an article by Evgenij Evtušenko appeared in *Literaturnaja Gazeta*, entitled "The return of Gumilev's poetry", from which readers learned that a volume of Gumilev's poetry was to be published in the series *Biblioteka poeta* (Bol'šaja serija). Since then *Novye knigi* has announced its publication, with the title *Stixotvornye proizvedenija*, in an edition of 100,000 copies, for the second quarter of 1988, as well as a volume entitled *Stixotvorenija i poemy* to be published by "Sovremennik" in the same quarter. (It appears that the article by A.Pavlovskij in *Voprosy literatury* No. 10, 1986, entitled "Nikolaj Gumilev", is based on his preface to the forthcoming *Biblioteka poeta* volume, and that Vladimir Karpov's *Ogonek* article referred to below may be the basis of *his* preface to the "Sovremennik" edition.)

Gumilev's "rehabilitation" has been launched; as yet, however, the word has to be used in quotation marks, since there is no indication at present that the Soviet authorities intend to investigate the alleged Tagancev conspiracy that caused the poet's arrest and execution.

The most significant piece to appear in the Soviet Union in the centennial year was the long article by Vladimir Karpov, newly elected First Secretary of the Writers' Union, which was published in *Ogonek* No.36, 1986, entitled "The poet Nikolaj Gumilev". It contained long extracts from letters by Gumilev and Axmatova not hitherto published in the Soviet Union, and was illustrated by similarly unpublished photographs. (Karpov dwelt at length and with sympathy on an aspect of Gumilev's life that has usually earned the scorn of Soviet commentators: his war record. Karpov, as a former Red Army officer who, like Gumilev, served as a scout [*razvedčik*], understood not only Gumilev's sense of patriotism but also the exhiliration the man of action feels on dangerous military sorties, and so vividly described by Gumilev in "Zapiski kavalerista".)

Towards the end of the centenary year more Gumilev poems were published in *Družba narodov* No.12, 1986; then in *Ogonek* No.11, 1987, others appeared side by side with a selection of poems by his fellow Acmeist Narbut.

These events in the national press were matched by publications in learned journals equally interesting for the specialist: the appearance of Gumilev compositions not previously published in the Soviet Union (*Otravlennaja tunika* in *Sovremennaja dramaturgija* No.3, 1986) or, indeed, anywhere (the play *Oxota na nosoroga* in *Russkaja literatura* No.2, 1987), as well as parts of Gumilev's correspondence: in *Novyj mir* No.9, 1986 ("Stixi i pis'ma. Anna Axmatova. N.Gumilev", published by Emma Gerštejn), in *Literaturnaja učeba* No.2, 1987 (subtitled "Po stranicam pisem N.S.Gumileva k V.Ja.Brjusovu", published by M.V.Tolmačev) and in *Izvestija ANSSSR*, 46, 1, 1987 ("Neizvestnye pis'ma N.S.Gumileva", published by R.D.Timenčik).*

But the most extraordinary publication was, again, in *Ogonek*: in Nos.14 and 15, 1987, they published part of a work which had been presumed lost, Gumilev's "African Diary", an account of his last visit to Abyssinia in 1913. Fascinating though that was, equally interesting was the information, casually inserted into the short introduction, that the manuscript of the diary fragment had been offered to the magazine by Gumilev's son, Orest Nikolaevič Vysotskij. Few people were aware that Gumilev had a second son, although Lidija Čukovskaja does refer to the fact in her book *Zapiski ob Anne Axmatove*, volume I, page 31. (Orest Nikolaevich was born in 1913, son of Gumilev and Ol'ga Nikolaevna Vysotskaja, a theatre director who in her youth studied with Evreinov and Mejerxol'd .)

What further revelations await the Gumilev specialist? When the enormous archives of the Lenin Library and Pushkin House (the latter closed to virtually all foreign researchers for several years now) also succumb to "openness" there will surely be many more interesting discoveries, and we shall find the answers to at least some of the questions that frustrate the would-be biographer of Gumilev.

The present volume is a collection of the papers given at the Gumilev Centenary Symposium at Ross Priory, the University of Strathclyde, in July 1986. The Symposium was the first international conference to be devoted to Gumilev. The papers cover a wide range of themes and approaches to the writer. Several challenge conventional views of Gumilev: Michael Basker and Raoul Eshelman, from different angles,

---

* Most of the letters in these three articles had already appeared in the West.

confront the cliché of the simple warrior-poet and explorer-poet to show how profoundly the mystical or occult beliefs prevalent in Gumilev's youth affected his poetry and how much more complex Gumilev's philosophy is than certain cold-warriors (on either side) make out. Ewa Thompson's provocative thesis is that Gumilev is not the "knee-jerk" patriot he has been praised or blamed for being, but that his attitude to Russia evolves, painfully, to a tragic acceptance of the good and the bad in his country's history.

Eulalia Papla sees Gumilev as essentially a Christian poet and she examines those poems in which religious motifs combine with the theme of pilgrimage (*peregrinatio vitae*).

Elaine Rusinko considers Gumilev's emphasis on the reader of poetry, on the communicative act between poet and perceiver, in which Gumilev anticipates the semiotic view of art; in particular she explores the parallel between Gumilev's poetics and the structuralist view of the creative personality propounded by Jan Mukařovský.

Focusing on areas hitherto insufficiently studied, Earl Sampson analyses Gumilev's prose, while Jean Bonamour examines his writings on French poets.

Anthony Parton describes the philosophical-artistic links that lie behind Gumilev's friendship with Natalija Gončarova and Mixail Larionov. Ben Hellman contrasts Gumilev's attitude to the First World War with that of other Acmeists, and in his appendix contributes to our scanty knowledge of Gumilev's biography. Inna Chechelnitsky presents the case for the "hidden presence" of Gumilev in Axmatova's *Poem without a Hero*. Louis Allain in his study of Gumilev's attempts at the epic poem contends that *Mik*, his "colonial" *poema*, is, among other things, a dialogue with Lermontov, author of *Mcyri*.

Denis Mickiewicz and Samuel Schwarzband take structuralist approaches to Gumilev's work: the latter considers *Kolčan* (and, by implication, all collections of poems by Gumilev and other Acmeist poets) as a coherent system and analyses the collection's composition in this light. Denis Mickiewicz constructs a poetics for Gumilev based on an examination of (almost a meditation on) the evolution of a poem, "Pered noč'ju severnoj, korotkoj...", written over several years.

I have pleasure in acknowledging the generous grant awarded by the Ford Foundation which made the Symposium possible, and the British Academy's help in financing the visit of one of our participants.

I wish to express my gratitude to Mr John Stuart for allowing me to reproduce the beautiful Gončarova portrait of Gumilev which is the frontispiece to this collection.

The editor and contributors extend their thanks to the Research and Development Fund of the University of Strathclyde for generously covering the cost of preparing the typescript of the *Proceedings*.

Finally, I should like to thank Louise Boyle, who prepared the camera-ready typescript with skill, patience and unfailing good humour.

University of Strathclyde SDG
Glasgow
October 1987

LA RECHERCHE DE LA FORME LONGUE
DANS LA POESIE DE N.S. GUMILEV

LOUIS ALLAIN

Toute sa vie, Gumilev, spécialiste incontesté du genre court en poésie, s'est intéressé à l'introuvable formule du poème russe.

Dès son premier recueil de vers, paru en 1905, et pratiquement jusqu'à la fin de sa vie, le poète n'aura de cesse d'explorer les recettes de la forme longue.

Ces recherches vont s'effectuer selon des orientations fort variées. Un premier type de poème s'ébauche lors de la période "symboliste" de Gumilev. Un second type verra le jour à l'époque "acméiste", ce qui constitue en soi une curiosité, puisque cette nouvelle poétique, fondée par Gumilev lui-même, semblait exclure *a priori* toute recherche en matière de forme longue. Enfin, il apparaît possible de définir une troisième catégorie, celle des oeuvres dramatiques dont l'originalité est encore insuffisamment appréciée.

Le premier type de poème mis au point par Gumilev peut être qualifié d'expérimental. On peut ainsi citer dans le recueil *Put' konkvistadorov*, paru en 1905, les trois poèmes "Deva solnca", "Osennjaja pesnja", "Skazka o koroljax"; dans le recueil *Žemčuga* (1910) "Vozvraščenie Odisseja" et "Kapitany"; dans le recueil *Cužoe nebo* (1912) "Bludnyj syn" et "Otkrytie Ameriki".

Dans ces premières tentatives, le poète éprouve une évidente difficulté à se dégager des influences croisées de Brjusov dans le domaine de l'inspiration exotique et de Bal'mont dans celui de l'écriture lyrique.

Ainsi dans le poème "Deva solnca" le "puissant roi" qui se présente lui-même sous les espèces du "fouet de Dieu", de la "voix de Dieu", et dont le but suprême est la recherche de la "fille du soleil", "fille du paradis flamboyant", autrefois apparue à lui en songe, fait-il partie du bric-à-brac ordinaire des images symbolistes. Sur le plan de l'écriture on relève des réminiscences parfois abusives.

Brjusov perce trop clairement à la strophe 10:

> Я стал властителем вселенной,
> Я Божий бич, я Божий глас,
> Я царь жестокий и надменный,
> Но лишь для вас, о лишь для вас. (I,14)(1)

Bal'mont se rappelle de trop près à la strophe 29:

> Он как гроза, он гордо губит
> В палящем зареве мечты,
> За то, что он безмерно любит
> Безумно-белые цветы. (I, 17)

Enfin, il n'est pas jusqu'à Blok qui ne pointe le bout de son nez à la strophe 27:

> И гордый царь опять остался
> Безмолвно-бледен и один,
> И кто-то весело смеялся,
> Бездонной радостью глубин. (I, 17)

"Osennjaja pesnja" est un poème onirique, sans trame bien définie, dont la clé nous est donnée par les deux derniers vers:

> ...И нет дриады, сна земли,
> Пред ярким часом пробужденья. (I, 26)

Le sujet, pour autant qu'on puisse le reconstruire, met en scène de "jeunes dryades":

>   В лесу, где часто по кустам
>   Резвились юные дриады,
>   Стоял безмолвно-строгий храм,
>   Маня покоем колоннады.
>
>   И белый мрамор говорил
>   О царстве Вечного Молчанья
>   И о полете гордых крыл,
>   Неверно-тяжких, как рыданье. (I, 18-19)

Dans son "Chant" une des jeunes dryades fait une déclaration d'amour au "prince du feu", son "fiancé", semblable à un "joyeux bûcher", auquel elle finit par s'unir:

>   Он совершен, великий брак,
>   Безумный крик всемирных оргий!
>   Пускай леса оденет мрак,
>   В них было счастье и восторги. (I, 25)

Quant à la facture, non linéaire, du poème, elle n'innove en rien par rapport à la recette du poème cyclique, ou segmenté, de Bal'mont qui aimait regrouper dans un ensemble unique une succession de pièces courtes, au lien thématique souple.

Construit selon le même principe, "Skazka o koroljax" est un poème fantastique dont la structure mythologique est mieux articulée, mais dont la langue n'arrive pas à se dégager des clichés à la mode:

>   "Кто узнает, что томится
>   За пределом наших знаний
>   И, как бледная царица,
>   Ждет мучений и лобзаний".
>   . . . .
>   Мрачный всадник примчался на черном коне...
>   . . . .   (I, 28)
>   "Путь к Неведомой Невесте
>   Наш единый верный путь ..."
>   . . . .
>   "Правду мы возьмем у Бога
>   Силой огненных мечей". (I, 30)

Si dans ses trois premiers poèmes Gumilev reste étroitement prisonnier de l'imagerie symboliste, il manifeste déjà plus d'autonomie dans les deux poèmes suivants.

"Vozvraščenie Odisseja" marque un très net tournant en direction du thème et du sujet dans une narration pregnante. Certes, sur le plan de la composition, ce poème ne constitue encore qu'une sorte de juxtaposition de trois pièces de vers proches du genre de la ballade ("U berega", "Izbienie ženixov", "Odissej i Laerta"), mais, à la différence de la ballade classique, ce n'est pas l'événement en lui-même, mais ce que Blok appelle "lirika slučaja", autrement dit la substance lyrique de l'événement, qui est promue au premier plan:

>   Что это? Брошены красные ткани,
>   Или, дымясь, растекается кровь?
>
>   Ну, собирайся со мною в дорогу,
>   Юноша светлый, мой сын Телемах!
>   Надо служить беспощадному богу,
>   Богу Тревоги на черных путях.
>
>   Снова полюбим влекущую даль мы
>   И золотой от луны горизонт,
>   Снова увидим священные пальмы
>   И опененный, клокочущий Понт. (I, 140)

Le retour au "sujet en vers" marque incontestablement le souci de trouver une nouvelle forme de poème, plus personnelle et surtout plus contraignante.

"Kapitany", qui reçut un accueil exceptionnel de la part des lecteurs, marque un nouveau progrès de la recherche expérimentale. Sans toutefois se démarquer encore suffisamment de la structure poétique mise au point par Bal'mont, ni surtout des thèmes exotiques exploités par Brjusov dans ses oeuvres de jeunesse, Gumilev commence à rompre avec l'imagerie trop allégorique du symbolisme. Le poète recourt de plus en plus au détail concret "pointu". Ainsi se manifestent les premières poussées de ce "chosisme" (*veščizm*), caractéristique de la maturité de Gumilev:

> Темнокожие мулатки
> И гадают, и поют,
> И несется запах сладкий
> От готовящихся блюд.
>
> А в заплеванных тавернах
> От заката до утра
> Мечут ряд колод неверных
> Завитые шулера.
>
> Хорошо по докам порта
> И слоняться, и лежать,
> И с солдатами из форта
> Ночью драки затевать. (I, 145)

L'avancée créatrice constituée par "Kapitany" sera suivie d'un recul. "Bludnyj syn", en 1912, n'est que l'ultime avatar d'un symbolisme désuet, celui de Brjusov et de Bal'mont, par opposition à celui de Vjačeslav Ivanov, de Blok et de Belyj, lui-même en profonde évolution. Les quatre monologues lyriques de "Bludnyj syn" n'ajoutent rien à la gloire du poète.

Ce recul est largement compensé par "Otkrytie Ameriki", publié dans le même recueil. Gumilev change à la fois de registre et de ton. Il se rapproche manifestement du style épique dont il stylise certains aspects. Le poème est composé de trois chants (le quatrième, publié dans l'édition en revue de 1910, n'est pas réintégré dans le recueil de 1912). Le poète s'adresse à plusieurs reprises à la Muse, qui sert à la fois de principe de construction et d'inspiration. Ainsi, dès la seconde strophe du chant I, le poète l'associe-t-il étroitement à son entreprise:

> Мы с тобою, Муза, быстроноги,
> Любим ивы вдоль степной дороги,
> Мерный скрип колес и вдалеке

> Белый парус на большой реке.
> Этот мир, такой святой и строгий,
> Что нет места в нем пустой тоске. (I, 200)

Si l'on prend en compte les quatre chants, le dessein de Gumilev paraît se résumer à la trame suivante: arrivé au pays "du nard, de l'or, du corail", Colomb est "abandonné par la Muse des Lointaines Errances" et quitte de lui-même la contrée qu'il vient de découvrir. Or, pour être traité dans sa vraie dimension, un tel sujet exigeait une autre approche du matériau historique, une autre écriture poétique. Malgré un louable effort de tonalité épique, les "chants" de "Otkrytie Ameriki" restent en effet prisonniers de la formule passablement usée du cycle lyrique. C'est peut-être le sentiment plus ou moins conscient de l'inadéquation de la forme et du fond, du sujet et du genre, qui fit renoncer le poète à publier le quatrième "chant" dans le recueil de 1912.

Quelles que fussent ses options poétiques nouvelles, Gumilev ne pouvait pas ne pas tenir compte, dès lors qu'il ne récusait pas expressément la notion même de "forme longue", de la tendance générale du poème à évoluer, depuis l'éclatement du symbolisme, de l'inspiration lyrique pure à l'épopée lyrique, voire même au principe épique.

C'est en 1914 que Gumilev "ose" pour la première fois aborder publiquement les problèmes théoriques posés par le genre épique dans le contexte actuel. Un compte rendu non signé, paru dans *Apollon* (1914, N° 1-2), indique que lors d'une séance de la Société des Propagateurs des Belles-Lettres (*Obščestvo revnitelej xudožestvennogo slova*)

> Н.Гумилев прочитал большую (960 строк) поэму свою "Мик и Луи", а затем изложил свои взгляды на эпический род, к коему он причисляет свою поэму, и на современные его возможности. Основная мысль сводилась к утверждению, что единственной областью, в которой еще

> возможно большое эпическое творчество,
> есть поэзия "экзотическая". (Действие
> прочитанной поэмы происходит в
> Абиссинии, которую Гумилев три раза
> посетил.)

Au cours de la discussion qui suivit

> бо́льшая часть высказавшихся, отдавая
> справедливость поэтическим достоинствам
> поэмы, оспаривала теоретические
> воззрения автора; вопрос о современной
> эпической поэзии остался открытым. (2)

Mik fut très vraisemblablement composé en 1913 après le dernier voyage de Gumilev en Afrique. Des extraits de ce "poème africain" furent publiés dans le recueil *Kolčan* en 1916 sous le titre "Dva otryvka iz abissinskoj poemy". Il ne devait paraître en édition séparée qu'en 1918. Une seconde édition vit le jour en 1922 après la mort du poète.

Le choix du mètre est en lui-même significatif. Gumilev a retenu le vers iambique à quatre pieds avec parallélisme des rimes masculines. C'est précisément le mètre utilisé par Lermontov dans *Mcyri* (ce mot géorgien signifie selon l'indication fournie par Lermontov lui-même: moine servant, novice). Dans ce poème dont le romantisme se pare tout naturellement d'exotisme, Lermontov oppose avec insistance la nature majestueuse du Caucase aux lois de la société qui entravent le libre épanouissement de la personnalité.

Une certaine orientation du poème de Gumilev par rapport à celui de Lermontov est, au début du moins, manifeste.

Mik raconte l'histoire d'un "fils de tsar", le jeune Mik, que le "chef des abyssins" Ato-Gano emmène en captivité dans son palais après la victoire qu'il vient de remporter sur la tribu rebelle des Gourabes. Ainsi se manifeste, dès le départ, une certaine similitude de destin avec le "novice" de Lermontov.

Le poème se compose de dix parties. Au fur et à mesure du déroulement de l'action, Gumilev rompt sa dépendance initiale du poème de Lermontov, illustrée par une réminiscence directe. La description de la lutte entre le roi de la tribu des Gourabes et le chef des troupes du Négus, Ato-Gano, n'est qu'une variante à peine déguisée du combat qui oppose Mcyri à la panthère au début de la strophe 18.

Chez Gumilev:

> Дубину поднял негр; старик
> Увертливый к земле приник,
> Пустил копье, успел скакнуть
> Всей тажестю ему на грудь. (II, 206)

Chez Lermontov:

> "Ко мне он кинулся на грудь;
> Но в горло я успел воткнуть
> И там два раза повернуть
> Мое оружье...." (3)

L'inspiration de Gumilev dans *Mik* procède du merveilleux et du fantastique et, en même temps, d'une sorte de réalisme minutieux. Mik, le jeune prisonnier, âgé d'environ sept ans, se lie d'amitié avec un "grand babouin velu", captif comme lui, et que personne ne réussit à approcher, sauf lui. Conversant tous deux dans "la langue des singes", ils finissent par concevoir un projet d'évasion au pays dont les villages n'appartiennent qu'aux singes. Ceux-ci, malheureusement, sont les seuls animaux à ne pas avoir de roi. Sur ces entrefaites, lors d'une réception offerte par le consul de France à Ato-Gano, Mik fait la connaissance de Louis, le fils du consul, qui "va avoir bientôt dix ans". Instruit du projet, Louis l'approuve car il a décidé de "devenir le roi des singes". Le trio s'enfuit et affronte de multiples aventures avant d'arriver dans la "ville des singes". Le vieux babouin propose à la "tribu des

singes libres" d'élire Louis roi, ce qu'elle décide.
Dans cette sixième partie du poème nous sommes déjà
très loin de Lermontov et par contre très près de
l'anglais Rudyard Kipling et sourtout du français
Louis Henri Boussenard, populaires à l'époque auprès
du public russe, et spécialistes incontestés de
littérature exotique de type "colonial". Cette partie
s'achève, au demeurant, par un clin d'oeil ironique
au dit Boussenard. Il manque, en effet, quelque chose
pour que le bonheur de Louis, devenu roi des singes,
soit complet:

> Чтобы сестра, отец и мать
> Его могли здесь увидать
> Хоть силою волшебных чар,
> И в "Вокруг света" обо всем
> Поведал мальчикам потом
> Его любимый Буссенар. (II, 223)

Cependant, le règne de Louis devait être bref
("vsë naskučilo emu"). Il rêve de devenir le roi,
non plus de "ces misérables grottes, mais des
léopards et des panthères". Tel "La chèvre de
Monsieur Seguin" (1866) d'Alphonse Daudet, Louis
repousse toute la nuit les assauts des panthères qui
l'ont entraîné dans un piège, et meurt au petit
matin. Alerté par les cris de douleur de Mik, "le
puissant Esprit des Forêts" apparaît à ce dernier
"monté sur un éléphant de feu" et lui propose
d'exaucer le voeu qu'il formulera:

> Мне видеть хочется Луи
> Таким, каким он в жизни был. (II, 229)

Pour revoir Louis, Mik va devoir

> Вдоль по течению ручья
> [идти] три дня, потом семь дней
> Через пустыню черных змей.
> Там у чугунной двери в ад,
> С кошачьей мордой, но рогат,

> Есть зверь, и к брату твоему
> Дорога ведома ему. (II, 229)

Après avoir surmonté divers obstacles et dissipé un impévisible malentendu, Mik s'assure le concours d'une alouette dont il finit par apprendre que Louis est au paradis des anges. Dans l'épilogue (dixième partie), le lecteur assiste au triomphe terrestre de Mik:

> В Аддис-Абебе не найти
> Глупца, который бы не знал,
> Что Мик на царственном пути
> Прекрасней солнца воссиял. (II, 237)

Malgré une incontestable beauté formelle, le poème est déroutant à plus d'un titre. Il y a en fait comme deux poèmes en un seul, ce qui crée une impression, moins de dualité que de dysfonctionnement au niveau de l'inspiration et de la construction.

Dans la première partie Gumilev innove en acclimatant en terre russe un style de littérature coloniale, sourcé hors des frontières de l'empire mais fortement enraciné en Occident, particulièrement en Angleterre. Cette littérature met au premier plan, comme dans la narration "primitive" telle qu'elle a été définie par Ejxenbaum en 1919, "une succession rapide et inattendue d'événements et de situations" dont "le principe organisateur" n'est qu'"une combinaison de motifs et de leurs motivations". A ce niveau, toujours selon Ejxenbaum, il ne saurait être question de "ton personnel de l'auteur", ni encore moins de tonalité épique.(4)

La deuxième partie rompt complètement avec la tradition précédente (si l'on excepte à la rigueur l'épilogue en trompe-l'oeil). Au centre se trouve la mort de Louis, victime des "forces d'en-haut", mais surtout de son orgueil et de sa démesure:

> Луи суровым был царем.
> Он не заботился о том,

> Чтó есть, где пить, как лучше спать,
> А все сбирался воевать;
> Хотел идти, собрав отряд,
> Иль крокодила из реки
> Загнать в густые тростники,
> Но ни за что его народ
> Не соглашался на поход,
> И огорченный властелин
> Бродил печален и один. (II, 223-24)

Sur le thème de la mort de Louis et de ses attendus se greffe celui de l'enfer et de la rédemption. A la question de Mik, l'Esprit des Forêts répond que Louis est "en enfer" et lui indique le moyen de s'y rendre sans lui garantir la possibilité d'en repartir après avoir revu Louis. Or l'enfer que va visiter Mik comporte deux parties. La première est peuplée d'ossements "de poissons, d'oiseaux, d'animaux et d'hommes":

> Как та страшна была тропа!
> Там бормотали черепа,
> Бычачьи двигались рога,
> Ища незримого врага.
> И гнулись пальцы мертвецов,
> Стараясь что-нибудь поймать... (II, 230)

Puis, au-delà d'un "vaste fossé", "il devient plus facile de respirer":

> Там им открылся мир иной,
> Равнина с лесом и горой,
> Необозримая страна,
> Жилище душ, которых нет.
> Над ней струила слабый свет
> Великолепная луна;
> Не та, которую ты сам
> Так часто видишь по ночам,
> А мать ее, ясна, горда,
> Доисторических времен,
> Что умерла еще тогда,
> Как мир наш не был сотворен. (II, 230-31)

Il s'agit, cette fois, d'un authentique royaume des ombres, semblable à celui de la mythologie grecque:

> ... тени мёртвых пастухов
> Пасли издохнувших коров.
> Там тень охотника порой
> Ждала, склоняясь над норой,
> Где сонно грызли тень корней
> Сообщества бобров-теней. (II, 231)

Dans cet étrange royaume

> Ни вздох, ни лепет струй, ни стук
> Не нарушал молчанья... (II, 231)

Dans ce paysage vide Mik reconnaît l'ombre de son père, le seul à émettre - ou est-ce une illusion? - un faible signe de vie:

> За тенью дикого волчца
> Он своего узнал отца,
> Сидевшего, как в старину,
> На грязной, бурой шкуре гну.
> Мик, плача, руки протянул,
> Но тот вздохнул и не взглянул,
> Как будто только ветерок
> Слегка его коснулся щек.
> Как мертвецы не видны нам,
> Так мы не видны мертвецам. (II, 231)

Mais Louis reste introuvable. La raison de sa non-présence en ces lieux tient au fait qu'il est blanc:

> Зверь поднял страшные глаза:
> "Зачем ты раньше не сказал?
> Все белые - как колдуны,
> Все при рожденьи крещены,
> Чтоб после смерти их Христос
> К себе на небеса вознес." (II, 232)

Mik, sur les conseils de la Bête, a donc recours à
une alouette magique qui, à sa demande, s'envole
trois fois vers le ciel. A la première fois,
l'alouette rapporte:

>". . . . . твой друг
>Попал в седьмой небесный круг,
>Перед которым звездный сад
>Черней, чем самый черный ад". (II, 233)

A la seconde fois:

>"Луи высоко, он в раю,
>Там Михаил Архистратиг
>Его зачислил в рать свою". (II, 233)

A la troisième fois, l'alouette tarde à revenir:

>Три дня ждал жаворонка Мик
>И к ожиданию привык,
>Когда свалился на песок
>Холодный пуховой комок.
>Такое видеть торжество
>Там жаворонку довелось,
>Что сердце слабое его
>От радости разорвалось. (II, 234)

Ainsi donc, le poème *Mik* est à la fois un poème
d'aventures dans le plus pur style de la littérature
coloniale, destiné à amuser des enfants ou à
distraire des adultes épris d'exotisme teinté de
fantastique, et un poème cosmique qui n'est
accessible qu'aux seuls initiés possédant le don de
voir de grands arcanes dans les aventures les plus
communes. Cette dichotomie entre les "aventures de
la jungle" et le "jardin des planètes" où se règle le
problème de la rédemption universelle, correspond
sans doute à la dichotomie du dessein de Gumilev qui
voulait réaliser le principe épique dans le cadre de
l'exotisme. Mais plus que de dichotomie, il s'agit
ici de mutation par rapport à la formule initiale du

poème. Le déroulement de la narration "primitive" tourne court et perd sa vertu attractive. L'aspect "métaphysique", à prétention épique, est quant à lui minoré, sinon étouffé par son contexte. Le principe épique qui eût exigé comme principe constructeur "le ton personnel" de l'auteur est contredit, à sa racine même, par un enchaînement mécanique d'épisodes destinés à divertir, péché mignon de tout type de littérature qui se compromet avec le style de facture coloniale, importé de surcroît.

Les trois ou quatre ébauches de poèmes conçus à la même période ("Poema Načala"; "Iz poemy *Dva sna*"; "V Kitae" etc) sont trop fragmentaires ou lacunaires pour être pris sérieusement en compte. Mais, apparemment du moins, ces ébauches ne s'écartent guère dans le principe de la formule de *Mik*: narration exotique avec mélange de mythologie et de cosmologie, ce qui annihile la recherche obstinée du souffle épique.

Or, si l'on considère que, dans le même temps, Gumilev a écrit six oeuvres dramatiques, sans parler de ses autres oeuvres littéraires, de ses articles critiques et de ses traductions, cet inachèvement répété revêt une signification particulière qui se situe à plusieurs niveaux. Certes la raison principale est à chercher dans ce qu'il faut bien appeler la "contradiction interne des genres". Mais il existe aussi d'autres explications, cette fois conjoncturelles. L'intérêt de la société russe pour l'exotisme oriental s'était paradoxalement épanoui à la faveur de la défaite de Port-Arthur. Cependant, les premiers revers de l'armée russe en 1914 portent un coup d'arrêt brutal à la mode des "japonaiseries".

Si bien qu'à l'époque où Gumilev compose ou publie ses poèmes "africains" ou "chinois", l'inspiration exotique ne trouve plus d'écho auprès du public, surtout si elle prétend sortir de son domaine propre (imitation ou stylisation) pour donner naissance à des récits en vers à prétention épique.

Il y avait, enfin, une troisième raison. Les principes affichés de la nouvelle école fondée par

Gumilev lui-même et par Gorodeckij étaient peu compatibles avec la recherche de la forme longue en poésie. La rupture avec l'idéologie poétique du symbolisme tout imprégnée de sacralisation signifiait *ipso facto* l'abandon des "élucubrations" philosophico-mystiques, le renoncement à tout type d'expression hiératique, la fin de genres comme celui de l'hymne ou du dithyrambe. Tout l'arsenal du bric-à-brac symboliste est remplacé par le culte de la chose, du détail concret et incisif, pris dans leur contexte historique. D'où un inévitable resserrement de la gamme poétique et l'attrait de plus en plus fort qu'exerce sur Gumilev le type de la ballade.

Si, malgré toutes ces raisons, Gumilev continue obstinément à s'intéresser au genre du poème (poème et "acméisme" sont tellement contradictoires que Gorodeckij, pour sa part, restera fidèle à la poétique du symbolisme dans les quelques poèmes qu'il écrira encore), c'est qu'il considère non sans raison que le principe épique transcende les écoles et les genres poétiques et que, dans le domaine russe, il constitue le point d'orgue de toute création majeure.

Mais il n'y a pas que dans le domaine lyrique ou épique que Gumilev se soit laissé tenter, avec des fortunes diverses, par la forme longue. Le principe dramatique devait lui aussi l'inspirer et non sans succès.

Gumilev a écrit six oeuvres dramatiques en vers. La première, *Don-Žuan v Egipte*, composée vraisemblablement en 1911, a été incluse en 1912 dans le recueil *Čužoe nebo*. La dernière, *Otravlennaja tunika*, a été conçue en 1917-1918 et publiée beaucoup plus tard à New York en 1952. Ainsi donc, pendant toute l'époque de sa maturité, le genre dramatique a été une constante de l'inspiration du poète.

Les trois premières pièces, *Don-Žuan v Egipte*, *Akteon* (1913) et *Igra* ("scène dramatique", 1916) sont des pièces en un acte. *Gondla* (1917) est un "poème dramatique en quatre actes". *Ditja Allaxa* (1917) est un "conte arabe en trois tableaux" destiné au théâtre de marionnettes. *Otravlennaja tunika* est une "tragédie en cinq actes".

À l'exception de cette dernière pièce dont V. Sečkarev a pu écrire:

> Нет сомнения, что "Отравленная туника" принадлежит к самым лучшим созданиям в истории русского театра вообще (III, xxvi),

l'oeuvre dramaturgique de Gumilev n'est pas vraiment d'essence théâtrale et lui-même n'a jamais particulièrement insisté pour que ses pièces fussent jouées.

M. A. Kuzmin, dans sa recension de l'unique représentation de *Gondla* à Petrograd en 1922, observe que les mots mêmes dont le dramaturge se sert

> не влекут за собою никакого жеста, никакого действия и нисколько не одушевлены театральной психологией и логикой. Из ограниченного количества неожиданных, необоснованных *поступков*, стихотворных *описаний* и лирических *сентенций*, неубедительных и часто друг другу противоречащих – никак не создать театрального впечатления. (5)

La critique de Kuzmin concernant l'aspect artificiel, voire contradictoire, des actions, des descriptions et des sentences lyriques, est sans doute excessive. Mais la critique ne porte que sur la théâtralité de la pièce, non sur la qualité du poème:

> ... поэма захватывает красотой языка, динамикой отличных трехстопных анапестов с перекрестной, звучной рифмой каждых четырех строк, с патетическим подъемом дикции. (6) ... язык "Гондлы" захватывает

> своим динамическим ритмом; особенно
> удачны его восторженные монологи и его
> [главного героя - L.A.] беспомощное
> возмущение. Хороши также "оссиановские"
> описания природы, как, например, в
> словах Вождя:
>
> Поднимается ветер вечерний,
> За утесами видно луну,
> И по морю из ртути и черни
> Мы отправимся в нашу страну.
>
> Поток мелодически инструментованных слов
> заставляет забывать встречающиеся иногда
> прозаизмы или слишком выспренный
> пафос.(7)

Gondla est en effet le meilleur, sinon le seul vrai poème de Gumilev. Sur le plan de la qualité, il est à la forme longue ce qu'est à la forme courte une poésie comme "Zabludivšijsja tramvaj".

Le "poème dramatique" *Gondla* est assorti de deux épigraphes qui en définissent d'emblée le ton et la structure. La première est une citation de S.N.Syromjatnikov, la seconde appartient à Ernest Renan. Toutes deux ont été puisées par Gumilev dans le livre de Syromjatnikov *Saga ob Erike Krasnom* (St.Petersburg, 1890). Syromjatnikov décrit dans son ouvrage la collision au IX° siècle, en Islande, de deux cultures spécifiques, la normande et la celte. Les Vikings étaient des guerriers armés de haches et d'épées, alors que les moines-ermites irlandais n'étaient forts que de leur seul bâton et de l'Evangile. Cette rencontre inopinée détermina tout le sort futur de l'île. Le combat entre le glaive et la Bible devait tourner à la déconfiture des rois guerriers et à l'émergence d'une population pacifique de bergers et de pêcheurs. La citation de Renan, que Gumilev a pu lire dans le livre de Syromjatnikov, fait partie de l'article "La poésie des races celtiques", paru initialement dans la *Revue des Deux Mondes* en 1854.(8). L'écrivain français y oppose la cruauté et la barbarie germaniques au legs spirituel des preux celtiques, fait de bienveillance et de compassion à l'égard des faibles.

Le ressort dramatique de *Gondla* est donc bien articulé. Il s'agit d'un conflit dialectique entre la civilisation et la barbarie, entre le "loup" et le "cygne", entre l'art, frère de l'amour des hommes, et un paganisme pervers aux pratiques sauvages.

L'intrigue est aussi foisonnante (à l'excès, selon certains critiques) que la finalité en est simple. Par un procédé habile, Gumilev ne nous apprend que progressivement la protohistoire du récit. La langue est somptueusement belle et musicale, dans la tradition spirituelle d'Ossian et de Richard Wagner. L'art de la métaphore comme transfert à partir du coeur des objets est inspiré à la fois par le style des sagas scandinaves et par une sublimation de l'expressionnisme symboliste.

Tant au point de vue de la langue que des situations, *Gondla* peut être considéré comme un dépassement moderniste du drame de Blok *Roza i krest*. Le personnage de Gondla est une subtile réincarnation de Rycar'-Nesčastje. Alors que ce dernier n'était que le messager de l'angoisse et de la souffrance comme sources de beauté, Gondla porte en lui-même spontanément cette "secrète beauté". Le même transfert s'opère à un autre niveau entre Izora et Lera-Laik. Ecartant résolument tout psychologisme, Gumilev lui substitue le dynamisme d'une action fertile en rebondissements.

L'intensité dramatique du poème est accrue par l'engagement de l'auteur lui-même, dont "le ton personnel" ne fait pas défaut. Gumilev met au premier plan l'idée de la mission hiératique du poète. Ici encore, le symbolisme est à la fois récusé et transfiguré, renaissant de ses cendres tel un Sphynx. Le hiératisme du poète était conçu par les symbolistes comme une sorte de sacerdoce exercé par un prophète ou un maître à penser. Gumilev, quant à lui, interprète dans *Gondla* ce hiératisme comme la révélation aux autres de la plus haute justification de la vie: l'art. Ce n'est que par l'art et le chant que Gondla, le héros, sort de son insignifiance corporelle. Bossu, craintif, presque pitoyable, il devient roi par un caprice du sort et renonce à son titre parce que dans son esprit il n'est rien de plus haut que le poète et son art. C'était, au demeurant, la conviction intime, poussée parfois jusqu'à la naïveté, de Gumilev lui-même. Elle est, dans son existence, le ressort secret de son éternel don-juanisme. Il considérait, en effet, que dans le coeur des femmes personne ne pouvait rivaliser avec un poète. Cette conviction se haussait au niveau de l'éthique, lorsqu'estimant que la pureté n'était pas de ce monde, il la cherchait avant tout dans la poésie, rêvant de se transfigurer à travers elle et de changer un monde fondamentalement hostile à l'homme.

Génie lyrique et dramatique, Gumilev n'avait pas la dimension épique à laquelle il aspirait tant. Ce "conquistador cuirassé de fer" était en réalité d'une très grande fragilité intérieure. Et c'est pour se protéger contre cette vulnérabilité dont il avait conscience qu'il s'était inventé une armure de théâtre, adoptant pour la vie une pose qui n'était qu'une seconde nature.

Pour autant, l'artiste, le "ménestrel", ne manquait ni de souffle, ni de puissance. La légende du luth enchanté qu'il a empruntée à la mythologie celtique dans *Gondla* correspondait tout à fait à sa vérité intime: celui qui s'est consacré à l'art ne connaît ni repos, ni retour en arrière. Et cette vérité a été si profondément - jusqu'à la douleur et au déchirement - vécue et ressentie par lui que son luth enchanté continue de jouer pour lui et pour nous au-delà de la mort. Il chante, ce luth, la mélodieuse prophétie du malheureux Gondla:

> И окажется правдой поверье,
> Что земля хороша и свята,
> Что она - золотое преддверье
> Огнезарного Дома Христа. (III, 54)

NOTES

1. N.Gumilev, *Sobranie sočinenij* (4 volumes), édit. G.Struve et B.Filippov (Washington, 1962-68), I, 14. Par la suite toutes les citations de l'oeuvre de Gumilev proviennent de cette édition avec, entre parenthèses, l'indication du volume et de la page.

2. Cité dans N.Gumilev, *Sobr. soč.*, II, 336.

3. M.Ju.Lermontov, *Izbrannye proizvedenija v dvux tomax* (M., 1959), I, 466.

4. B.Ejxenbaum, *O proze* (L., 1969), 306.

5. Cité dans N.Gumilev, *Sobr. soč.*, III, 238-9.

6. V.M.Sečkarev, "Gumilev-dramaturg", dans N.Gumilev, *Sobr. soč.*, III, xxi.

7. Ibid., p.xxvi.

8. Voir N.Gumilev, *Sobr. soč.*, III, 41, pour la citation de Renan.

"STIXI IZ SNOV": ART, MAGIC AND DREAM IN GUMILEV'S *ROMANTIČESKIE CVETY*

MICHAEL BASKER

1

This paper examines the themes of art, of magic and occultism, and of dream and the dream-inducing, in the poetry of Gumilev's second collection, *Romantičeskie cvety*.(1) It maintains that magic and dream are inextricably linked in *Romantičeskie cvety* through the doctrines of occultism (or 'secret knowledge'), and that they are also integral to the concept of art which both underlies these poems and receives significant thematic elaboration within them. In conjunction, the themes of art, magic, and dream are found to pervade the entire collection, lending it a fundamental unity, and providing a vital key to its meaning. The main object of the paper is therefore to suggest an overall approach to the appreciation and coherent interpretation of a volume of Gumilev's verse in which previous critics have discerned little of intrinsic interest, for *Romantičeskie cvety* has hitherto been treated almost exclusively as a derivative phase in Gumilev's lengthy poetic apprenticeship, and still awaits thorough critical appraisal.(2) It is also hoped that an examination of these themes in a single early collection will contribute towards establishing their more widespread and enduring importance to Gumilev's art, for his concern with magic, occultism, and dream has in general been underestimated, and often discounted or ignored.

The dominant critical view of Gumilev has undoubtedly been of a poet principally concerned with the concrete realities of the external, physical world, and not with any penumbral realm of dream and the occult. Clearly indicative of this is the tenaciously persistent stereotype of the poet-warrior, "independent, energetic, not remotely a dreamer",(3) who writes "consistently in the major key"(4) of manly endeavour, heroic exploit and physical adventure. With similar implication, Gumilev has also been regarded as a "poet-geographer", enamoured of the "Muse of Distant Travels".(5) In the recent opinion of Georges Nivat, for example: "Tout Gumilev est diurne, coloré, impregné de poésie géographique et toponymique."(6) Accepted notions of Acmeism, and Gumilev's own apparent rejection in his manifesto of the Symbolist thematics of "mysticism, occultism and theosophy" (IV,174), likewise suggest a poetry that is essentially diurnal. "The avowed aim of the new school", writes Renato Poggioli, "was ... a beauty to be wrought out of the substance of things rather than out of the shadow of dreams". And with reference to the domain of magic, Gumilev, he says, "rejected the temptation to wander into the metaphysical and the occult, and ventured instead into the material and physical world".(7) Similar perceptions have led others to doubt the profundity of Gumilev's work.(8) Even his Acmeist colleague, Sergej Gorodeckij, who noted with seeming approbation that his poetry is devoid of "mysticism, magic, cabbalism and theosophy", added waspishly that "there are many abysses of the spirit of which it has no suspicion".(9) And Aleksandr Blok, in his article "Bez božestva, bez vdoxnovenija", used the imagery of dream to make a similar point in forthright condemnation:

> N.Gumilev and certain other "Acmeists" ... sleep an interminable sleep without dreams; ... in their poetry they stifle

the most important thing, the only thing of value: *the soul*.(10)

The principal departure from such attitudes has been the view adopted by Gleb Struve, Earl Sampson and others, who have perceived in Gumilev's *later* work a significant shift in preoccupations, an increased depth, and a new element of mysticism. Struve, for example, in one of his many articles on Gumilev, finds in *Koster* and *Ognennyj stolp* "unexpected notes aligning him above all with Tjutčev - the poet of second sight and secret hearing" (*tajnovidenija i tajnoslušanija*);(11) and elsewhere he refers to the "magical" poems and new "visionary quality" (*vizionerstvo*) of Gumilev's last collection.(12) Similarly, Goleniščev-Kutuzov, Ocup, and Klenovskij, in articles which, albeit lacking in detail, make a general case for the presence of magical and occult themes in Gumilev's work, all direct their attention almost exclusively to the late poetry. It is indicative of the resistance to such opinions that Klenovskij's argument, that "the basic meaning of Gumilev's work" resides in a "small but extremely valuable group of poems containing occult motifs", elicited an editorial disclaimer on the appearance of his article in *Grani*.(13) The topic of dream has not been the subject of any separate study of Gumilev's poetry, although many critics have noted in passing the presence of dream motifs in individual poems. Recent sophisticated analyses of "Zabludivšijsja tramvaj" and, in the present volume, of "Duša i telo" have finally (and from very different standpoints) given detailed consideration to the treatment both of dream and of certain occult doctrines in two of Gumilev's most important late poems;(14) but here again, the presence of comparable themes in his early work has not been seriously examined.

Although Blok's already quoted article, "Bez božestva, bez vdoxnovenija", has generally been regarded as the culminating expression of his long-standing hostility towards Gumilev and his poetry,(15) other comments by Blok nevertheless suggest the basis for the different reading of Gumilev which is advanced below. In March 1919 Blok presented Gumilev with a copy of his *Third Volume*, inscribed "To ... the author of *Koster*, read not only 'by day', when I 'do not understand' verse, but also by night, when I understand".(16) And this intimation of a complex, night-time poet, perhaps closely attuned to Gorodeckij's "abysses of the spirit", might be compared with Blok's well-known comments on Mandel'štam's reading of his verse at the *Klub poetov* in October 1920. "At first", Blok remarked, "the ubiquitous notes of Gumilev [*obščegumilevskoe raspevanie*] sound intolerable". But, he continued:

> One gradually becomes accustomed ... the performer is visible. His poems arise out of dreams - extremely idiosyncratic ones, lying in the realm of art alone. Gumilev defines his path: from the irrational to the rational (the opposite of my own).(17)

These observations on Mandel'štam's "stixi iz snov", in which Blok detected clear echoes of Gumilev, hold unerringly true for the poems which Gumilev himself produced at the outset of his career, in *Romantičeskie cvety*.

2

The best-known and most widely anthologised poem of *Romantičeskie cvety* is undoubtedly "Žiraf". Indeed, several critics, acquaintances, and parodists have taken the poem as in some sense epitomizing Gumilev's writing;(18) and it forms an appropriate point of departure for the analysis of his second collection:

Сегодня, я вижу, особенно грустен твой взгляд,
И руки особенно тонки, колени обняв.
Послушай: далеко, далеко, на озере Чад
Изысканный бродит жираф.

Ему грациозная стройность и нега дана,
И шкуру его украшает волшебный узор,
С которым равняться осмелится только луна,
Дробясь и качаясь на влаге широких озер.

Вдали он подобен цветным парусам корабля,
И бег его плавен, как радостный птичий полет.
Я знаю, что много чудесного видит земля,
Когда на закате он прячется в мраморный грот.

Я знаю веселые сказки таинственных стран
Про черную деву, про страсть молодого вождя,
Но ты слишком долго вдыхала тяжелый туман,
Ты верить не хочешь во что-нибудь, кроме дождя.

И как я тебе расскажу про тропический сад,
Про стройные пальмы, про запах немыслимых трав
. . .
Ты плачешь? Послушай ... далеко, на озере Чад
Изысканный бродит жираф.

(I,76-7)

As Ralph Matlaw has already argued, "Žiraf", "like all [Gumilev's] early 'animal poems', turns ultimately into a picture of an inner or psychological state or episode". At the same time, however, Professor Matlaw has adopted the view that, in contrast to "certain poems of the later collections" in which visionary and magical elements are strong, the early poems are "essentially depictive and emblematic"; and that "Žiraf" is the "most 'parnassian' of those poems".(19) Yet the striking adjective *izyskannyj*, "very much commented upon at the time of the appearance of *Romantičeskie cvety*, because people could not imagine a giraffe to be dainty [*sic*] and thought the epithet somewhat *recherché*",(20) hints from the outset that Gumilev's true concern is not at all the Parnassian objectivity with which his early verse is commonly associated.(21) In fact, the initial emphasis of the description is wholly upon the aesthetic, and the magic:

> Ему грациозная стройность и нега дана,
> И шкуру его украшает волшебный узор...

From the magic the poem proceeds to the miraculous ("Ja znaju, čto mnogo čudesnogo vidit zemlja"); and it moves on through "fairy-tales" of "mysterious" lands to the "scents of the inconceivable". It seems, therefore, that even Brjusov for once missed the point when he objected (in the margin of his copy of *Romantičeskie cvety*) that there are no marble grottoes on the shores of Lake Chad.(22) The setting of Gumilev's poem is indeed "daleko, daleko"; for "brightly-coloured" though it may be, it does not belong to the world of "geography and toponymy" at all. One might hesitate, at this stage, to relate it specifically to the realm of dream, but it is surely the idiosyncratic product of an aesthetic imagination, and not the accurate record of empirical observation.

It is also readily apparent from a reading of "Žiraf" that the sunlit realm of Lake Chad is contrasted with the more colourless and humdrum world of immediate phsyical reality, neatly rendered through the experience of the sad-eyed woman to whom the impassioned "African" description is addressed: she has "breathed in the stifling fog for too long", and "will not believe in anything other than rain". This contrast between dull reality and a more exciting "non-present" occurs repeatedly in the poems of *Romantičeskie cvety*, and lies at the core of the romanticism proclaimed by the collection's title. Of particular interest in "Žiraf", however, are the motive and form of its elaboration; and insight into these aspects of the poem may be derived from

Gumilev's comments on the very dissimilar poetry of Innokentij Annenskij, included some two years after the publication of *Romantičeskie cvety* in his important theoretical article, "Žizn' stixa". Annenskij, writes Gumilev,

> loves exclusively "today" and exclusively "here", and this love prompts him to the suppression not only of theatrical props [*dekoracii*], but of all decorativeness [*dekorativnost'*]. Because of this, his verses torment, they inflict incurable wounds on the soul, and it is necessary to struggle against them with incantations of time and space [*zaklinanija vremen i prostranstv*] (IV,166).

In complete contrast to this, "Žiraf" (like the "verses" of *Romantičeskie cvety* in general) is emphatically "decorative";(23) the poet, as has been seen, is scarcely enamoured of the present, and it might tentatively be inferred that Gumilev, who had set out for Paris in 1906 with the intention of studying occultism, and who wrote early in 1908 of the influence of the French occultists on his theory of poetry,(24) regarded his own art in these early years precisely as one potential means of occult, "incantatory" resistance to the wounds of here and now. "Poetry should hypnotise", he began a review in 1910, "in this lies its strength" (IV,247). The "poem within a poem" in "Žiraf", with the *plavnyj beg* of its five-foot amphibrachs, and its emphasis on mystery and magical pattern, might consequently be interpreted as the dramatic representation of an attempt at hypnotic-incantatory artistic performance. (The performer, to adapt Blok's phrase, is prominently visible). And although, by a neat touch, its success in this particular case seems less than assured, the very presence of the unreceptive female addressee serves to indicate that such "romantic incantation" is no merely escapist art for art's sake. The woman, ensnared in her *segodnja* from the opening word of the poem, is a victim of the here and today, who suffers the wounds of spiritual limitation. The motive for the hypnotic performance (if it is not to be dismissed as mere cynical seduction ploy!) must lie, therefore, in the conviction that art can comfort, can strengthen one to cope with the afflictions of the present, and so, ultimately, enlarge mental and spiritual horizons, and enrich the personality.

This interpretation of the function of art implicit in "Žiraf" finds substantial corroboration in a letter to Brjusov of March 1907, in which, significantly, Gumilev expressly refers to himself as an "adept of occultism". Describing the effect that he "dreamed" (*mečtal*) of attaining in his own poetry, and had most often experienced at first hand when reading the verse of Brjusov, he informs the elder poet that certain of his lines

> have entered as a constituent part not into my outlook upon the world (that would be too little), but into the formulation of the obscure desires of my astral body, and hence into my true personality.(25)

Furthermore, this same concept of the power of art was in essence reiterated, in terms less obviously redolent of occultism, in "Žizn' stixa":

> Outstanding [*prekrasnye*] poems, like living beings, can enter into the circle of our lives; they can teach, or call, or bless.... Under their influence people love, hate and die. (IV,163)

The artist's magical incantations, that is to say, might lead in the first instance away from the here and today; but their relevance is ultimately to the present.

3

The artistic performance enacted in the central stanzas of "Žiraf" has a close parallel in another poem of *Romantičeskie cvety*, on the Japanese theatre celebrity, Sada-Yakko. Her versatile repertoire - performed to the flickering of shadows upon the *polotna dekoracij* - culminates in a form of verbal incantation which is in this instance entirely successful in captivating and transporting her audience from familiar, waking reality into an unfamiliar realm of aesthetic artifice:

> Вы бросали в нас цветами
> Незнакомого искусства,
> Непонятными словами
> Опьяняя наши чувства,
> И мы верили, что солнце
> Только вымысел японца.
>
> (I,60)

More frequently, however, the apparent focus of the poetry centres upon a different means of transcending time and space: upon dream rather than art. But just as art and magic are closely inter-related (art is a form of magic, and magic is one of the subjects of Gumilev's art), so, too, are art and dream, and dream and magic.

The convergence between art and dream, like that between art and magic, is readily perceptible in the superficial sense that dream is often the overt source as well as the chief setting and substance of the poetry. However, it also finds a deeper, theoretical sanction in the doctrines of occultism. According to Papus - a disciple of Eliphas Lévi, whose work Gumilev is known to have studied,(26) and an eminent occultist in his own right - it is by the concept of the astral body, or that same sphere which

Gumilev, in the letter to Brjusov already quoted, envisaged as susceptible to art, that "occultists account for visions and actions at a distance, presentiments, prophetic ecstasy, dreams and madness".(27) Furthermore, whilst art, even as incantation or hypnosis, is evidently a deliberate and active process, so, for the "adept of occultism", is dream. Implicit in this same doctrine, therefore, is a close analogy between artist and magus; while dream is in turn not only a subject for the artist and an analogue of art, but also a chief instrument of the magician. Thus, Lévi emphasises that the ability to avail oneself directly of the astral light is "the source of all real, effective, occult magic". To this end, the adept of occultism is able to "magnetise himself", entering into "an abnormal condition ... a kind of lucid and waking somnambulism" in which his will remains active, giving direction to his "dream", "which then transforms into [astral] vision". Such "magnetism of a person by himself, accomplishing his own lucidity and directing himself at will, is the perfection of magical art".(28)

Whether or not Gumilev wholeheartedly subscribed to such ideas, the concept of the deliberately directed "magnetic" (or, to use the more familiar modern term, "hypnotic") dream finds significant reflection in the poems of *Romantičeskie cvety*. A form of self-magnetism is evidently practised, for example, by the "junyj mag" of "Zaklinanie", who intones "nezdešnie slova" and burns magical grasses, thereby transcending space and inducing a dream-like state:

> Аромат сжигаемых растений
> Открывал пространства без границ,
> Где носились сумрачные тени,
> То на рыб похожи, то на птиц.
>
> (I,66)

The presence in this poem of an unnamed "*carica bezzakonij*" by the emerald waters of the Nile might be interpreted as another element of the magnetic dream, and thus as a further consequence of the young magician's wilful magical practise; for as Gumilev indicated in a review published in 1909, the love of Queen Cleopatra was a supremely tantalizing prize even for the modern-day occultist (IV,218). The concepts of magnetic dream and waking somnambulism also provide an essential key to narrative events in such poems as "Maskarad" and "Peščera sna". In the former, the strange "theatrical props" of a masked ball - which the opening lines again locate explicitly in the "here" and "today" - rapidly cast a magnetic spell over the participants:

Над ними повисли тяжелые чары,
Высокие свечи горели, краснея,
И в темные сны погружалися пары...(29)

The lyric narrator, who also experiences this mesmeric effect, nevertheless retains his lucidity, and continues to dance, to converse, and to recollect. In "Peščera sna" (I,63-4), too, the setting - "Tam, gde poxoronen staryj mag" - is admirably suited to the engenderment of dream; and there is a strong element of wilful control in the achievement of a state of "waking somnambulism". The main narrative is here in the future tense, for the lyric narrator of this poem apparently possesses the power of the true adept - to foretell those visions which will be induced when the quiet of evening descends upon his carefully selected, potently magnetic surroundings.(30) The narrator and his partner will see before them the shade of the dead magus (at the end of the proceedings he will "again become a corpse") and, in the rather timid figure of Lucifer and his attendant shadows, in Queen Mab and the Wandering Jew, those spirits over whom it may be supposed that he once wielded his occult power.(31) Throughout the course of these astral visions (and it is precisely as such that, in occult theory, the dead manifest themselves from beyond the grave)(32) the living witnesses will remain able not only to see and hear, but also to choose silence and prudent concealment; and at dawn they will record the experience of their "somnambulism" in song. "To see in the astral light", as Lévi puts it, "is to dream awake."(33)

The most complex and impressive elaboration of the theme of occult dream is to be found, however, in "Karakalla" (I,84-6). At first sight, Gumilev's subject is an unlikely one. The Roman Emperor Caracalla was an infamous tyrant, whose reputation for treachery, wanton cruelty and profligate extravagance led Gibbon to describe him as "the common enemy of mankind";(34) and indeed, two distinct aspects of this historical image find imaginative elaboration in Gumilev's "Imperatoru" (I,83-4) and "Moreplavatel' Pavzanij" (I,86-7), poems which in the 1908 edition of *Romantičeskie cvety* were formally linked with "Karakalla" as the first and third parts of a single cycle.(35) "Imperatoru", like "Peščera sna", "Zaklinanie" and "Giena" (I,67-8: another of Gumilev's variations on the Cleopatra motif) contains a strong element of necromancy.(36) It presents Caracalla as dread autocrat who, even after death, has power to command the obedience of the "bednyj brodjačij pevec" who encounters his awesome shade:

> Призрак какой-то неведомой силы,
> Ты ль, указавший законы судьбе,
> Ты ль, император, во мраке могилы
> Хочешь, чтоб я говорил о тебе?

"Moreplavatel' Pavzanij", on the other hand, offers a glimpse of Caracalla's fabled prodigality. Located "V dni bezumnyx/ Izvraščenij Karakally", its chief subject is the extravagant reception which the Emperor himself, to the prayers of sacred prostitutes in the presence of vast, carefully regimented crowds, accords to a large, emerald crocodile, brought to Rome from the banks of the distant Nile. Yet against this background, in the much longer central poem Gumilev chooses to present a strikingly different, "internalised" portrait of Caracalla, not as a tyrant but as dreamer, magus, and artist.

His Emperor is, in consequence, a sharply divided soul; and "Karakalla" begins accordingly with the indication of an emphatic split between the office and the man:

> ...О, каким бы стал ты властелином,
> Если б не был ты самим собой!

It is next intimated that Caracalla possesses a "quiet secret" beside which the images of the great potentates of Rome now seem a pale and insignificant shadow (stanza 3). The obvious implication is that he possesses the Secret Knowledge of occultism; and in what follows he foresakes both enticing day-dreams of military conquest and glory (stanzas 5 and 6), and the no less powerful sexual allurement of his empress, "Strastnaja, kak junaja tigrica/ Nežnaja, kak lebed' sonnyx vod" (stanza 7), for the pursuit of protracted night-time visions in his exotic gardens (stanzas 8-14). Here, with the onset of evening and contemplation of his dancing girls, whose movements are perhaps more hypnotic than erotic, something like the patterned skin of the "gracefully shapely giraffe" ("... slovno zoloto na černi,/ Vidny nogi strojnyx tancovščic"), he shows himself well able to enter into that magnetic state of "lucid and waking somnambulism" which is the *sine qua non* and very pinnacle of occult operations. Though "pierced by the arrow of dreams", he is thus capable, for example, of disputing with Phoebus (appropriately enough, not only the deity of light, but also the soothsaying god and ruler over the inner world of fantasy), and in the subsequent course of his reverie he is likewise able to abjure the moon in words "terrifying and forbidden". The lines on Phoebus also suggest an explanation for the elaborate ceremonial devoted to the arrival of the Egyptian crocodile in "Moreplavatel' Pavzanij". The outlandish reptile was evidently prized by Caracalla not as a mere plaything, but as a potently magnetic instrument of dream-inducement, and as such it finds an important place in his gardens:

> Как и ты стрелою снов пронзенный,
> С любопытным взором [Феб] застыл
> Там, где дремлет, с Нила привезенный,
> Темно-изумрудный крокодил.

In all probability, however, it is also to be understood that the carefully staged importation of the crocodile was by no means the Emperor's most elaborate step towards the engenderment of his own dreams. According to tradition, he was himself the founder and architect of the royal gardens, stocked in the poem, "Slovno prixotlivye kamei", with an improbable and bizarre array of flora and fauna, which provide both the setting and content of his night-long reverie.(37)

Further reliance on extra-textual information proves to be a significant feature of Gumilev's early poem cycle. Thus, idiosyncratic though his portrait of Caracalla may be, several points of detail apparently stem from the account of his reign given in the *Roman History* of Dio Cassius. Here Gumilev would have found considerable substance for the Emperor's day-dream, in "Karakalla", of "subjugating the rebellious Parthians", and a basis for the relatively minor incident of the Emperor's neglect of his consort's sexual invitation: according to Dio, Caracalla was "disgusted with his wife, who was a most shameless creature". In addition, Dio's passing reference to Caracalla's longing for "sole knowledge and power", and to his "gratification of his curiosity to the neglect of affairs of state" perhaps contains the seeds of Gumilev's description of his "insatiable thirst for dream" (I,84) and of the

penchant for the rich and strange so amply reflected
in the contents of his gardens.(38) Of particular
note, however, is a brief passage in Dio on the minor
Germanic tribe of the Alamani, an obscure people,
conquered by Caracalla, who practised magic to his
detriment:

> The enchantments of the enemy had made
> Antoninus [Caracalla] frenzied and *beside
> himself*; at any rate, some of the
> Alamani, on hearing of his condition,
> asserted that they had employed charms *to
> put him out of his mind*. For he was sick
> not only in body ... but in mind as well,
> suffering from *certain distressing
> visions* ... Therefore he *called up
> spirits* to find some remedy against them.
> [Emphasis mine.](39)

Gumilev must almost certainly have known this passage,
for in "Igry" (I,82-3), another "Roman poem" of
Romantičeskie cvety, he depicts a bold *vožd' alamanov*
who is at once both dangerous adversary of Rome –
"ubijca s glazami gieny" – and magician: "zaklinatel'
vetrov i tumanov". The poem's narrator admiringly
describes a provincial circus, a three-day orgy of
butchery scarcely equalled even in Rome, and eagerly
anticipates its climax in the slaughter of the Alaman
chieftain by the blood-crazed beasts that have
survived. But his expectations are thwarted when the
chieftain appears in the arena:

> Но, прижавшись к перилам дубовым,
> Вдруг завыл он, спокойный и хмурый,
> И согласным ответили ревом
> И медведи, и волки, и туры.
>
> Распластались покорно удавы,
> И упали слоны на колени,
> Ожидая его повелений...

In this the Alaman chieftain gives dramatic demonstration of what Lévi terms one of the Seven Secondary Powers of the True Magus: "To subdue the most ferocious animals and be able to pronounce the words which paralyse and charm serpents".(40) His occult abilities are in no doubt, and the poem concludes with the provincial narrator's agitated apostrophe of "The Consul and the Eternal Gods".(41)

The implication which may be drawn from "Igry" is that Gumilev's Caracalla (who, as Dio informs us, had a bloodthirsty love of the circus, which he indulged at the expense of local officials even on provincial tour)(42) is indeed bewitched by the formidable magic of the conquered Alamani. The extremes of his divided nature and, to the extent that it might be regarded as a sickness, his extravagant and insatiable "thirst for dream" thus find explanation on an occult level. But Caracalla is also a considerable magician in his own right; and Dio refers to his exercise of magic in the attempt to remedy his predicament. How far his single-minded cultivation of the magical dream might also therefore be construed as an effective cure for his afflictions will be examined in detail below. At this point it is sufficient merely to note, as some measure of Caracalla's success, that at dawn he is able to record his visionary experiences in measured and "flowery" verse. As in "Peščera sna", that is, Gumilev's dreamer and magician is also an artist. It might be added, in the light of Blok's characterisation of Mandel'štam, that his poetry in a most literal sense "arises out of dreams". And in so far as Caracalla's dream gardens are his own artistic construct, these idiosyncratic dreams "lie in the realm of art alone".

4

Comparison with the small group of poems dealt with in the previous section will next serve to demonstrate the more widespread presence of dream motifs in *Romantičeskie cvety*. Gumilev's introduction of such motifs is occasionally emphatic, but it is more often unobtrusive or indirect and, particularly where the "abnormal condition" of waking dream is concerned, interpretation may be dependent on the context provided by other poems.

It is indicative of Gumilev's relatively undemonstrative methods that apart from "Peščera sna" - where, as Earl Sampson has remarked, "the title is the only direct indication that the fantastic figures in the poem are dream images"(43) - "Mečty" (I,58) is the only poem whose title makes explicit reference to dream. A dream framework is also invoked by the first lines of two other poems: "Mne snilos', my umerli oba" (I,59) and "Strannyj son uvidel ja segodnja" ("Jaguar", I,69-70). More typically, however, Gumilev relies in "Princessa" on an unemphatic simile in mid-poem to indicate that the central narrative event takes the form of "astral vision":

Стало тихо тишиной виденья.
(I,62)

Similarly, in "Krest" he uses an apparent cliché which perhaps arrests attention only in the broad context of other poems:

Я чувствовал, будто игра эта - сон.
(I,62)

And in "Užas", too, the key motif of dream is introduced obliquely as one in a series of images in the second stanza:

В угрюмом сне застыли вещи,
Был странен серый полумрак,
И точно маятник зловещий,
Звучал мой одинокий шаг.
(I,71)

This is analogous to a line from "Karakalla":
Беспокоен смутный сон растений
(I,85)
and similar examples could be adduced from "Otkaz" (I,56-7) and "Za grobom" (I,71-2).

Elsewhere, even such unobtrusive reference is omitted, and the presence of a dream setting is indicated primarily by the recurrent imagery and vocabulary of the collection. So, for example, comparison with the shadowy dream creatures, half bird, half fish, which are evoked by the magus in "Zaklinanie", suggests that an otherwise unremarkable metaphor in "Neoromantičeskaja skazka" also places within the realm of dream the distant and dangerous journey which the young prince undertakes despite his elderly major-domo's wise advice:

"Не ходи за те границы,
Помни старые законы,
Видишь, траурные птицы,
В небе *плавают вороны*."
(I,296)

The image of the (*plavajuščie pticy*) is inverted in "Korabl'" (I,68-9), where strange "flying fish" ("letučie strannye ryby") bear similar connotations of magnetic vision; and it is also unobtrusively incorporated into "Žiraf", with the consequent implication that Gumilev's giraffe, too, is fundamentally a creature of dream:

И бег его плавен, как радостный птичий полет.(44)
(I,76)

This is perhaps confirmed by the improbable marble grotto that is its shelter by night, for in both "Za grobom" and "Peščera sna" ("gde zijaet v mramore peščera") the cave is the location and probably the magnetic instrument of dream. The corridor(45) and the garden(46) perform similar functions in other poems of *Romantičeskie cvety*.

Another common signal of the dream state are the fogs which in "Karakalla" "swim like dreams". Fleeting "belesovatye tumany" thus form part of the "Egyptian" setting of "Giena" (I,67-8), in conjunction with other dream elements such as the cave, or the butterflies that also figure in "Karakalla" and "Peščera sna". And mists occur once more at the beginning of the original published version of "Ozero Čad", together in this case with an echo of the snakes that hang (*svisajut*) to the ground from the darkened palms of Caracalla's garden, or wind their way, "kak sny neobyčajny", through the cannibal's kingdom in "Neoromantičeskaja skazka" (I,296):

> На таинственном(47) озере Чад
> Повисают, как змеи, лианы,
> Разъяренные звери рычат
> И блуждают седые туманы.
> (I,78/311)

A further variation on this imagery is also found in "Nosorog", where the dream motif is implicit from the first word:

> Видишь, мчатся обезьяны
> С диким криком на лианы,
> Что свисают низко, низко...
> (I,77)

Amongst other elements in Gumilev's intricate network of imagery and vocabulary indicative of dream, mention need be made only of his persistent allusion to temporal background. Night, and particularly the transitional periods at evening and before dawn, with their attendant mists, are naturally the time of dream and magic, and almost a third of the poems of *Romantičeskie cvety* are set against the contrast of night and day. These generally conclude with dawn and a return to the waking present.(48) Night is also the setting for intense imaginative experience, alien to the ordinary "here" and "today", in poems such as "Krysa" (I,48) or "Dumy" (I,51-2) where no other dream signal appears to be included.

An evident consequence of Gumilev's extensive recourse to dream motifs is the very consistent 'deconcretisation' of geographical and historical settings, and the internalisation of his poetry within the mind and the imagination. The exotic landscape of Lake Chad thus closely resembles that of Imperial Rome or of ancient Egypt, because in sharp contrast to the Parnassian poetry with which Gumilev's early verse is frequently compared, all are of the same inner, psychical realm referred to in one poem as the "gardens of the soul" (I,73-4). The "non-physical", "non-geographical" setting of "Žiraf" is indeed therefore thoroughly typical of *Romantičeskie cvety*, and vocabulary, imagery and setting all bring significant unity to the collection.

The question which now remains to be examined is how far this unity also obtains at a deeper level of meaning.

5

Gumilev's use of recurrent motifs indicative of dream is not, of course, a recipe for drab monotony. The pattern of recurrent imagery and vocabulary is shifting, its constituent elements, as has been seen, often unobtrusive, and a further guarantee of diversity is the considerable fluctuation in the mood and effect of the dreams Gumilev depicts. Dream can delight, as in "Sady duši" or disturb, as in "Za grobom" (I,71-1). Its potential variety of mood is intimated by the narrator's anticipation of vision in "Peščera sna":

> Будем слушать серебристый смех
> И бессильно-горькое рыданье.
> (I,63)

And whereas in this poem dream provides strength to meet the day, in "Rassvet", for example, a resplendently colourful nocturnal vision leads at dawn only to weakness and fear (I,49-50). Clearly, too, the relationship between the inner world of dream and the outer world of "here" and "today" by

which it is repeatedly framed is by no means
constant, and it is rarely so straightforward as in
"Mečty", where the dreams of the "staryj voron s
oborvannym niščim" are constructed in diametrical
contrast to their humble waking condition (I,58).(49)
Concepts of time and space do, nevertheless, provide
an important clue to the function of dream in
Romantičeskie cvety: for the dream states depicted,
quite irrespective of their temporal setting, show an
almost unfailing orientation towards the past.

In certain of the poems already discussed the
evocation of the past in dream takes the form of
necromancy, the magnetic conjuration of the shades of
the dead. Other poems involve recollection, although
only in a few instances, such as "Vospominanie"
(I,57) or "Korabl'" (I,68-9), can this be
convincingly interpreted as a reflection of the
protagonist's own waking experience. More often, the
process of dream recollection must be regarded as a
function of what Gumilev himself later termed the
"protomemory" (*prapamjat'*).(50) This may relate to a
past existence of the protagonist - most strikingly,
perhaps, in "Smert'", which appears to record the
persona's recollection of a previous encounter with
death (I,50) - or to the collective, frequently
prehistoric past of mankind. Like the presence of
dream, attunement to the latter is often signified by
key-words and phrases - "drevnij" (I,53,82,311),
"namek starinnoj tajny" (I,73), "s nezapamjatnyx por"
(I,51), and so on.

Not surprisingly, Gumilev's representation of the
protomemory finds extensive sanction in the theories
of occultism. Even Eliphas Lévi, who as a professed
Catholic was something of an exception amongst
contemporary occultists in repudiating the
Pythagorean doctrine of metempsychosis, found it
"probable that [Pythagoras] came upon former memories
in dreams", for "the real life of our individuality
consists in memory alone".(51) The explanation lies
once more in the concept of the astral light which is
variously the province of art, magic, and dream.

"Every act, and will, remains imprinted in the astral light"; and the images of the past, "only effaced by the more powerful impressions of reality during waking hours", are in their entirety potentially accessible to the occult vision of the skilled adept.(52) In moving from description to interpretation of the poetry, however, it is helpful also to note a substantial correspondence between the workings of the protomemory in *Romantičeskie cvety* and the later theories of Jung's analytical psychology. (These, according to Jung, had important historical parallels in the works of the medieval alchemists which in another context had been influential upon Lévi and the French occult revival of the nineteenth century.) "The main task of dreams", Jung has stated, "is to bring back a sort of 'recollection' of the prehistoric, as well as the infantile world, right down to the level of the most primitive instincts."(53)

The workings of both collective and personal aspects of the protomemory are apparent in "Maskarad" (I,52-3 and 293-4). In his condition of "waking somnambulism", the lyric persona of this poem first experiences bewilderment and an inexplicable sense of the familiar:

> О чем-то грустил я, чему-то смеялся,
> И что-то казалось мне странно-знакомо.
> (I,53)

The compound adjective, as it transpires, here signifies the stirrings of "protorecollection" and anamnestic identification; and in the next lines an encounter with a "Queen of Sodom" is described in terms of a still elusive collective archetype. "Mne dušu izmučila večnaja tajna", exclaims the protagonist in the original version (I,293); while in the later redaction the element of recollection involved is rendered more explicit: "Ty tak mne napomnila drevnjuju skazku" (I,53). Yet when the Queen eventually reveals her face the protagonist's confused feelings and dim recollections crystallise into a sudden recognition of her identity which apparently relates to a previous personal existence:

> Я вспомнил, я вспомнил ... такие же тени,
> Такую же дикую дрожь сладострастья
> И ласковый, вкрадчивый шопот: "Воскресни,
> Умри и воскресни для неги и счастья".
> (I,294)

It might be added that the dream events are charged throughout with intense emotive significance, and that the precious moment of recognition entails a far-reaching, intuitive illumination:

> Я многое понял в тот миг сокровенный.
> (I,54,294)

This insight, it seems reasonable to assume, retains its significance into the waking present, the "here" and "today" with which the poem opens.

In "Jaguar" (I,69-70), "Giena" (I,67-8) and "Orel Sindbada" (I,75-6), the dream encounter with ancient images of the lover or traveller brings about comparable moments of dramatic insight, a perception of identities presumably inaccessible to the waking consciousness, and hence, perhaps, a lasting increase of self-knowledge. "Princessa" (I,62-3), however, introduces a slight variation into the function of the retrospective dream. The heroine of this poem is helplessly lost in a dark wood until a workman finds her and leads her to his hut. He falls peacefully asleep; but the silence of the night, the deep shadows, and the flickering light of a dim icon-lamp appear to induce in the princess a "magnetic" state of vision, based on recognition, of which the contents of the hut form the subject:

> Неужели это только тряпки,
> Жалкие, ненужные отбросы,
> Кроличьи засушенные лапки,
> Брошенные на пол папиросы?
>
> Почему же ей ее томленье
> Кажется мучительно знакомо,
> И ей шепчут грязные поленья,
> Что она теперь лишь вправду дома?

Even the most banal of objects are here imbued with vibrant psychic intensity and, as in "Maskarad", the waking vision is an experience of acute but elusive significance. Its meaning, however, is implicit in the very terms of the princess's incomprehension, and relates in this case not so much to true identity as to spiritual *rodina*, her true place in the scheme of existence. Her tormenting sensation of familiarity, conveyed by a compound epithet that closely resembles the "stranno-znakomo" of "Maskarad", might be interpreted here too as a product of the protomemory. In other words, on the inchoate level of protorecollection she has indeed experienced this place before, and is indeed "truly home". In "bringing back a sort of 'recollection' of the prehistoric" (to use Jung's expression) the dream thus reveals a state of completeness, of integration into a more primitive and psychically colourful world in which the princess, or - since her memory is presumably not of her own present life - mankind in general had formerly participated. Finally, however, the poem which began with the princess's disorientation and tears comes full circle. She returns from the forest in the early dawn, and the poem ends with her abiding sense of loss, as she sheds tears "about the hut" during many lonely nights ("gluxie noči"). Dream symbols, according to Jung, can evoke "our original nature"; but modern man "feels himself isolated in the cosmos, because he is no longer involved in nature and has lost his emotional 'unconscious identity' with natural phenomena".(54)

This interpretation of "Princessa" may also be extended to other poems of the collection. A comparable perception of vivid, primeval intensity is conveyed on a vaster scale by the vision of the animated heavens in "V nebesax" (I,50-1)(55) and "Rassvet". And just as the princess must leave the hut at morning, so in "Rassvet" the mist of daybreak eclipses the colourful, picturesque vision of the fantastic constellatory beasts. Man is remote from the primitive grandeur of natural phemomena, and quite literally "isolated in the cosmos":

> Что нам в бледном утреннем обмане?
> И Павлин, и Змей - чужие людям.
> Вот они растаяли в тумане,
> И мы больше видеть их не будем.
>
> Мы дрожим, как маленькие дети,
> Нас пугают времени налеты...
> (I,49-50)

The notion that the consciousness of modern man has lost the "mystical participation"(56) of the primitive psyche also affords an interpretation of "Ozero Čad" (I,78-80) perhaps more satisfactory than that of the transition from innocence to experience proposed by Matlaw,(57) and sheds further light on the artistic performance in "Žiraf". The priestess-heroine of "Ozero Čad" is first seen in her native environment, the primeval dream-world of "mysterious Chad". In this her "true home" (in the 1908 text she is the "favourite daughter of mighty Chad") her hieratically ordered actions have an inherent, sacred significance, and even the rain serves as numinous background for her celebration of ancient ritual ("tajny drevnego obrjada": I,311). But a European warrior entices her away, and in his civilised, modern world she loses her sacred, inner identity:

> Словно вещь, я брошена в Марселе.
> (I,79)

She is debilitated (*obessilena*), beset by troubles and haunting remorse, and so comes to experience the inner dislocation typical of "here" and "today". Moreover, a reading of this poem in conjunction with the thematically related "Žiraf" now seems to suggest that the purpose of the incantatory artistic performance there directed at the civilised, neurasthenic heroine whose perception of the rain differs so pointedly from that of the priestess of Chad, is specifically to reverse the process which brings the latter to her suffering and sense of loss. In other words, it is the endeavour of the artist and magus to heal the wounds of present-day disorientation, limitation, and unfulfilment by seeking to renew the link with the almost forgotten condition, intimated in dream by the protomemory, in which man felt himself psychically integrated (at home) into a "theatrically decorative" or primitively vivid universe, where objects and actions were endowed with numinous, as if magical significance, and all relationships gave the same "tremor to the soul" (IV,590) as the dream encounter with a Cleopatra or a Queen of Sodom.

6

Gumilev's prehistoric dream world is nevertheless no lost Eden. If in "Princessa" or "Žiraf" it seems enticingly calm and unforbidding, elsewhere, by contrast, it is characterised by that troubled darkness which Blok apparently discerned in Gumilev's work. It can inspire the primordial instinct of fear, and the poems make reference to "drevnjaja zloba" (I,81), and "zverinaja zloba ... s nezapamjatnyx por" (I,51). To seek imaginative and emotional communion with the primitive condition of "our original nature" is therefore a potentially dangerous, sometimes terrifying enterprise, which demands a particular form of courage.

The element of risk involved in transcending the narrow confines of the familar, waking world is implicit, for instance, in "Vljublennaja v D'javola", where there is a sharp contrast in spiritual capacity between the passionate girl who "dreams always" and is "enamoured of the Devil", and those inhabitants of her oppressively gloomy world who attempt to exorcise the exhilarating danger and restore normality (I,64-5). Another contrast in perceptions is of crucial importance in "Axill i Odissej" (I,267). For the first four stanzas of this poem Odysseus reproaches Achilles with his lapse into idle luxury and apparent effeminacy ("... zavivajet, kak deve, nevol'nica/Černyx kudrej tvoix dlinnye prjadi"), and recounts the Achaeans' many setbacks in battle in an attempt to shame him into returning to the war. But the poem develops into a notable depreciation of the conventionally heroic, manly warrior. The powerfully laconic reply of the perfumed and elegant Achilles comes in the fifth and final stanza:

> Брось, Одиссей, эти стоны притворные,
> Красная кровь вас с землей не разлучит,
> А у меня она страшная, черная,
> В сердце скопилась и давит и мучит.

Despite his effete exterior, Gumilev's Achilles is no weak-willed coward; and his words reveal a spiritual complexity and depth which make him more than a match for the brave Odysseus. (Significantly, the last lines of the poem refute Odysseus's more simplistic analysis: "Serdce bezgnevno i vzor tvoj lileen".) Achilles' comparison between his own black and terrifying blood and that of Odysseus perhaps suggests a foreknowledge of his impending death, and thus a gift of insight that extends into the province of occult vision,(58) but it is his conscious recognition of the terrible darkness *within* him ("V serdce skopilas' ..."), together with his aesthetic appreciation of exquisite refinements so distasteful to the forthright warrior ("vmesto dospexov mexa leoparda ..."; "zapax ne krovi, a narda"; "sladkie vina"), which is the source of his forceful superiority. The soul of the aesthete is tormented and sharply divided, for, much more than the physical man of action, he is susceptible to the "wounds of the present"; but it is his strength that he seeks breadth of experience, mental confrontation with both "černaja gibel'" and "nevedomoe sčast'e",(59) and the expansion of consciousness into "prostranstva bez granic" (I,66).

Like Achilles, Caracalla, too, is a complex, introspective aesthete, a connoisseur of the bizarre who neglects the ordinary "masculine" duties of warrior and lover for psychical rather than physical adventure; and in "Karakalla" the confrontation with inner darkness, clearly connected with the protomemory, reveals its full positive value. The significance of Caracalla's waking dream is most explicit in the poem's early drafts. Thus, in one version:(60)

> И под этим замолчавшим небом
> Ты с великой тайною - одно.

And, at somewhat greater length, in a second:(61)

> Стон земли несется из тумана,
> Стон земли, больной от диких чар.
>
> И великой мукою вселенной
> На минуту грудь свою омыв,
> Ты стоишь, божественно-надменный,
> Император, ты тогда счастлив.

Clearly, Caracalla here achieves that "emotional identity with natural phenomena" generally lost to civilised man, and in this "oneness" finds relief from the dualities by which he is beset. But this is not, in the final analysis, a pantheistic communion of spirit with nature. As has been seen, the primeval landscape of Caracalla's garden, which has numerous parallels in *Romantičeskie cvety*, is one of the inner realm of dream; and thus Caracalla's contentment is in the sense of completeness brought about through the union of consciousness (for the magnetic dream is consciously directed) with the "velikaja tajna" of his own being, the inner *vselennaja* of his unconscious mind. Such an alignment of conscious and unconscious elements is described by Jung as the "transcendent function", and constitutes the essential act in the individuation process, the "rounding out of the personality into a whole", central to his thought.(62)

In the final published version of the poem, the dark-emerald crocodile of the Nile is crucial in pointing a similar meaning. "Čuždyj ljudjam i prirode",(63) the freak embodiment of fantastic *skazka* and "destroyer of harmony" (I,87), it evidently conveys something akin to the primal groans of the sick earth in the earlier drafts. At the same time, this disturbing, prehistoric beast forms an anamnestic link between the conscious mind of the emperor-aesthete and its darkest, primitive depths. As amphibious reptile (broadly analogous, incidentally, to the emerald flying fishes in "Korabl'" and to the emerald-backed dolphins that are the link between the "seashore" and the enchanted dream realm of the prince in "Otkaz"),(64) the crocodile may be seen in Jungian terms as one of those creatures, symbolic of transcendence, "with the ability to live in two environments, in water or on the earth":

> These creatures, coming from the depths of the ancient Earth Mother, are symbolic denizens of the collective unconscious. They bring into the field of consciousness a special chthonic (underworld) message.(65)

In such symbols the union of conscious and unconscious contents is consummated,(66) and Caracalla's strange encounter with the moon, which descends to him "Moloda, svetla, i vljublenna", to be dismissed by his words of black magic, "ešče strašnee i zapretnej", confirms his determination to pursue the uniquely powerful "chthonic message" without distraction from the higher, conventionally romantic, and ideal. He is intent on fathoming those "abysses of the spirit" which in Gorodeckij's opinion had no place in the poetry of Gumilev.

Naturally the message that emerges symbolically from the underworld of the psyche is not rationally articulated; but its result, at the end of the poem, is much as in the earlier drafts:

> Медленно, как следует царю,
> Ты, неверный, пышными стихами
> Юную приветствуешь зарю.
> (I,86)

Again, that is, the previously disoriented emperor has at least temporarily "found himself". The epithet "nevernyj" indicates a less than complete transformation, but the poetry that he composes to meet the dawn no less certainly suggests that, unlike in "Rassvet" or "Princessa", something of the dream encounter with the alien (*čužoe*) and prehistoric depths has been successfully assimilated to bring strength and solace into the waking present. The refined aesthete's conscious confrontation with the troubled forces, in one sense perhaps conjured upon him by his enemies, but ultimately of his own being, is thus an effective means of occult resistance to the wounds of the here and today, a source of enrichment of personality and of growth towards self-fulfilment. In Jungian terms, through "integrating a part of his unconscious personality and bringing it into real life", Caracalla moves along the path towards the "full realisation of the potential of his individual Self" which is the end point of the individuation process.(67) Within the context of *Romantičeskie cvety* the pattern of loss of identity, disorientation and inner fragmentation, perhaps most fully described in "Ozero Čad", is entirely reversed; and the way of the artist, magus and dreamer, whose goal is intimated in "Žiraf", finds its most thorough vindication.

Although the value of Caracalla's experience is offset by other poems of the collection, it might be added that it is on this positive note that the last authorized edition of *Romantičeskie cvety* closes. The three poems on Lake Chad are followed by the seven "Roman" poems, culminating in "Igry" and the "Karakalla" cycle, and the collection is rounded off by "Neoromantičeskaja skazka". This concluding poem describes the journey of a young prince, "scarcely out of the nursery", beyond the confines of his known world into the dangerous dream realm of the rhinoceros and the cannibal.(68) With the help of his major-domo's magic, the prince vanquishes the cannibal lord of "evil and incantations" and returns victorious. The cannibal is brought back a captive, and afterwards tamed and transformed to act out a peaceful role in the friendly waking kingdom. With rather more ease than the Roman Emperor, the fairy-tale prince assimilates to the good a part of the darkness within, and so develops towards maturity. Thus the direction of Caracalla's achievement is finally echoed in a lighter key.

7

While the colouration and impact of dream may fluctuate considerably from poem to poem, it is now clear that in terms of meaning as well as of expression Gumilev's preoccupation with dream and magic, and with art and the figure of the artist-aesthete, brings to the poetry of *Romantičeskie cvety* a strong underlying unity. The poems do not formulate a single, consistent message;

instead, as with the imagery, a consistent inner thematic core is constantly rearticulated in a series of shifting, often diametrically opposing patterns, and as a result interpretation of individual poems is ultimately dependent upon the context of the whole. The organisation of the poetic *sbornik* as a coherent system, which, as Dr S.Schwarzband demonstrates in the present volume, formed a distinctive feature of Acmeist poetics, is already therefore significantly foreshadowed in Gumilev's second collection.

To return once more to the remarks of Aleksandr Blok, it might also now be suggested that the "path" of Gumilev's idiosyncratic dream poetry, like that of Mandel'štam's in 1920, is indeed the very opposite of Blok's. In contrast, at least, to the typical movement of Symbolist poetry, *a realibus ad realiora*, Gumilev's early poetry moves first inwards into the realm of the psyche - colourful and enticing or dark and forbidding as it may be - and thence back once more into present reality. (Like the art it so resembles, dream enters as a formative influence "into the circle of our lives".) Though Gumilev adopts the characteristically Symbolist thematics of dream and magic, the immediate focus of his poetry is thus *within* rather than *beyond*, and its ultimate concern is with the real rather than the Ideal. In these respects, too, already consonant with the precepts of Acmeism, it is anthropocentric, and constitutes a meaningful "return to this earth". In further contradistinction to Symbolism, it might also be termed "existential" rather than "philosophical". In general, like Caracalla's crocodile, Gumilev's dreams and dream poetry are primarily expressive not of an "outlook upon the world" (*mirosozercanie*) - which, in the words of his letter to Brjusov of March 1907, "would be too little" - but of various facets of man's "true personality". The main axis of meaning is thus different in kind, and in a sense more elusive, than in Symbolism. Partly for this reason, one suspects, Gumilev's verse has sometimes been dismissed as lacking in depth. In fact, virtually from the outset it reveals a very considerable sophistication and profundity.

Among the more specific connections between *Romantičeskie cvety* and Gumilev's later work, it might be noted in conclusion that his attention to "true personality" and the development of the individual towards self-fulfilment directly anticipates that concern with the complete "flowering of all physical and spiritual forces" he once advanced as a definition of Acmeism (IV,309). A direct descendant of Caracalla is accordingly Cadmus, the royal architect, magus and visionary who is the hero of Gumilev's programmatically Acmeist drama, *Akteon*.(69) Yet just as Caracalla succeeds only where others fail, so Cadmus is the representation of an ideal. Much of Gumilev's poetry thus continues to deal with the predicament of alienation in the civilised world, with modern man's sense of incompleteness and loss of place. A continuing strong element of primitivism is the reverse of this same coin. Furthermore, in each subsequent collection of Gumilev's verse it is again possible to trace his enduring preoccupation with aspects of occultism, with art as enchantment, hypnosis, "zloveščix, nočnyx videnij tetrad'" (II,19); and not only with dream, but with dream as protorecollection and with the notion of previous incarnations.(70) The motifs of magic, occultism and dream are not specific to *Koster* and *Ognennyj stolp*, or indeed to any single period of Gumilev's career, and in this respect at least his poetry is considerably more homogeneous than the view of his creative path advanced by Struve and others would suggest. Throughout, its main emphasis is internal, and the "manly adventure" and distant travels it depicts remain essentially inner ones, more suited to the broad and complex aesthete than to the forthright warrior and curious geographer.

NOTES

1. First published in Paris in the early weeks of 1908 and subsequently reissued by Gumilev in a condensed version, incorporated into *Žemčuga* in 1910, and in an enlarged and revised version in 1918. The present article is largely based on the fullest, 1918 text, which is reproduced in N.Gumilev, *Sobranie sočinenij v četyrex tomax*, ed. G.P.Struve and B.A.Filippov (Washington, 1962-8). References to this edition will appear in the text by volume and page number. Where appropriate, however, account is also taken of earlier variant readings, and six poems from the 1918 edition have been excluded from consideration on chronological grounds: "Sonet", "Ballada", and "Ossian" (I,45-7), which first appeared in *Put' Konkvistadorov* (1905), and "Vybor", "Osnovateli", and "Manlij" (I,55,81-2), which were composed after the first publication of *Romantičeskie cvety*.

2. The fullest account to date is in E.D.Sampson, *Nikolay Gumilev* (Boston, 1979), pp.56-63. See also Ju.Verkhovskij, "Put' poeta: o poezii N.S.Gumileva", *Sovremennaja literatura* (Leningrad, 1925), pp.93-111, which discusses *Romantičeskie cvety* in conjunction with Gumilev's other early collections.

3. E.Aničkov, *Novaja russkaja poezija* (Berlin, 1923), p.108.

4. D.S.Mirsky, *A History of Russian Literature* (London, 1964), p.486. M.Slonim, *From Chekhov to the Revolution* (New York, 1962), p.215 also states: "Most of [Gumilev's] poems are in a major key."

5. The image of the poet-geographer was of course combined with that of poet-warrior in Julij Ajxenval'd's well-known intepretation of Gumilev's work ("Gumilev", in his *Siluety russkix pisatelej*, vol.3 [4th edn, Berlin, 1923], pp.265-78).

6. G.Nivat, "L'Italie de Blok et celle de Gumilev", *Revue des Etudes Slaves*, LIV, (1982), 707.

7. Renato Poggioli, *The Poets of Russia, 1890-1930* (Cambridge, Mass., 1960), pp.215-16,226.

8. See the summary of such views in S.Monas, "Gumilev: Akme and Adam in Saint Petersburg", in N.S.Gumilev, *Selected Works*, trans. B.Raffel and A.Burago (New York, 1972), p.13.

9. S.M.Gorodeckij, review of *Čužoe nebo* in *Reč'*, 15(28).X.1912, p.5.

10. A.A.Blok, *Sobranie sočinenij v vos'mi tomax* (Moscow-Leningrad, 1960-3), VI, 183.

11. G.P.Struve, "Gumilev", *Rossija i slavjanstvo*, No.144 (29. VIII. 1931), p.3.

12. "Tvorčeskij put' Gumileva", in Gumilev, *Sobranie sočinenij*, II, xxxiii-xxxiv. See also, for example, E.D.Sampson, "In the Middle of the Journey of Life: Gumilev's *Pillar of Fire*", *Russian Literature Triquarterly*, 1 (1971), 287.

13. I.Goleniščev-Kutuzov, "Mističeskoe načalo v poezii Gumileva", *Rossija i slavjanstvo*, No.144 (29.VIII.1931), p.3; N.Ocup, Introduction to N.S.Gumilev, *Izbrannoe* (Paris, 1959), pp.27-8; D.Klenovskij, "Okkul'tnye motivy v russkoj poezii nashego veka", *Grani*, 20 (1953), 129-37. (The editorial note of dissociation from Klenovskij's views appears on p.129.)

14. On the former, see I.Masing-Delic, "The Time-Space Structure and Allusion Pattern in Gumilev's 'Zabludivshiisia Tramvai'", *Essays in Poetics*, vol.7, 1 (1982), 62-83; and E.Rusinko, "Lost in Space and Time: Gumilev's 'Zabludivšijsja tramvaj'", *Slavic and East European Journal*, vol.26, 4, (1982), 383-402. Masing-Delic, like R.Eshelman in his essay on "Duša i telo", gives consideration to the concept of the "astral body" which is also of relevance in *Romantičeskie cvety*. Rusinko, however, bases her analysis on Bergsonian philosophy rather than occult doctrine, and rejects the "understanding of the poem as a return to mysticism" (p.399). Each of these valuable studies is testimony to the scope for further enquiry along similar lines.

15. See the summary of such views in A.Pyman, *The Life of Aleksandr Blok*, vol.II (Oxford, 1980), pp.348-9.

16. *Aleksandr Blok: Novye materialy i issledovanija* ("Literaturnoe nasledstvo", vol.92), bk.3 (Moscow, 1982), p.56.

17. *Sobranie sočinenij*, VII, 371.

18. See, for example, A.M.Remizov, "Krjuk (pamjat' peterburgskaja)", *Novaja russkaja kniga*, 1922, 1, p.8; V.I.Ivanov-Razumnik, "Izyskannyj žiraf", *Znamja*, 3-4 (1920), cols.51-2, and the comments and parodies in N.Gumilev, *Neizdannoe i nesobrannoe*, compiled and ed. M.Basker and S.Graham (Paris, 1986), pp.188,288; and Ju.Rakitin, "Dve teni: Blok i Gumilev", *Vestnik russkogo xristianskogo dviženija*, 147 (1986), p.174.

19. R.E.Matlaw, "Gumilev, Rimbaud, and Africa: Acmeism and the Exotic", in *Actes du VIe Congrès de l'Association Internationale de Littérature Comparée* (Stüttgart, 1975), pp.654-5.

20. L.I.Strakhovsky, *Craftsmen of the Word: Three Poets of Modern Russia* (Cambridge, Mass., 1949), p.15.

21. These views might ultimately be traced to V.Ja.Brjusov's review of *Romantičeskie cvety* in *Vesy*, 1908, 3, 77-8. See also, for example, Sampson, *Gumilev*, pp.59-60, and *Istorija russkoj poezij*, II (Leningrad, 1969), p.376.

22. V.Puriševaja, "Biblioteka Valerija Brjusova", in *Literaturnoe nasledstvo*, vol.27-8 (Moscow, 1937), p.674.

23. It is noteworthy that I.F.Annenskij used both *dekoracija* and *dekorativnyj* in his short review of *Romantičeskie cvety* (reprinted in G.P.Struve, "Innokentij Annenskij i Gumilev: 'Neizvestnaja' stat'ja Annenskogo", *Novyj žurnal*, 78 (1965), 285-7).

24. *Neizdannoe i nesobrannoe*, p.99; N.S.Gumilev, *Neizdannye stixi i pis'ma* (Paris, 1980), p.37.

25. *Neizdannye stixi i pis'ma*, p.14.

26. See Gumilev, *Neizdannoe i nesobrannoe*, p.100.

27. Papus [Dr. Encausse], *What is Occultism: A Philosophical and Critical Study*, trans. F.Rothwell (London, 1913), p.18. Brjusov, in a pseudonymous review of S.Tuxolka, *Okkul'tizm i magija*, (*Vesy*, 1907, 7, p.81) refers to the Russian translation of this work as a standard authority.

28. Eliphas Lévi [A.Constant], *Transcendental Magic: Its Doctrine and Ritual*, trans. A.E.Waite (London, 1896), pp.97,113,63.

29. The quotation is from the first published version of the poem (I,293-4), which appeared in *Vesy*, 1907, no.7. Explicit reference to dream is omitted from the more polished version included in the 1918 edition of *Romantičeskie cvety* (I,53-4), but the bizarre "dream" background is there more vividly described.

30. The ability of the "true Magus" to foresee future events is described in Lévi, *Transcendental Magic*, p.12.

31. The power of the magus to "command the spirits" is described in Papus, *What is Occultism?*, pp.63-5. The devil is described as a frequent agent of the magician in Lévi, *Transcendental Magic*, p.29.

32. Lévi, *Transcendental Magic*, pp.273-4.

33. Ibid., p.113.

34. E.Gibbon, *The Decline and Fall of the Roman Empire*, vol.1 (2nd edn, London, 1909), p.148.

35. For further details, see I, 312.

36. As a biographical aside to this theme, it may be noted that according to the unpublished memoirs of D.Kardovskij, Gumilev himself attempted to evoke the spirits of the dead during his student years in Paris. To his apparent horror, he claimed at least one partial success (communicated by R.D.Timenčik). His method appears to have been closer to the high magical practices involving techniques of self-magnetism, described for example, in the

chapter on necromancy in Lévi, *Transcendental Magic*, pp.111-19, than to the more banal procedures of spiritualism.

37. See, for example, Shelley's celebration of the gardens in the Preface to his *Prometheus Unbound*. Gumilev might have known Shelley at this time from Bal'mont's translation.

38. Dio Cassius, *Dio's Roman History*, with an English translation by E.Cary (9 vols; London, 1927), IX, 341-3, 243, 303, 325. Caracalla's attitude to his wife would also conveniently correspond to Lévi's notion of the true initiate as one who has freed himself from enslavement to physical passion (*Transcendental Magic*, pp.28,32).

39. *Dio's Roman History*, IX, 315, 317.

40. *Transcendental Magic*, p.12.

41. According to *The Oxford Classical Dictionary* (2nd edn, ed. N.G.L.Hammond and H.H.Sullard [Oxford, 1980], p.280), "under the Empire ... the Emperors either recommended the candidates or themselves assumed the consulship". The relevance to Caracalla remains direct.

42. *Dio's Roman History*, IX, pp.291, 297-9, 331.

43. Sampson, *Gumilev*, p.61.

44. Compare also the line from "Sady duši": "Ee flamingo plavaet v lazuri" (I,74).

45. See I, 70, 72, 292.

46. See I, 73, 77, 85.

47. *Tainstvennyj / tajnyj* might also be regarded as words significant of dream: cf. I,56,63,66,71,73,75,84,85,88.

48. Unambiguous examples are "Rassvet" (I,49-50), "V nebesax" (I,50-1), "Krest" (I,52-3), "Umnyj D'javol" (I,56), "Princessa" (I,62-3), "Peščera sna" (I,63-4), "Ljubovniki" (I,65-6), "Zaklinanie" (I,66-7), "Ozero Čad" (I,78), "Karakalla" (I,84-6), "Odinoko-nezrjačee solnce" (I,269), and "Nevesta l'va" (draft version: *Neizdannye stixi i pis'ma*, pp.106-7).

49. Despite its title, this poem describes genuine dream and not mere day-time imaginings. See the raven's observation: "Čto emu na razvalinax bašni/ Nebyvalye snilis' viden'ja".

50. "Prapamjat'" is the title of a poem in *Koster* (II, 21).

51. *The History of Magic*, trans. A.E.Waite (London, 1913), p.99.

52. Lévi, *Transcendental Magic*, pp.82,63. Implicit here is a close connection between necromancy and protorecollection, of particular relevance to a consideration of "Giena" and "Zaklinanie".

53. C.G.Jung *et al.*, *Man and his Symbols* (London, 1964), p.89. On the importance which Jung attached to the "historical parallels" he elaborated in such late works as *Psychology and Alchemy* or "Commentary on the 'Secret of the Golden Flower'", see his *Memories, Dreams and Reflections* (London, 1963), pp.192-3.

   There is, of course, no question here of any direct influence of Jung on Gumilev. In 1908 Jung was at the start of his career, and had published only specialist clinical studies.

54. *Man and his Symbols*, p.85. "Princessa" would also readily admit of a more detailed Jungian interpretation. Briefly, the workman might be regarded as an animus figure, guiding the ego, or Princess, through the forest of the unconscious psyche towards the psychic "centre" of the Self, symbolized by the hut. Such a journey would represent the inception of the process of individuation central to Jungian psychology.

55. Originally entitled "Skazočnoe" (I,291) and thereby, perhaps, immediately established as a dream poem. Compare the title "Neoromantičeskaja skazka", and the use of *skazka* in connection with "primitive" dream motifs in I,53,63,65,76.

56. The term is Jung's, in *Man and his Symbols*, p.31.

57. "Gumilev, Rimbaud, and Africa", p.656. The lyric heroine's consciousness of her sexual charms, and her adulterous anticipation of future luxury, especially pronounced in the 1908 text (I,311-12), cast some doubt on Matlaw's reading.

58. See above, note 30.

59. The phrases occur in "Nas bylo pjat' ... my byli kapitany" (I,268).

60. Moscow, Gosudarstvennaja biblioteka SSSR imeni Lenina. Rukopisnyj otdel, f.386, k.86, ed. xr.20, 1.36.

61. Gumilev, *Neizdannoe i nesobrannoe*, p.230.

62. C.G.Jung, *Collected Works* IX, pt.1 (London, 1959), para.524.

63. In a draft version of "Moreplavatel' Pavzanij": Gumilev, *Neizdannoe i nesobrannoe*, p.231.

64. Line 8 of "Otkaz" (I,56-7) originally read: "Oni predlagali svoi izumrudnye spiny" (GBL, f.386, k.84, ed. xr.18, 1.43). The adjective "gljancevitye", mistakenly listed as an earlier variant in Gumilev, *Neizdannye stixi i pis'ma*, p.108, was a later substitution.

65. Jung *et al.*, *Man and his Symbols*, p.153.

66. Jung, *Collected Works*, IX, pt.1, para.524.

67. See Jung *et al.*, *Man and his Symbols*, pp.191,146.

68. On the journey as another common symbol of transcendence, see Jung *et al.*, *Man and his Symbols*, pp.146-50.

69. See M.Basker, "Gumilev's 'Akteon': A Forgotten Manifesto of Acmeism", *Slavonic and East European Review*, vol.63, 4 (1985), 498-517.

70. This, of course, finds mention even in Gumilev's Acmeist manifesto (IV, 174-5).

REMARQUES SUR GUMILEV,
CRITIQUE DE LA POESIE FRANÇAISE

JEAN BONAMOUR

Gumilev est l'un des poètes russes du XXème siècle les plus liés à la poésie française. Dès 1908, à propos de *Romantičeskie cvety* Brjusov évoquait Leconte de Lisle et les Parnassiens, et le nom de l'école parnassienne restera associé à celui de l'acméisme. Traductions, oeuvres originales ou écrits théoriques, c'est l'ensemble de l'oeuvre de Gumilev qui peut être considéré comme une approche, indissolublement créatrice et critique, de la poésie française.

Les remarques qui suivent n'ont pas pour but de traiter cet immense sujet; une synthèse serait d'ailleurs prématurée dans l'état actuel de nos connaissances.(1) Nous voudrions seulement montrer, à l'aide de quelques exemples, combien les jugements critiques de Gumilev sur la poésie française sont solidaires des choix et de la stratégie du poète russe.

Premier point: jusque dans ses écrits critiques Gumilev ne se veut à aucun degré historien de la poésie française et ne vise aucunement à en donner une vue synthétique. S'il cite une cinquantaine d'écrivains français, presque tous poètes, c'est généralement à propos de compte-rendus critiques ou de traductions. Ajoutons que les références aux autres littératures européennes (anglaise notamment, mais aussi italienne et allemande) sont nombreuses, comme chez beaucoup d'écrivains de l'"âge d'argent". Parmi les noms cités prédominent les poètes français contemporains: Banville, Baudelaire, Gautier, Hugo, Mallarmé, Verlaine. Mais la part du hasard reste grande, et beaucoup de noms n'apparaîssent qu'une fois: des écrivains classiques (Boileau, Corneille, Du Bellay, etc.) mais aussi des modernes: ainsi Rimbaud, cité pour sa prose. Ceci réduit évidamment la signification qu'il convient d'accorder à la présence ou à l'absence d'un nom. D'autre part la défiance de Gumilev vis-à-vis des théorisations de l'histoire littéraire est manifeste: il ironise sur l'entreprise de Brjusov publiant une anthologie des lyriques français du XIXème siècle et se plaît à brouiller les généalogies littéraires.(2) Il y a là, plus profondément, un certain scepticisme sur l'histoire littéraire en général.(3)

Gumilev critique n'est donc pas historien, mais lecteur, et surtout poète lecteur de poètes; c'est de ce point de vue qu'on analysera ses articles sur Gautier et Baudelaire.

Particulièrement révélateur est le grand article sur Gautier paru dans *Apollon* (1911), qui constitue en lui-même un véritable manifeste. Consacré "parnassien", auteur de traductions de Gautier avant celle, trois ans plus tard, d'*Emaux et Camées*, Gumilev à travers Gautier livre beaucoup de lui-même et de ses idées sur la poésie. Gautier n'est pas seulement le poète "impeccable", il est le poète exemplaire, "[zaključivšij] v odnom sebe vozmožnosti francuskoj poezii na pjat'desjat let vpered",(4) et ce n'est pas un hasard si Gumilev place son article sous le signe d'une citation de Puškin ("Lis' junosti i krasoty poklonnikom byt' dolžen genij"). C'est ce caractère exemplaire qui suscite un jeu d'inclusions et d'exclusions: poète de la forme, Gautier est aussi le poète de la vie, de la gaieté rabelaisienne: "Sekret Got'e ne v tom, čto on soveršenen, a v tom, čto on moguč, zarazitel'no moguč, kak Rable, kak Nemvrod, kak bol'šoj i smelyj lesnoj zver'":(5) ici apparaît l'idée "adamiste" (cf. "Nasledie simvolizma i akmeizm"), l'exaltation de l'énergie vitale qui est l'une des constantes de la personnalité poétique de Gumilev.

Le problème fond/forme s'élargit ainsi en une réflexion sur les rapports vie/art dont l'oeuvre de

Gautier donne l'image exemplaire: "on uže poznal veličestvennyj ideal žizni v iskusstve i dlja iskusstva". L'amour de la vie n'est pas seulement épicurisme, il implique la reconnaissance de notre finitude et du caractère inépuisable de la vie. C'est le tort du romantisme français – des émules maladroits de Hugo - que d'avoir voulu réviser les valeurs éthiques au nom des valeurs esthétiques: il y avait là une mutilation de la réalité, de la vie qui, en fin de compte, était vouée à mutiler l'art lui-même. C'est uniquement par la perfection de la forme que le poète doit dominer la vie, et seule la rigueur formelle peut lui permettre de la recréer dans son intégrité. La virtu du conquistador est aussi une vertu de l'artiste: tel est le sens de la formule critiquant implicitement Baudelaire:

> Учитель и друг Бодлера, он не поддался соблазну безобразного, очарованию сплина, а странное и экзотическое любил только до тех пор, пока оно не теряло пластичных форм.(6)

On retrouve quelques échos de cette réserve implicite dans la préface récemment publiée sur Baudelaire.(7) La généalogie poétique que donne Gumilev de l'oeuvre baudelairienne est sans surprise, et fondée sur de nombreux textes du poète lui-même: Sainte-Beuve et Gautier en France, de Quincey et Poe dans la littérature de langue anglaise. Mais cette typologie permet d'imputer à "l'imagination anglo-saxonne" la sensibilité et le système des images baudelairiens, en privilégiant, du côté français, l'exigence de "clarté" et le travail sur la forme (cf. l'emploi révélateur de la formule: "filologičeskoe gurmanstvo"). Ceci conduit Gumilev à définir précisément – peut-être trop précisément – la place de Baudelaire dans la poésie française du XIXème siècle. Certes, en faisant la conquête d'un nouveau territoire poétique, Baudelaire est fidèle au génie de son siècle et même, plus profondément, à la vocation de la poésie selon Gumilev (cf. les images de la conquête et de l'exploration géographique). Mais les phrases citées par Gumilev de la préface aux *Fleurs du Mal*(8) ont une nuance de défi sarcastique, sensible dans l'ensemble du texte, à l'adresse du public confondant morale et littérature, et ne définissent nullement le projet baudelairien dans sa totalité. La seconde citation sur les rapports entre poésie et musique(9) vise à parfaire l'image d'un poète voué au culte de la forme, quitte à négliger la dimension métaphysique de son projet.(10)

Le souci est donc évident de présenter Baudelaire exclusivement dans ses rapports avec le matériau poétique qu'est la langue, et telle est bien la signification du rapprochement opéré avec Gautier et Verlaine. Si Baudelaire n'est pas exclusivement un poète de la forme, c'est en vertu d'un principe général, "pour la simple raison que de tels poètes n'existent pas ni ne peuvent exister".(11) Mais dans cette unité du fond et de la forme, la forme commande le fond, et Gumilev n'est pas loin de déduire la thématique baudelairienne de particularités formelles; de même le goût de Baudelaire pour un vocabulaire mêlé s'explique par son intérêt linguistique pour le latin vulgaire.(12) La distinction entre moi biographique et moi du poète, ainsi que la notion de "masque" relèvent du même souci.

Quel que soit l'intérêt de cette approche, en quelque sorte formaliste, pour la connaissance de Gumilev, elle rend difficilement compte de l'originalité de Baudelaire. Romantique, Baudelaire ne peut l'être que dans un sens large d'appartenance à une génération.(13) Son culte de la forme en fait un parnassien, et Gumilev a, fort logiquement, une certain difficulté à le dissocier du Parnasse:

> Для парнассцев он был слишком нервен, слишком причудлив, и он говорит не столько о вещах мира, сколько о вызываемых ими ощущениях.(14)

Cette dernière formule, pourtant proche de définitions courantes du symbolisme,(15) ne suffit pas à faire de Baudelaire un symboliste:

> ... Ни ощущения многопланности бытия, ни желанья дать почувствовать за словами абсолютное у него не было.(16)

On peut penser que cette interprétation assez conservatrice(17) prive Baudelaire de ce qui fait sa voix propre pour le lecteur contemporain. En ce sens Gumilev se montre meilleur critique de Baudelaire dans ses admirables traductions. Mais, plus que jamais dans la tragédie historique de la Russie d'après-guerre, le modèle reste pour Gumilev le poète qui par la maîtrise du vers domine la vie - son époque, la condition humaine - dans un effort où l'union forme/fond est aussi une union de l'éthique et de l'esthétique.

Ces pages sur Baudelaire montrent la permanence des valeurs "parnassiennes" dans le système de références de Gumilev critique. Mais cette permanence elle-même, et avec elle celle de la poésie et de la littérature françaises, ne s'explique que par le rôle qu'elle joue dans le système de la réflexion théorique de Gumilev. A cet égard le fameux manifeste "Nasledie simvolizma i akmeizm" constitue un bon exemple: certes, la tradition française y est interprétée avec une certaine approximation historique,(18) mais il est d'autant plus clair que la place qu'elle occupe est éminente parce qu'exemplaire, et exemplaire parce que s'insérant dans un système d'oppositions (symbolisme français opposé aux symbolismes allemand et russe) qui a valeur fondatrice pour l'acméisme. Gumilev se sert de la littérature française pour créer, par un système de références souple, son propre espace culturel, et la filiation toute idéale qu'il instaure avec la tradition française - définie par des qualités au fond universelles - lui permet sans sacrifier son indépendance d'affirmer l'originalité acméiste. En ce sens les choix du critique ne font que refléter la stratégie du poète théoricien, toujours liée au contexte de la vie littéraire russe.

NOTES

1. Du seul point de vue de l'histoire littéraire, G.Struve mentionne quelques lacunes de notre information concernant la première période ("Tvorčeskij put' Gumileva" *in* N.Gumilev *Sobranie sočinenij*, 4 volumes, Washington 1962-1968, t.II, pp.vi-vii. Ci-dessous: Gumilev, *Sobr. soč.*)

2. Gumilev, *Sobr. soč.*, t.IV, pp.384-386. Noter que la suggestion de Gumilev de considérer Vigny comme un symboliste est assez originale (en dépit ou à cause de l'usage rhétorique des symboles chez Vigny) et qu'elle peut avoir été empruntée à J.Moréas, cité dans le même texte ("... pour suivre l'exacte filiation de la nouvelle école, il faudrait remonter jusques à certains poèmes d'Alfred de Vigny, jusques à Shakespeare ...") *Le Figaro*, 18 Sept. 1886 (d'après J.Moréas, *Les premières armes du symbolisme*, M.Pakenham édit., University of Exeter, 1973).

3. Cf. l'usage que fait Gumilev de typologies a-historiques (typologies de tempéraments individuels : ainsi Brjusov, dans le même texte, est un classique "éternel", ou encore typologies nationales).

4. Gumilev, *Sobr. soč.*, t.IV, pp.386-387.

5. *Ibidem*, p.388.

6. *Ibidem*, p.387.

7. Publiée par S.Graham *in Le Messager. Vestnik russkogo xristianskogo dviženija*, 144, Paris,

I-II, 1985. (Ci-dessous: *Vestnik*).

8. Voir le texte de Baudelaire: "Des poètes illustres s'étaient partagé ..." dans Charles Baudelaire, *Oeuvres complètes* en 3 vol., édit. Yves Florenne, Paris, Club du livre, t.I, 1966, p.1024. (Ci-dessous *Baudelaire*).

9. *Ibidem*, p.1026: "Comment, par une série d'efforts déterminée, l'artiste peut s'élever à une originalité proportionelle..."

10. Il est caractéristique, par exemple, que Gumilev ait omis la phrase suivante: "[la phrase poétique] peut monter à pic *vers le ciel*, sans essoufflement, ou descendre perpendiculairement *vers l'enfer* avec la vélocité de toute pesanteur". (C'est nous qui soulignons. *Baudelaire*, p.1026.).

11. *Vestnik*, 157.

12. *Ibidem*. Il y a là sans doute une allusion à la note des *Fleurs de Mal*: "Franciscae meae laudes", qui est une analyse du latin de l'antiquité tardive comme reflet de la spiritualité de l'époque. Le point de vue de Baudelaire est donc en fait inverse de celui de Gumilev. (Cf. *Baudelaire*, p.1031).

13. C'est le sens de l'apparente contradiction du texte entre: "ego po spravedlivosti pričisljajut k romantikam" (*Vestnik*, 154) et plus loin: "... dlja togo, čtoby byt' romantikom, emu ne xvatilo ..." (*ibidem*, 158).

14. *Vestnik*, 158.

15. Elle est proche, notamment, de la définition, au reste banale, donnée par Gumilev lui-même: "... on [simvolizm] javilsja sledstviem zrelosti

čeloveceskogo duxa, provozglasivšego, čto mir est' naše predstavlenie" (Gumilev, *Sobr. soč.*, t.IV, p.170).

16. *Vestnik*, 158.

17. C'est à certains égards celle de Sainte-Beuve. Noter que Gumilev oppose bien rapidement Baudelaire à Claudel qui l'admire, et, plus généralement, à l'"esprit du temps". Les réflexions de Proust sur Baudelaire dans ce qui sera le *Contre Sainte-Beuve* précèdent d'une bonne dizaine d'années la préface de Gumilev.

СКРЫТОЕ ПРИСТУСТВИЕ Н. ГУМИЛЕВА В *ПОЭМЕ БЕЗ ГЕРОЯ* А. АХМАТОВОЙ

ИННА ЧЕЧЕЛЬНИЦКАЯ

> И ведаю, что обо мне далеком
> Звенит Ахматовой сиренный стих.
> Н.Гумилев, 1915

К периоду 40-х годов, кроме создания *Реквиема* и *Поэмы без героя*, также относятся статьи Ахматовой о Пушкине, которые своим стилем приближаются к "ахматовской прозе"(1) и, во многом, перекликаются с ее поэмами и стихотворными циклами тех лет. Эти годы были одним из плодотворных периодов творчества Ахматовой, время творческих поисков и прозаических "автопризнаний": "Стихи раскрывают поэта в глубинных пластах, а автопризнания касаются жизненных установок, взглядов, вкусов, тяготений. Они служат биографическим ключом...".(2)

Заглядывая в "творческую лабораторию" Пушкина, Ахматова не только находила ответ на вопросы, волновавшие ее, но и разгадывала его трагическую судьбу, узнавая в ней судьбу своих героев и свою собственную (статья "Невское взморье"). Для того, чтобы понять психологический импульс создания, Ахматова, пользуясь методом "образной системы",(3) сопоставляет известные календарные события в жизни Пушкина и его произведения.(4) Постижение Ахматовой "тайнописи" Пушкина - это и оправдание собственного метода "криптограммы", "зеркального письма", "симпатических чернил", на которые она "набрела", "чудом", в своей Поэме.(5) Страшась очередных упреков, она ссылается на Пушкина, на тайну его созданий, на его подтекст, доказывая тем самым возможность соединения жизненной тайны и "тайнописи" как творческого метода.(6) Особенно, это заметно в ее пушкинских статьях, в которых поражает насколько то, что она говорит о Пушкине, приложимо к ее собственному творчеству: "Проза тогда (1830) была новым способом выражения для Пушкина, и ему в ней было почему-то (говорю так пока, и отчасти по собственному опыту) удобнее произвести свое замечательное, беспримерное заклинание судьбы. (Даже трудно это как-то иначе назвать.)"(7)

Этим "автопризнанием" Ахматова сама дает нам право изучения ее "творческой лаборатории", ее "тайнописи", ее прозы, сознавая, что это приведет к расшифровке не только текстов, но и раскроет тайну жизненных взаимоотношений, ставших импульсом создания тех или иных строк *Поэмы без героя*, то-есть "проза... вернет нам стихи обновленными и как бы увиденными в ряде волшебных зеркал".(8)

В связи с изучением роли Николая Гумилева в творчестве Анны Ахматовой, я хотела бы обратить внимание исследователей на возможный ключ или один из возможных подходов к этой теме, - через ахматовские статьи к ее стихам. Там мы находим не только перекличку двух поэтов, но и направление мысли, внутреннего психологического замысла, наконец, причину создания того или иного стихотворения, цикла стихов, которые в свою очередь приведут нас к *Поэме без героя*, где мы можем проследить гумилевский слой или, как назвала это Ахматова, "линию отсутствующего героя".(9)

Одно из ее последних, известных нам обращений к творчеству Пушкина можно считать статью "Пушкин и Невское взморье" (1963).(10) Своей статьей Ахматова не только заставила пушкинистов взлянуть по-новому на произведения Пушкина 30-х годов, но и сопоставила строки различных произведений этой последекабристской поры с ею найденными документами, подтверждающими его скрытую тайну - поиски могилы декабристов. "Невероятно, - пишет Ахматова - чтобы Пушкин в первый раз, когда он был в Петербурге сразу после казни ... не искал место могил на Невском взморье."(11) Установив, что в произведениях Пушкина той поры речь идет о "безымянной могиле" декабристов,(12) Ахматова раскрывает свою собственную тайну — поиски могилы расстрелянного поэта —, нечаянно обмолвившись о том, что "часто там бывала", а также, что знает историю этого места неслучайно. Сопоставив воспоминания друзей Ахматовой и ее произведения 20-х годов, находим ответ или объяснение ее прогулок по местам, которые затем были тщательно описаны в статье.

Однако, вернемся к датам, к которым у Ахматовой было особое пристрастие. Дата, число, — для Ахматовой это и символический день памяти — "поминальные даты" — и обозначение неназванного героя; дата раскрывает героя, день встречи или разлуки с ним; дата — это и указатель времени, для стихов; возвращение к дате — это возвращение к памятному событию, которое всегда связано с близким человеком или героем Поэмы. Играя порой с датами, поэт дает читателю ключ как к Поэме, так и к отдельным произведениям прошлого.

Каждое посвящение в Поэме имеет свою дату: памятный день разлуки или невстречи с героем. Первое: годовщина дня смерти О.Мандельштама.(13) Второе: символический день смерти Ольги Глебовой-Судейкиной.(14) Третье: день разлуки с "героем будущего"(15) и, наконец, последнее, которое я предлагаю рассматривать, как своеобразное четвертое посвящение Николаю Степановичу Гумилеву, с датой его смерти, 25 августа: Вступление к Поэме.(16) Эта часть Поэмы никогда, в течение многих лет работы и различных добавлений, не изменялась. Кроме того Первое посвящение, Первая часть ("1913 год") и Вступление относятся к первоначальному замыслу и символически все три части связаны одним, сороковым, годом. Можно предположить (а даты позволяют нам это сделать), что год сороковой был годом памяти по погибшим, или "панихидой",(17) и что в их честь Автор зажигает "заветные свечи" и обращается к памяти близких. А через 23 года после того, как она рассказала миру в своей Поэме о поэтах и о своем трагическом поколении, она гасит "заветные свечи" и, подводя итоги, прощается со своими героями, и уже Поэма и ее даты становятся в свою очередь Памятью. Чтобы доказать, какое место в Поэме занимает Осип Мандельштам, я уже воспользовалась сопоставлением дат Поэмы и стихотворения "Через 23 года".(18) Поэтическая перекличка поэтов еще раз подтвердила значение Дат. В настоящей работе приведу лишь тексты, которые подтверждают возможность использования этого метода и для доказательства "линии Гумилева" в *Поэме без героя* (курсив здесь и в дальнейшем мой - И.Ч.):

Я зажгла заветные свечи,
Чтобы этот светился вечер,
И с тобою, ко мне не пришедшим,
Сорок первый встречаю год... (58-61)

Поэма без героя (1940)

Осип Мандельштам, "В Петербурге мы сойдемся снова..." (1920):

Что ж, гаси, пожалуй, наши свечи,
В черном бархате всемирной пустоты...

Анна Ахматова, "Через 23 года" (13 мая 1963):

Я гашу те заветные свечи,
Мой окончен волшебный вечер...

Напомним, что в первых редакциях Поэмы первая часть начиналась строками, к которым мы уже обращались: "я зажгла заветные свечи", и заканчивалась: "'я к смерти готов'".(19) Последней фразой этой части, при помощи самого автора, а именно - в ее воспоминаниях, был обнаружен "слой Мандельштама",(20) который автор долгое время сохранял на "втором дне шкатулки".(21) В тех же воспоминаниях о Мандельштаме Ахматова пишет: "В 1925 году ... в Царском Селе я жила с Мандельштамами ... Там он диктовал мне свои воспоминания о Гумилеве."(22) Воспоминания Мандельштама о Гумилеве остались неизвестны, но движущей силой создания Поэмы были, возможно, и эти воспоминания. Тем самым мысли Мандельштама и его память о Гумилеве дали право Ахматовой соединить, слить эти два образа в Поэме.(23)

Этих трех людей объединяло внутреннее единство, которое Мандельштам вкладывал в значение "наши свечи" и его "Мы". В это "Мы" входила группа людей, центральной фигурой которой являлся Н.Гумилев. С его смертью группа распалась, а дружба Ахматовой с Мандельштамом, возобновившаяся в середине 1920-х годов, сохраняла старое единение, и в нем всегда присутствовал Гумилев, с которым велся воображаемый разговор. Мандельштама, - вспоминает Надежда Яковлевна, - "не оставляла ностальгическая тоска по этому 'Мы', в которое входила и одна женщина - Ахматова."(24)

Отметим, как неожиданно Ахматова в своих воспоминаниях о Мандельштаме приводит одно единственное письмо Мандельштама к ней. В письме он еще раз признается в своей верности этому "Мы": "Дорогая Анна Андреевна, ... Хочется домой, хочется видеть Вас. Знайте, что я обладаю способностью вести воображаемую беседу только с двумя людьми: с Николаем Степановичем и с Вами ..."(25) Письмо это было написано к годовщине смерти Николая Степановича Гумилева, 25 августа 1928 года. С этой датой связаны и многие произведения Ахматовой, написанные в 1921 году, в цикле стихов *Anno Domini*: "Пока не свалюсь под забором..." (30 август 1921), "Чугунная ограда, сосновая кровать..." (27 август 1921), "Долгим взглядом твоим истомленная..." (25 август 1921), и, наконец, "Пророчешь, горькая, и руки уронила..." (27 августа 1921). Не случайно в своих воспоминаниях Ахматова приводит письма Мандельштама о Гумилеве; это ни что иное, как намеренное сопоставление двух имен,(26) неразрывная связь с которыми "не прерывалась" до конца жизни Ахматовой, всегда сохранявшей преданность "заветным свечам", заветным страницам, оставленным ей с сознанием того, что она будет той, кто сохранит память о них, так как она была "последняя из тех, кого он [Мандельштам] включал в это 'Мы'".(27) В разные годы, обращаясь к Ахматовой, ее герои с надеждой говорили, "Сохрани меня, моя царица" (Гумилев), "Сохрани мою речь навсегда за привкус несчастья и дыма..." (Мандельштам).(28) И ответом на их мольбу, возможно, звучит ее *Поэма без героя*; а даты, связанные с их гибелью - 27 декабря [1940] и 25 август [1941], - и, как мы заметили выше, 13 мая, и, как мы увидим, 3 августа - становятся символическими и несут тот трагизм, которым пропитано ее творчество. Эти даты стали своеобразным тонким трагическим "узнаванием"(29) ее героев в Поэме. Одним из таких "узнаваний" Гумилева, через Дату, и является Вступление к Поэме, а дантовское звучание ниже приведенных строк можно отнести к тому же разряду поэтической перелкички поэтов, которое отмечалось выше, в связи со "слоем" Мандельштама:

> Из года сорокового
> Как с башни, на все гляжу.
> Как будто прощаюсь снова
> С тем, с чем давно простилась,
> Как будто перекрестилась
> И под темные своды схожу.
>
> 25 августа 1941
> Осажденный Ленинград

Ср. у Н.Гумилева:

> Они ликуют, эти звери,
> А между них, потупя взгляд,
> Изгнанник бедный, Алигьери
> Стопой неспешной сходит в Ад.
>
> Флоренция, 1912(30)

Необходимо обратить внимание на первые варианты Поэмы, где Вступление имеет подзаголовок *Набат*, выделенный курсивом в некоторых рукописных редакциях самим автором.(31) Возможно, уместно именно здесь привести строки известного пророческого гумилевского "Мужик" (1916), где слышен тот же предупреждающий "набат": "Над потрясенной столицей/ Выстрелы, крики, *набат...*"(32) Нельзя не учесть также важное совпадение строк Вступления - "Как с башни на все гляжу" - в Поэме и в повести Шелли "Ченчи" - "I see as from a tower the end of all".(33) Та же тема - начало конца - будет повторена Ахматовой через двадцать лет в "Царскосельской оде" ("И тому переулку приходит конец..."), датированной 3 августа 1961 - то есть, написанная в памятную годовщину ареста Гумилева, ровно через сорок лет после трагического события, с которым, как мы увидим, связана ее статья "Пушкин и Невское взморье".

Как уже отмечалось выше, обращение Ахматовой к поискам Пушкиным "безымянных" могил декабристов перекликается не только с ее собственной судьбой, но и с идеей Поэмы. Пушкину "не надо было их вспоминать: он просто не забывал ни живых, ни мертвых"; она знает, что он не мог не начать поиски "места их погребения".(34) Слухи о могилах казненных посылали его на остров Голодай;(35) еще раз, с упорством, Ахматова повторяет: "Я не допускаю мысли, чтоб место их погребения было для него безразлично."(36) В этом видит она причину посещения Пушкиным заброшенного острова "за Невой", а затем, очень подробно, описывает место, которое указано в пушкинском "Домике":

> Кроме Голодая на взморье много мелких островков. На них действительно сидят морские птицы - чайки, утки; сушатся рыбачьи сети, иногда догнивает дырявая лодка, чернеют следы костров. Так во всяком случае, было *в начале XX века, когда я часто там бывала.*(37)

Частое посещение этого заброшенного места за Невой, о котором говорит Ахматова, давая пространное обозначение - "в начале XX века", и есть та самая тайна, которая скрывается и в стихах и в Поэме. В 1921 году Ахматова, как бы от имени друга, рассскрывает причину своих частых прогулок:

> Я с тобой, мой ангел, не лукавил,
> Как же вышло, что тебя оставил
> За себя заложницей в неволе
> Всей земной непоправимой боли?
> Под мостами полыньи дымятся,
> Над кострами искры золотятся,
> Грузный ветер окаянно воет,
> И шальная пуля за Невою
> Ищет сердце бедное твое.
> И, одна в дому оледенелом,
> Белая лежишь в сияньи белом,
> Славя имя горькое мое.
>
> 7 декабря 1921, Петербург(38)

Эти слова могли быть обращены только к одному человеку, тому, кто оставил ее вдовою, кого "шальная пуля", как она думала тогда, нашла "за Невою", и чью могилу она разыскивала там, где Пушкин разыскивал могилы казненных. Именно тогда, "сразу после казни", слухи о могиле казненного посылали ее на остров Голодай. В воспоминаниях вдовы Осипа Мандельштама мы находим то, что скрыто в статье о Пушкине: "Хорошо жить в маленькой стране, где можно громко заявить о своем праве и выкрасть запретное мертвое тело, а не бродить, *как Пушкин*, а потом *мы втроем с Ахматовой по острову Голодаю* и странным рощам под Петербургом, *куда молва посылала нас в поисках могилы расстрелянного поэта*."(39)

Это воспоминание раскрывает для нас не только адресата вышеприведенного стихотворения Ахматовой 1921 года, но и причину посещения ею этого острова; ведь и "вдова" одного из декабристов (Рылеева) "точно знала место могилы",(40) утверждает Ахматова в статье; но сама она только через девять лет узнала настоящее место казни Гумилева. Причина обращения Пушкина к памяти казненных декабристов — в его вере в "высокое верование античности в то, что могила праведника — сокровище страны и благословение богов".(41) Ахматова находит в пушкинских произведениях примеры, подтверждающие как его тайную мысль, так и тему, скрытую в *Поэме без героя*. Примеры из пушкинских произведений еще раз подтверждают ее мысль: Дуня приезжает на могилу станционного смотрителя; "Марья Ивановна перед отъездом из крепости идет проститься с могилами родителей (*Капитанская дочка*)"; "Татьяна говорит, что готова отдать 'всю ветошь маскарада' ... за смиренное кладбище."(42) Явно обращаясь к своей современности, утверждая вслед за Пушкиным, что могилы праведников — "сокровище страны",(43) Ахматова говорит, что этим он (Пушкин) "несомненно, горько попрекает Николая I, который не только не вернул родным тела казненных декабристов, но велел закопать их на каком-то пустыре".(44)

Как верный друг, вдова, сестра, подобно Антигоне, борется она за право похоронить "милого брата". Можно сказать, что ей, как и Пушкину, "безымянная могила на Невском взморье должна была казаться ... собственной могилой".(45) Именно эта трагическая тайна — "обнаженная нетерпимость страдания ..., стон",(46) который она почувствовала у Пушкина, и был ее собственный, а поэтому, найдя причину, она смогла определить импульс, движущий Пушкиным в создании таких стихов как "Домик" (1828), "Когда порой воспоминанье ..." (1830), "Петербургская повесть" ("Медный всадник") 1833, — где он в последних строках хоронит своего героя "ради Бога".

Также "трижды"(47) возвращается Ахматова к "безымянной могиле" расстрелянного: в 1921 году в *Anno Domini* ("сразу после казни"); в последний период творчества в 60-е годы; и в сороковые годы в своей "Петербургской повести",(48) где кроме Дат есть еще Числа, несущие в себе все тот же знак, дающий при сопоставлении событий прошлого и настоящего Таинственную Дату. Это также один из приемов, использованных Ахматовой для создания "криптограммы". Числа требуют подсчета или отсчета, как и даты. Одно такое число запрятано в последние строки "Решки" с датой *5 января 1941*:

> А твоей двусмысленной славе,
> *Двадцать лет* лежавшей в канаве,
> Я еще не так послужу,
> Мы с тобой еще попируем,

> И я царским моим поцелуем
> Злую полночь твою награжу.

Отсчитывая от Даты двадцать лет, мы получаем ту же "незабвенную дату"(49) - 1921; эти строки, как и Число, уже не напоминание, не обращение к его Памяти, как во Вступлении, в них чувствуется некая торжествующая и величественная легкость, может быть, потому, что они стали ответом на незаслуженное недоверие ее верности, - ведь Гумилев, обращаясь к своей жене, в тяжелый год перед разлукой (разводом), поведал ей и о своем будущем:

> И не узнаешь никогда ты,
> Чтоб не мутила взор тревога,
> В какой болотине проклятой
> Моя окончилась дорога.
>
> "Прощенье", 1917(50)

Но его вдова, начавшая свои поиски "сразу после казни" на Невском взморье, все же нашла его "безымянную могилу":

> - Я про Колю знаю, - ответила Анна Андреевна. - Их расстреляли близ Бернгардовки, по Ирининской дороге. У одних знакомых была прачка, а у той дочь - следователь. Она, то есть прачка, им рассказала и даже место указала со слов дочери. Туда пошли сразу, и была видна земля, утоптанная сапогами. А я узнала через 9 лет и туда поехала. Поляна: кривая маленькая сосна; рядом другая, мощная, но с вывороченными корнями. Это и была стенка. Земля запала, понизилась, потому что там не насыпали могил. Ямы. Две братские ямы на 60 человек. Когда я туда приехала, всюду росли высокие белые цветы. Я рвала их и думала: "другие приносят на могилу цветы, а я

> их с могилы срываю"... Приговоренных
> везли на ветхом грузовике, везли долго,
> грузовик останавливался.(51)

Вопреки пророчеству Гумилева, она нашла его могилу и рассказала о ней в Поэме, справила панихиду в годовщину его смерти, через двадцать лет.

Но не только Датой и Числом пристутствует Гумилев в Поэме, строки его стихов и посланий стали для автора знаками памяти.

Обратимся к одному стихотворению Ахматовой, написанному через *сорок* календарных дней и возвращающему нас к тем же событиям 1921 года: "Царскосельская ода" (3 августа 1961), с подзаголовком "Девятисотые годы":

> Настоящую оду
> Нашептало... Постой,
> Царскосельскую одурь
> Прячу в ящик пустой,
> В роковую шкатулку,
> В кипарисный ларец,
> А тому переулку
> Наступает конец...(52)

Это стихотворение не имеет посвящения, но эпиграфом к нему служит строка из стихотворения Гумилева "Заблудившийся трамвай" (1921): "А *в переулке* забор дощатый...". Этот эпиграф, как и дату стихотворения, можно считать своеобразным Посвящением. Уже первые строки оды возвращают читателя к прошлому, а отклик автора к герою или его обращение к нему начинается, как и обращение в первой главе к главному герою: "*Постой*,/ Царскосельскую одурь/ Прячу в ящик пустой... (Ср. *Поэму без героя*: "Постой,/ Ты как будто не значишься..." [156-157]).(53) Следующая строка оды уже прямой ответ-перикличка с Гумилевым: "А тому переулку/ Наступает конец...". Как и стихотворение "Через 23 года", так и Поэма и ода связаны с Памятью о роковых днях и посвящаются тем, на кого указывают даты. Значение "роковой шкатулки" Ахматова раскрывает в своей статье о "Каменном госте"

Пушкина, где она пишет: "... как глубоко Пушкин запрятал свое томление по счастью, своеобразное заклинание судьбы, и в этом кроется мысль, - говорит Ахматова, в очередной раз прикрываясь именем Пушкина, как надежным заслоном, и раскрывает свою собственную тайну, - *так люди не найдут, не будут обсуждать, что невыносимо... спрятать в ящик с двойным, нет, с тройным дном*".(54) (Ср.: "И смущенье свое не прячу... /У шкатулки ж тройное дно" [Поэма, 570-571].)(55) Ахматова предупреждает читателя, в то же время подсказывая "подтекст": "дно", "шкатулка", "ящик". Втайне надеясь на поиски, указывает направление, которое приводит нас к оде, к Дате и, наконец, к "заветному месту" прошлого, - "призрачному" миру юности или к эпохе сказочного "Великана-кирасира",(56) т.е. к эпохе 90-х годов - времени царствования Александра III-го; иными словами, это "первый (нижний) пласт" памяти,(57) то есть, ее царскосельская юность и все, что с этим периодом связано. Сплетение времен: 90-е годы, первое десятилетие XX века, *Кипарисовый ларец* Анненского(58) - все это ассоциативно соединяет память о Царском, о юности, а тем самым о Гумилеве.

В своих комментариях Э.Герштейн отмечает один из методов ахматовского исследования: соединив элегическое послание Пушкина ("Царское село", 1819 года) и последнюю царскосельскую сцену *Капитанской дочки*,(59) Ахматова нашла "заветное место" Пушкина в Царском селе, и "это - определяет Герштейн, - дает Ахматовой ключ к истолкованию автобиографических мотивов в историческом повествовании".(60) Повидимому пушкинское царскосельское "заветное место" - в дворцовом саду: "Марья Ивановна ... пошла в сад ["Царское Село" - "Под липовые сени"]. Солнце освещало вершины лип, пожетлевших уже под свежим дыханием осени ["Царское село" - "и дряхлый пух дерев..."]. Широкое озеро сияло неподвижно ["Царское село" - "и в тихом озере ... Станицу гордую спокойных лебедей"] ... лебеди важно выплывали ... Марья Иванова пошла около прекрасного луга ["Царское село" - "Да вновь увижу я ковры густых лугов..."]." Предположим, что именно таким переплетением текстов нашла Ахматова "заветное место" Пушкина, но в этих поисках она пользуется своей собственной памятью, у которой есть свое "заветное место", в том же Царском. Э.Герштейн в комментариях о художественном методе Ахматовой обращает наше внимание на строки в "Автобиографии" и строки Поэмы, считая прозаическую заметку художественным импульсом к строкам Поэмы.(61) Заранее соглашаясь с исследователем, и использовав вышеприведенный метод переплетения текстов, мы обращаемся к тем же царскосельским строкам Поэмы, которые должны привести к месту переходящему, как у Пушкина, из одного произведения в другое, из прошлого в настоящее. Обратим внимание на лирическое отступление в третьей главе Поэмы, где автор ведет нас "Камероновой Галереей/ В... таинственный *сад* ... там за *островом*, там за садом/ Разве мы не встретимся взглядом/ Наших прежних ясных очей ..." (428-435) ... А теперь бы *домой* скорее ..."(427).(62) Если Пушкин восклицает в своей элегии "веди, веди меня под липовые сени...", то стремление Автора Поэмы "домой" - в Царское, к тому месту, которое стало ее "заветным местом", в Дом "в переулке", "с дощатым забором", о котором вспоминает Ахматова и в своей автобиографической прозе: "По одной стороне этого переулка домов не было, а тянулся очень ветхий некрашенный *дощатый забор*."(63) В сороковые годы в царскосельских стихах те же мотивы и регалии ахматовского "заветного места", которые затем вошли в "шкатулку" "Царскосельской оды". В них запрятана тема героя Поэмы, и при этом каждое стихотворение имеет пушкинский знак-эпиграф или нераскрытую цитату. Некоторые из них относятся к периоду создания "Поэмы без героя": "Ива" (1940), с эпиграфом из пушкинского "Царского села",(64) также "Мне ни к чему одические рати..." из цикла "Тайны ремесла" (1940), где роль пушкинского эпиграфа несет вторая строка: "И прелесть элегических затей...."(65)

В 1961 году "дощатый забор" в Оде становится эпиграфом из гумилевского "Заблудившегося трамвая" (1921),(66) где одна из тем, как и у Ахматовой, - тема "заветного места" - перекликается с пушкинской повестью *Капитанская дочка*. Сходство тем повести и поэмы Гумилева было впервые отмечено в комментариях Г.Струве, определившего связь строк "Заблудившегося трамвая" с известным эпизодом в повести Пушкина.(66) Эта близость не могла быть незамеченной Ахматовой, включившейся в эту перекличку поэтов. Тема последних глав повести и строки "Заблудившегося трамвая" стали скрытыми темами ее творчества и вошли как в Оду, так и в Поэму, где поэтические регалии имеют биографическую основу.(67) В *Капитанской дочке* Машенька Миронова - невеста арестованного государственного преступника, просящая о милосердии. Гринев "не изменник", при этом, "*не был свидетелем событий*", другими словами, отсутствовал, не был свидетелем страданий и унижений любимой, но как бы "*невидимо присутствовал*".(68) (Напомним, что "линией отсутствующего героя" назвала Ахматова слой Гумилева в Поэме.) То же "невидимое присутствие" мы находим в поэме Гумилева, где повествование, как и у Пушкина, идет от лица героя, возвращающегося в своих воспоминаниях к "заветному месту" в Царском: "А в переулке забор дощатый,/ Дом в три окна и серый газон...", к невстрече с своей возлюбленной: "Машенька, ты здесь жила и пела...", "ты стонала в своей светлице... Я же ... не увиделся вновь с тобой". В "Заблудившемся трамвае", как и в Поэме и в Оде, историческое прошлое переплетается с настоящим, с воспоминаниями юности, со звуками и "с чувствами разных временных слоев".(69) "Царскосельская ода" 1961 года, как книга с шифровкой, вместила в себя знаки прошлого: девяностые годы или "баснословные года", которыми Ахматова обозначает время своей юности. Это знак царскосельского прошлого, ставший знаковым эпиграфом ко всему гумилевскому циклу 1921-го года;(70) через двадцать лет переходит в Поэму, но уже как двойной знак - царскосельский и гумилевский - открывает тему заключительных строк "Решки": "Вовсе нет у меня родословной/ Кроме солнечной и баснословной,/ И привел меня сам Июль" (605-607). В двух предшествующих строках мы находим предполагаемый ответ Блоку.(71) Такое соседство двух поэтов не впервые в творчестве Ахматовой; то же можно сказать и об *Anno Domini*. Может быть, соседство их поминальных дней (август 1921), или их могил, дало право на близкое расположение строк в Поэме.

Указания на заветные места - т.е. тайные опознавательные знаки поэмы - составляют добавочный пласт произведения; например, дом в Безымянном переулке, где "у дощатого забора" росли сорняки.(72) Этот знак известен только посвященным, то есть тем или тому, кто может понять значение эпиграфа к Оде. Это место - условное обозначение переклички Автора Поэмы и ее героя.

А в *переулке* забор дощатый,
Дом в три окна и серый газон...

"Заблудившийся трамвай", август, 1921

А веселое слово - *дома* -
Никому теперь не знакомо.

Поэма без героя, Эпилог (668-669), 1941-42

А тому *переулку*
Наступает конец.

"Царскосельская Ода", 3 август 1961

Итак, в Поэме Ахматова возвращается к прошлому, к своим героям, справляет панихиду в "поминальный день" - 25 августа - по казненному. А, разыскав его могилу, переносит ее силой своего поэтического слова и глубокой верности назад в Царское, где на могиле, по православному обычаю, справляет тризну: "Пили допоздна водку, /Заедали кутьей..." (ведь и могила Блока была перенесена на Волково кладбище, назад в Питер: см. Эпилог, 555-557).

А в Поэме автор спускается к могилам умерших, как в подземную часовню или место погребения христианских мучеников (kryptē):

> из года сорокового,
> как с башни, на все гляжу.
> Как будто прощаюсь снова
> с тем, с чем давно простилась,
> как будто перекрестилась
> и под темные своды схожу.

> 25 августа 1941

Отслужив панихиду, она торжественно отмечает святое место знаками Памяти, известными только посвященным (эпитеты, числа, даты):

> А твоей двусмысленной славе,
> Двадцать лет лежавшей в канаве,
> Я еще не так послужу,
> Мы с тобой еще попируем,
> И я царским моим поцелуем
> Злую полночь твою награжу.

> 5 января 1941

Через двадцать лет, боясь, что осталось немного тех, кто сможет разгадать тайный смысл (kryptos) *Поэмы без героя*, а значит найти святое место погребения, она вкладывает знаки "криптограммы" в "Царскосельскую оду" 1961 года, надеясь, что знаки, прежде разбросанные в стихах и в прозе, приведут к "заветному месту":

> А теперь бы домой скорее
> Камероновой Галереей
> В ледяной таинственный сад,
> . . . .
> Там за островом, там за садом
> Разве мы не встретимся взглядом
> Наших прежних ясных очей ...

Все это дает нам право наметить три части Поэмы, обращенные к памяти Гумилева: Вступление, с датой 25 августа 1941, строки "Решки", с числом двадцать и перекличкой с произведениями Гумилева, указывающие на ту же дату - 1941 год, и, наконец, лирическое отступление с царскосельским мотивом и "заветным местом" юности.(73) Все при части, по своему расположению и своими темами, находятся как бы вне повествования или, лучше сказать, за чертой "Петербургской повести", но, несмотря на это, дают нам возможность дальнейшего поиска "линии Гумилева" в центральной канве Поэмы.

Своим внимательным отношением к биографии Пушкина, к событиям его жизни, отраженным как в прозе, так и в поэзии, Ахматова открыла для читателей свой творческий метод. Она еще раз утвердила читателя в возможности соединения биографии Поэта и его поэзии. Атрибуты жизни или быта, даты и числа, частички воспоминаний, статьи и письма, если они остались, черновики, если они сохранились, могут раскрыть самые глубинные пласты биографии поэта и помочь в поисках ключа к поэтическому наследию. Возможность использования исследовательского метода Ахматовой, в применении к ее собственной судьбе и ее поэзии, открывает те невидимые, намеренно скрытые слои, из которых составлена *Поэма без героя*. Путь, намеченный Ахматовой в ее исследовательской работе, приведет к раскрытию ее "творческой лаборатории". Недаром, заключая статью "'Каменный гость' Пушкина", она с некоторой долей надежды пишет: "самопризнания ... незаметны и обнаружить их можно лишь в результате тщательного анализа".(74) Эти слова не оправдание своего подхода к исследованию, а "автопризнание" поэта, доверяющего своему читателю.

П Р И М Е Ч А Н И Я

1. Э.Г.Герштейн. Послесловие в книге: *Ахматова о Пушкине*, Л., 1977, 284. В дальнейшем: *Ахматова о Пушкине*.

2. Н.Я.Мандельштам. *Вторая книга*, Париж, 1972. В дальнейшем: *Вторая книга*.

3. *Ахматова о Пушкине*, 286.

4. Статья "Болдинская осень (8-ая глава 'Онегина')", там же, 185. См. также эпиграф к Третьему Посвящению в Поэме, о встрече с адресатом посвящения, в книге: Л.К.Чуковская. *Записки об Анне Ахматовой*, Париж, 1980, т.2, 171. В дальнейшем: *Записки*.

5. Анна Ахматова. *Поэма без героя*. В сборнике: *Стихотворения и поэмы*, Л., 1977, 373, 430. В дальнейшем: *Стихотворения*.

6. В этом также проявляется несогласие с Блоком, ответ на его упрек об "уравнении с десятью неизвестными". А.С.Блок, *Собрание сочинений в 8-и томах*, М-Л, 1960-1965, т.8, 459. Поэма во многом упрямый спор с Блоком; об этом в моей диссертации "*Поэма без героя*" *Анны Ахматовой*, Brown University, 1982.

7. *Ахматова о Пушкине*, 260.

8. там же, 222.

9. Р.Д.Тименчик, В.Н.Топоров, Т.Г.Цивьян. "Ахматова и Кузмин", *Russian Literature*, №6, 1978, 300. В этой работе авторами было найдено впервые большое количество реминисценций творчества Гумилева в *Поэме без героя*. В дальнейшем: "Ахматова и Кузмин".

10. Статья впервые опубликована в юбилейном журнале *Прометей*, №10, М., 1974, 226-234.

11. *Ахматова о Пушкине*, 258.

12. Там же, 158.

13. В связи с последними исследованиями, эта дата, 27 декабря, связанная с именем О.Мандельштама, не вызывает более споров у исследователей *П.б.г.*

14. Примечание В.Жирмунского к *П.б.г.* в кн. *Стихотворения*, 513. О.Глебова-Судейкина родилась 27 мая 1887 [?] года в Ярославле, умерла 20 января 1945 года в Париже. Возможно, Ахматова намеренно соединила даты рождения-смерти в своем Посвящении.

15. Amanda Haight *Anna Akhmatova. A Poetic Pilgrimage*, New York-London, 1976, 168.

16. Несмотря на различные воспоминания современников, для Ахматовой даты: арест Гумилева, 3 августа, и расстрел, 25 августа 1921 г., никогда не изменялись, что легко проследить по ее воспоминаниям.
   а) В первых редакциях Поэмы дата была неполная (см. *Стихотворения*, 432). (25 августа появилось только в издании 60-х гг.)
   б) Б.Филиппов, говоря о "панихиде на сороковой день", также отмечает, что Вступление написано не в сороковом календарном году, а *25 августа сорок первого года* (выделено Б.Филипповым). В этом, по словам автора, замечена "Магия Чисел". В кн.Анна Ахматова. *Сочинения*, Мюнхен, 1968, т.2. 86, а также Б.Филиппов, *Статьи о литературе*, Лондон, 1981, 122.

17. *Стихотворения*, 307-308. Впервые опубликовано В.Жирмунским по рукописи (ЦГАЛИ) с примечанием: "Варьируется с началом 'Поэмы без героя'." Там же, 501.

18. Воспоминания о Мандельштаме в кн. *Сочинения*, 181: "13-го мая 1934 года его арестовали. В этот самый день я приехала к Мандельштамам." О месте Мандельштама в Поэме см. в моей диссертации (см. прим. 6).

19. Первые редакции *П.б.г.* в кн. *Стихотворения*, 431-442; а также в кн.: Анна Ахматова *Стихи, переписка, воспоминания, иконография*, Анн Арбор, 1977, 52-72.

20. Amanda Haight. Указ. соч., 152.

21. "[У шкатулки] двойное дно" заменено на "тройное дно". Запись от 20 апреля 1960 года. Л.Чуковская, *Записки*, т.2, 309.

22. *Сочинения*, т.2, 176.

23. Нельзя не согласиться с авторами статьи "Ахматова и Кузмин" (см. прим. 9), где рассматривается возможное сплетение двух образов в Поэме (Мандельштам и Гумилев) как и "склеивание" (Гумилев и Князев): "Пары связаны не только 'сходством' и 'дружбой', но и 'противоположностью...'"; с.254.

24. Н.Я.Мандельштам. *Вторая книга*, 66.

25. Листки из дневника, в сборнике: *Сочинения*, 177-178.

26. Отметим соединение (Мандельштам и Гумилев) в прозе Марины Цветаевой, "История одного посвящения", 1931, в кн.: Марина Цветаева, *Избранная проза в 2-х томах*, Нью-Йорк, 1979, т.1, 351-352.

27. Н.Мандельштам, *Вторая книга*, 66.

28. Н.Гумилев, "Ангел боли", 1917-1918 в кн.: Н.Гумилев. *Собрание сочинений в 4-х томах*, под редакцией Г.П.Струве и Б.А.Филиппова, Вашингтон, 1964, т.2, 170-171. О.Мандельштам с посвящением А.Ахматовой, 1931 г., в кн.: О.Мандельштам. *Сочинения в 2-х томах*, под редакцией Г.П.Струве и Б.А.Филиппова, Вашингтон, 1964-66, т.1, 154. В дальнейшем тексты по этим изданиям.

29. Мандельштамовское значение "узнаванья" (*Tristia*, 1918) я предлагаю ввести как необходимый термин при расшифровке *П.б.г.*

30. Н.Гумилев. *Собрание сочинений*, т.2, 131.

31. Ранняя редакция Поэмы, подаренная автором Н.Я.Мандельштам в Ташкенте; в кн.: Анна Ахматова. *Стихи, переписка*, 57.

32. Указ. соч., т.2, 13.

33. "Ахматова и Кузмин", 298.

34. *Ахматова о Пушкине*, 152.

35. "Северная оконечность Васильевского острова"; там же, 152.

36. там же, 154.

37. там же, 257. Курсив мой. В черновиках Ахматовой найдена запись рассказа Н.Лернера в книге: *Каторга и ссылка*, 1931 (*Ахматова о Пушкине*, 258), подтверждающая версию Ахматовой о поисках Пушкиным могилы декабристов уже в 1828 году. К сожалению нам неизвестна дата черновых набросков, но известны воспоминания Н.Я.Мандельштам, где она пишет, что "в период ежовщины" Ахматова "только и читала *Ссылку и каторгу* Ключевского". (Н.Я.Мандельштам. *Воспоминания*, Нью-Йорк, 1970, 259); мы можем предположить, что в те же годы Ахматова обратилась и к записям Н.Лернера, в книге с идентичным названием, а значит, что начало работы над статьей относится к 30-ым годам, периоду создания "Реквиема" и началом работы над *П.б.г.* (1937-1940), а не к 60-ым. В связи с этой темой см. также: "Вдали виднелось смоленское кладбище... за кладбищем был известный курганчик над телами казненных декабристов... на острове Голодае" - из книги, изданной в 1926 году - в предисловии к упом. статье Э.Г.Герштейн, *Прометей*, 219.

38. *Стихотворения*, 150.

39. *Вторая книга*, 165. Курсив мой. Западная часть Васильевского острова "была заболоченной, заросшей кустарником. Она получила название Смоленское кладбище... позднее это поле служило местом казней". *Путеводитель по Ленинграду*, Л., 1957, 328.

40. *Ахматова о Пушкине*, 152.

41. *Ахматова о Пушкине*, 156.

42. там же, 156.

43. там же, 156. Ту же мысль о "Доме Поэмы" - доме святого праведника - Ахматова повторит в "Античной страничке" (1961), а также в "Слове о Пушкине" (1961).

44. *Ахматова о Пушкине*, 154.

45. там же, 158.

46. там же, 151.

47. там же, 157.

48. Подзаголовок *П.б.г.* "Петербургская повесть" появилась в 60-е годы, то есть, в одно время с работой над статьей. Р.Д.Тименчик, А.В.Лавров. "Материалы А.А.Ахматовой в рукописком отделе Пушкинского дома", *Ежегодник рукописного отдела Пушкинского дома на 1974 год*, 1975, 78.

49. "Опять подошли 'незабвенные даты'..." *Стихотворения*, 260.

50. Указ. соч., т.2, 162.

51. Л.Чуковская, *Записки*, т.2, 432.

52. *Стихотворения*, 262.

53. В черновиках Ахматовой; из книги Н.Лернера, касающаяся небольшого черного ящика, в котором хранились пять щепок от пяти виселиц декабристов, собранные Пушкиным в одну из прогулок "за Невой". *Прометей*, 225.

54. Из записок 1957 года в сборнике: Анна Ахматова. *Стихи и проза*, Л., 1976, 548. В дальнейшем: *Стихи*.

55. Строка появилась только в 1955 году, как сообщает Л.Чуковская в своих *Записках* (т.2, 96); в редакция 40-х годов было: "У шкатулки двойное дно".

56. Автопризнание в кн. Л.Чуковской, *Записки*, 399.

57. *Стихотворения*, 507.

58. См. комментарии к оде В. Жирмунского в кн. *Стихотворения*, 432.

59. А.С.Пушкин. *Полное собрание сочинений в 10-и томах*, М., 1964. "Царское село" (1819), т.1, 371; *Капитанская дочка* (1833), т.6, 535-536.

60. *Ахматова о Пушкине*, 311.

61. там же, 314.

62. Символическое значение "Дома" в поэзии Ахматовой уже в ранние периоды ее творчества рассматривается как символ внутреннего одиночества Поэта в кн.: Sam Driver. *Anna Akhmatova*, New York, 1972, 66-69. Ср. также "И, раз проснувшись, видим, что забыли/ Мы даже путь в тот *дом уединенный*... ("Есть три эпохи у воспоминаний...")

63. *Стихотворения*, 492.

64. "Самоповторения" Пушкина замечены Ахматовой в ее ранних работах. См. статью "Заметки Ахматовой о Пушкине" Э.Герштейн, В.Вацуро, *Временник Пушкинской комиссии*, 1970. Л., 1972, 38. В примечаниях В.Жирмунского (*Стихотворения*, 478) даны воспоминания или автокомментарии к *дому*: он "летом ... зарастал сорняками - репейником, ... крапивой, лопухами; об этом я сказала в 40 г., вспоминая пушкинский 'ветхий пук дерев'"; имеется в виду все то же пушкинское "Царское село" 1819 года, доработанное им в 1823 г., в ссылке.

65. *Евгений Онегин*, глава 6, XLIV: "Без элегических затей/ Весна моих промчалась дней..."; т.5, 138. Можно предположить, что Ахматова пользуется пушкинской цитатой в тексте как определенным указателем темы; см. тоже в ее Посвящении к "Реквиему" - "каторжные норы" "тюремные затворы", обращающие читателя к "Посланию в Сибирь" Пушкина, ассоциативно переходящее к женам ссыльных ("невольные подруги") - центральной теме "Реквиема".

66. Н.Гумилев, т.2, 48-50.

67. В 60-е годы Ахматова записывает суждения первых читателей Поэмы, в данном случае замечание М.А.Зенкевича: "Слово акмеистическое, с твердо очерченными границами. По фантастике близко к 'Заблудившемуся трамваю'". Р.Д.Тименчик, А.В.Лавров, "Материалы", 76.

68. А.С.Пушкин, т.6, 532.

69. *Ахматова о Пушкине*, 314.

70. Впервые с этим эпиграфом в сб. *Бег времени*; см. *Стихотворения*, 471. Напомним важный для Ахматовой факт: "Тютчев умер в Царском". ("Из рукописного наследия А.А.Ахматовой", публикация А.Л.Мандрыкиной, *Нева*, №6, 1979, 197. (См.

также: "В разговоре Ахматова обмолвилась: 'У нас в России у всех память баснословная'." Н.Струве, "Восемь часов с Анной Ахматовой" в кн. *Сочинения*, т.2, 333.

71. Соседство строк можно объяснить и соседством дат смерти и соседством могил. А.Блок был похоронен на Смоленском кладбище 10 августа 1921 года. См. "А Смоленская нынче именинница..." (10 авг. 1921) из цикла *Anno Domini*. *Стихотворения*, 171.

72. "Семья Горенко в самом начале девятисотых годов жила на углу Широкой ул. и Безымянного переулка" примечание В.Жирмунского, *Стихотворения*, 171.

73. Мои предположения не отрицают прежде исследователями признанного склеивания (Гумилев и Недоброво) в этом лирическом отступлении.

74. *Сочинения*, т.2, 274.

"DUŠA I TELO" AS A PARADIGM OF GUMILEV'S MYSTICAL POETRY

RAOUL ESHELMAN

Introduction

"Duša i telo", the fourth poem in Gumilev's *Ognennyj stolp*, his last and most important book of poetry, belongs to a larger group of poems expressing a mystical world view, among them "Zabludivšijsja tramvaj", "Šestoe čuvstvo", "Pamjat'", "P'janyj derviš", "Slovo", "Estestvo" and many others.(1) These poems are mystical because they not only express piety or religious sentiment, but are also concerned with the notion of experiencing Godliness immanently in some way - whether in the form of a vision ("Duša i telo", "Zabludivšijsja tramvaj"), in an eschatological apprehension of reunion with God ("Šestoe čuvstvo", "Pamjat'"), in the form of a drunken ecstasy ("P'janyj derviš") or through the Word, the absolute expression of God's will and authority ("Slovo", "Estestvo"). Taken together, they form a mystical world view which draws its inspiration and ethical guidelines solely from the inner, spiritual world, a world which knows only one higher authority - that of God. In doing so, Gumilev participates in and extends a tradition going back to Neoplatonic philosophy and rooted in the Christian and Islamic Middle Ages: in this tradition, the individual attempts to reach God through a regimen of purification, concentration and, in certain cases, through the visionary experiencing of the Godhead.(2)

This study seeks to demonstrate the importance of this mystical world view using one of Gumilev's most striking poems - the curious dialogical "triptych", "Duša i telo".

Although "Duša i telo" is indeed exemplary of the mystical attitude which is characteristic of the late poems, it does not "stand for" the whole of Gumilev's mystical world view or somehow represent it in microcosm. Rather, it is a discrete whole contiguous to others within his late work; it is a speculative postulate in the form of a poem. In general, Gumilev's world view can be said to consist of such heterogeneous postulates which, although sharing certain common elements, remain as discrete units within his greater system of thought. For this reason it is useless to reduce his religious or mystical poetry to one set of themes or motifs that would "unite" these wholes in a satisfactory way. As a whole (or, more precisely, as a set of wholes) Gumilev's mystical poetry exemplifies the tension between the striving for unity and the limited means that man - who for Gumilev exists in a fragmented, catachretic world - has of achieving it.

"Duša i telo" consists of a curious ontological dialogue between the soul, the body and a lyrical persona. The lyrical persona addresses the soul and asks it to answer the (implicitly stated) question as to what it is. To this the soul replies with a self-descriptive soliloquy. The persona then turns to the body and asks it to reply to the soul. Here, too, the body "answers" by describing its own condition. Finally, as the "word of God shines from the heights in the form of *Ursa major*", the soul turns back to the lyrical persona (the "interlocutor") and asks who *he* is. The persona answers by identifying himself as an entity that is diffused throughout the cosmos and infinitely superior to body and soul, which are described as the "faint reflection of a dream running along the bottom of his consciousness". The identity of this third entity, which is apparently capable of transcending the opposition between body and soul, represents the most puzzling aspect of the poem.

While it is possible to find many individual structural elements that recur in other poems (the antinomic semantic structures, the theme of sensual male vs. indifferent female, references to Nordic mythology, apocalyptic allusions, etc.) it is difficult to correlate these motifs systematically with other poems: they are all subordinated, it would seem, to the unique postulate set forth in "Duša i telo" - namely that the traditional body and soul opposition can be resolved by this enigmatic third force. As is often the case with Gumilev's poetry, we must pay scrupulous attention to both the individual details of the poem and to its sources in speculative thought before further conclusions can be made.

The Tradition of Disputes between Body and Soul

One can make the peculiar nature of Gumilev's poem clearer by comparing it to the medieval tradition of dialogues between body and soul. This thematic sub-genre of the poetic dispute or *Streitgedicht* was widespread in the Middle Ages (and also in the Baroque) and there exist a great number of poems on the subject in almost all European languages.(3) Since the majority of these can be traced back to a single Latin poem, it should suffice to outline briefly the argumentation contained in this original text.

The poem, which is often titled "Visio Philiberti",(4) takes the form of a vision in which the lyrical persona sees how his soul, which has departed his body after his death, returns to the body to castigate it for its misdeeds in life:

> Noctis sub silentio tempore brumali
> Deditus quodammodo sompno spirituali
> Corpus carens video spiritu vitali
> De quo mihi visio fit sub forma tali.

(In the silence of a winter's night/ While given somehow to a spiritual dream/ I saw the body losing its vital spirit/ And a vision about this came over me.)

The soul excoriates the body's exploitative, materialistic ways while it was alive and asks sardonically:

> Ubi nunc sunt praedia quae tu congregasti?
> Celasque palatia, turres quas fundasti?
> Gemmae, torques, anuli, quos digito portasti?
> Et nummorum copia quam nimis amasti?

(Where is the booty now which you amassed?/And where are the high palaces and towers which you built?/ The gems, the necklaces, the rings that you wore on your fingers?/ And the heaps of money that you loved so much?)

Now that the body is dead - says the soul- these material possessions are no longer of any use to it: "Now you are food for the worms: such is divine might;/ Such is the ruin awaiting sinners like you!" After the soul has finished with its list of the body's sins, the body replies using the following, equally convincing logic:

> Ergo si tu domina creata fuisti,
> Et dabatur ratio, per quam debuisti
> Nos in mundo regere, cur mihi favisti
> In rebus illicitis, et non restitisti?

(Thus when you were created mistress/ And given reason, through which you were supposed/ To rule us in this world, why did you favor me/ In my illicit doings instead of trying to resist me?)

The rest of the poem (which is almost 100 quatrains long) repeats these diatribes in colourful detail, with neither body nor soul able to convince the other of its superiority. After initially assuming an intransigent posture, both, however, concede a certain truth to the other's arguments and in the end arrive at a common, bitter conclusion - namely that both will suffer eternal damnation for the sins they have committed in life. As the body puts it: "And I know, moreover, that I will arise/On the Day of Judgement and with you will endure/ Perpetual torments: O death so cruel,/ Death interminable, death without end!"

The medieval poem is above all addressed to the dualist (and also heretical) assumption that body and soul are wholly separate entities bearing separate responsibility for their actions. However, this potentially dangerous speculative problem is defused by recourse to the dogmatic logic of Christian eschatology: because both parties have sinned together, both will have to account for it later in hell. What is important for our purposes is that the original dualism is rendered void by the introduction of a third, transcendent principle based on the dogmatic logic of Christianity: the poem refutes the heretical notion that the immortal soul is superior to the mortal body, that the soul is a divine spark and the body an evil shell holding it prisoner. It is this aspect of the poem that is of the most importance for Gumilev, who, as I wish to show further on, argues in a similar way against the dualistic "heresy" propagated by his Symbolist predecessors like Belyj and Blok.

Formal and Semantic Aspects

From the general structure of Gumilev's poem it is evident that he was familiar with the traditional genre of body and soul disputes, even if "Duša i telo" does not directly quote "Visio Philiberti" or other poems in this tradition.(5) In the following analysis, in addition to treating the formal and semantic elements of "Duša i telo", I wish above all to show how Gumilev fills out the medieval dispute with peculiar elements of his own world view and how he "resolves" the dualistic quandary of the body and soul dispute by recourse to mystical tradition.

In formal terms, "Duša i telo" does not contain any unusual technical features. The meter is iambic pentameter, a relatively neutral verse form often found in Russian philosophical poetry. The number of realized stresses in each line varies for the most part between three and four, with some five-stressed lines. This creates a balanced rhythm which is neither monotonous nor conspicuous. Similarly, most sentences correspond precisely to the length of the stanzas and stay grammatically in close conjunction with line length. In general, one can say that the metric scheme and rhythmic structure of the poem are subordinate to the exposition of the various positions taken by the three voices. Much the same can also be said about the prosodic make-up of the poem, which is orchestrated primarily through the careful use of assonance and alliteration, i.e., through the repetition of discrete sounds with an emphatic intent, for example:

    Безумная, я бросила мой дом...

    К какому каторжник прикован цепью...

These accumulated euphonic repetitions, however, remain confined to one line or sometimes pairs of lines:

    Я пьяно, будто близится гроза,
    Иль будто пью я воду ключевую...

Here a whole series of phonological repetitions, built primarily around "a" and "u" as well as "p," "b" and "v" (ja, p'ja, bu, bli, ra, za/Il', bu, p'ju, ja, va, du, lju, vu) create a certain euphonic interference (*paromoiosis*) that emphasizes in iconic fashion the ecstatic state about which the body is speaking. The phonological (and formal) scheme of the poem thus works to emphasize certain words or phrases, but does not associate words having similar formal aspects but different semantic meanings. In fact, throughout the poem we are faced with precisely the contrary phenomenon, namely that entire words are repeated for emphasis; the repetition of sounds is due to the repetition of identical or morphologically related words (polyptoton) that do not provide us with "new" information. This tendency towards lexical repetition dominates our attention much more than does the alliteration and assonance noted above:

> А *ты, душа, ты* все-таки молчишь,
> Помилуй, Боже, мраморные *души*...
>
> Которая туманит *вновь* и *вновь*...
>
> То есть *горе*, мой надежный щит,
> Холодное, презрительное *горе*...
>
> И *тело мне* ответило *мое*,
> Простое *тело*, но с горячей кровью...
>
> Не *знаю* я, *что* значит бытие,
> Хотя и *знаю*, *что* зовут любовью...
>
> С *вопрос*ом, - кто же *вопрошатель*, ты?...
>
> Ужели вам допрашивать *меня*,...
> *Меня*, кому единое мгновенье...
> [...]
>
> - *Меня*, кто словно древо Игдразиль...
>
> *Поля* земные и *поля* блаженных...
>
> А *вы, вы* только слабый отсвет сна...

These insistent lexical repetitions (I have counted seventeen in all) are not only typical of Gumilev's ornamental or "rhetorical" style, but also have an added iconic function: they suggest the "doubleness" and tedium of existence — *taedium* of course also being the immediate rhetorical effect caused by such repetitive figures.

Following Boris Ejxenbaum, Denis Mickiewicz has called this general type of semantics "intensive".(6) Intensive semantics (in opposition to the "extensive" semantics of Symbolism or Romanticism, which creates a fluid web of sounds associating semantically different words with one another) creates a "lumpy" or heterogeneous texture in which such sound associations are avoided and in which lexical (or, one might add, accumulated cultural) meaning is allowed to dominate.

While this distinction cannot be reviewed in detail here, it does have far-reaching implications for both poetic interpretation and theory. This is because it implies two fundamentally different modes of producing meaning, depending on whether meaning is guided primarily by the association between lower-level text signs (i.e., equivalence relationships between the formal or sub-semantic elements of the text) or whether the "higher" levels of the text (allegorical constructs, argument, theme) are dominant. This second state of affairs - which would appear to be a necessary consequence of intensive semantics - is of crucial importance for understanding Gumilev, for whom the most important unit of the text is not the paradigmatic recombination of sign parts (semes or formal elements of the sign) but rather the syntagmatic alignment of complex semantic units (phrases, images, themes, myths) in the text.(7) In other words, Gumilev returns to a pre-Romantic, rhetorical mode of creating meaning that stresses theme and argumentation over metaphor and association and that is similar in its techniques to (pre-modern) emblematical or allegorical poetry. This problem will be treated later when I turn to the question of Gumilev's emblematical imagery and allegorically structured argumentation, which are both of crucial importance for "deciphering" his poetic message.

Imagery, Allegory and Theme

The formal-functional aspects of Gumilev's poem are, as noted above, of secondary importance for interpreting its greater meaning. Instead, the text's main semantic potential is provided by the syntagmatic combination of its imagery and the speculative background of the main arguments. Since the basic tripartite "structure" of the text is already given by Gumilev, I will examine its three elements consecutively in order to preserve the sequentiality of Gumilev's argumentation.

The Soul

The opening lines of the poem ("Over the city flows nocturnal silence/ And every rustle is dampened") place "Duša i telo" in the tradition of "nocturnal" speculative poetry, in which the conventional (daytime) rules of the world are suspended in favor of visionary poetic imagination. Although this visionary ambience of nighttime and silence is traditional (it can, for example, also be found in the first line of "Visio Philiberti"), Gumilev's reference to the "city" as an artificial construct created by man may go back to the opening lines of Tjutčev's "Bessonica":

> Ночной порой в пустыне городской
> Есть час один, проникнутый тоской,
> Когда на целый город ночь сошла
> И всюду водворилась мгла... (8)

In accordance with mystical tradition, the "nocturnal silence" which "flows over the city" represents the objective external condition necessary for a visionary state: the mystic is in this sense not solely an agent striving towards God but also the passive recipient of a divine message or experience which is revealed to him in the *unio mystica*, in the temporary mystical union with God.(9)

It is thus all the more significant that in spite of these favorable conditions the soul - which is normally the center of spirituality - does not react and must be brought to speak: "And you, soul, you nonetheless remain silent./ Have mercy, God, on marble souls." At first glance, the soul's answer to the implicit question posed by the persona consists of an obscure allegory ("Out of my mind, I left my house,/ Striving for another grandeur") and of mythopoeical elements common to Gumilev's figure of the cold and indifferent female ("Oh, I hated love", "...Sorrow is my reliable shield,/ Cold, contemptuous sorrow"). From the very beginning the poem thus presents us with an allegorical puzzle which is based not so much on the relatively "clear" semantic paradigms which compose it ("coldness", "sorrow", "spirituality", "immortality", etc), but on the unknown quality of the story (the metaphorical syntagm or allegory) related by the soul. In other words, the difficulty that the poem creates for us is not caused by the interplay of formal equivalences and the semantic and thematic paradigms based on them, but rather by the "crossing up" of the paradigmatic elements of the poem by a complex and (as we shall soon see) esoteric syntagm or allegory. In this way clarity and obscurity coexist in Gumilev's poetry.

The soul's monologue would appear to be based on the gnostic myth of Sophia and her fall from the spiritual domain into the material world. As the "Prekrasnaja dama" (among other names for her) Sophia is of course a central fixture of Symbolist poetry, and it is precisely this Symbolist notion of Sophia that Gumilev seeks to relativize. To be more specific, the first stanza of "Duša i telo" is an intertextual paraphrase of one of Blok's poems on the *Prekrasnaja dama* ("Ja ždu prizyva, išču otveta...")(10) which also plays on the question and answer theme: in Blok's poem the persona searches in vain for an answer to his (implicit) question about the meaning of life. The relevant stanza in Blok's poem is as follows:

> Я жду – и трепет объемлет новый
> Все ярче небо, молчанье глуше...
> Ночную тайну разрушит слово...
> Помилуй, Боже, ночные души!

There can be little doubt that this is a direct citation: Gumilev not only paraphrases the last line, but also uses the rhyme "gluše/duši". At the same time, it is also clear that Gumilev's intent runs counter to that of the original: he both reverses the situation (it is nighttime instead of just before daybreak, as in Blok's poem) and replaces "nocturnal" with "marble". Thus, whereas in Blok's poem the "nocturnal secret" will be "destroyed by a word", the external conditions in Gumilev's poem are ideal; similarly, the searching "nocturnal soul" of Blok becomes the spiritually frigid "marble" soul. As I will show in more detail, the notion of Sophia as used by Gumilev is a conscious revision and relativization of the Symbolist Sophia and the dualist philosophy that she represents. In the process, Gumilev harks back not to the Symbolist reworking of the Sophia myth but to the gnostic "original", which among other things serves to diminish the authority of the Symbolist concept: his argumentation is not "dialogical" - whereby the "alien" perspective would somehow be preserved - but rather dogmatic and definitive.

The gnostic myth on which the soul's monologue is based could have been derived from any number of sources;(11) however it appears to follow most closely the myth of Sophia as depicted in the so-called Valentinian tradition, which is also one of the best known. Since the myth in question is highly complicated and full of anthropomorphic embellishments I have confined myself to those aspects which are directly pertinent to Gumilev's poem.

The myth begins by assuming the existence of an unknowable, perfect and nameless Father (a deity comparable in scope to the transcendent God of conventional monotheism). The Father projects a thought out of himself which begets a number of secondary deities called Aeons, the youngest of which is Sophia, the Divine Wisdom of God in female form. Taken together, the Aeons make up a divine realm known as the Pleroma, which, although spiritually perfect, is not directly connected to the unknowable Father. In this heavily anthropomorphized myth, the perfection of the Pleroma is disrupted when Sophia is seized by a desire to know the Father, to comprehend his incomprehensible greatness: she tries to duplicate the creative act of the Father by conceiving another Aeon without the help of her male counterpart. The result, however, is a disaster, since as a female hypostasis Sophia can only project matter passively and not form it. The result is a shapeless lump, and Sophia goes out of her mind from passion and sorrow. In the process, the material world is formed out of these passions (grief, fear, bewilderment and ignorance). Consequently, the attitude of gnosticism towards the material world is extremely negative, whereby Sophia, who exists in both the divine and material spheres, acts as a mediator between the divine realm and gnostic or pneumatic man, whose soul (pneuma) is imprisoned in the material world. In the Valentinian myth, Sophia's (and man's) final salvation takes place when all the pneumatic (spiritual) elements in the world have been formed by knowledge and perfected. After this Sophia can reenter the Pleroma, unite in marriage with Jesus (who plays a secondary role) and re-establish the original harmony. The Symbolists, and in particular their spiritual father Vladimir Solov'ev, used this myth as the foundation of their poetic mysticism: the poet-theurge of Symbolism attempts to find the wandering Sophia in order to unite with her in erotic-spiritual union and bring about the perfecting of the world.(12)

There can be little doubt that in Gumilev's poem the soul's self-description is based on the gnostic myth. The soul, like Sophia, is "out of her mind" (*bezumnaja*), and has "left her home" (which may be interpreted as the pleroma) to strive for "another grandeur" (the Father). This precipitates her fall from grace and her indirect or passive participation in the creation of the material world ("And the earth's globe became a ball/ To which the convict was attached with a chain"). The imagery of this last line is of particular interest. Traditional religious imagery (as, for example, in "Visio Philiberti") depicts the soul as being fettered to the body — something which is evidently not the case here: it is not the soul itself, but the "convict" who is chained to the ball of the earth. In terms of the above-mentioned gnostic myth, one could interpret the "convict" as man, who is bound to the material world and awaiting salvation.(13) As in the gnostic myth, Sophia exists both in the macrocosmic and microcosmic spheres: she is not only the World Soul, but also the soul of man who opens her eyes "in the despised human body". The World Soul element returns in the line where the soul states that "the world is foreign to me, but well-formed (*strojnyj*) and beautiful": the World Soul, although a spiritual entity, protects or oversees the natural world (in much the same way as does the Greek goddess Ceres, from whom she is in part derived).

What we are thus dealing with here is a complex catachretic allegory in which the soul is simultaneously depicted as existing on two levels (something which would not be possible in a figural representation). This, in essence, is what is "modern" about Gumilev's allegorical imagery: while suggesting unity it is ultimately always catachretic or internally contradictory (something which is incompatible with traditional instructions for producing successful allegory). For Gumilev, unity is a postulate, but it is not something that can be realized in either the world or in poetry.

It might also be added that nothing in these lines is accidental. Thus, even embellishments like "the distant harps" and the "planetary choir" have precedents in hermetic tradition: visionary states are often described as being accompanied by angelic music or song (the harps being of course an emblem of this) and the planetary choir is a Pythagorean notion that can be found often in speculative literature.(14) These embellishments add to the obscurity of the poem's iamgery by their seemingly unmotivated presence. On the other hand, they have typical attributes of what Angus Fletcher has called *kosmos* (usually translated in Latin rhetoric as *ornatum*): they are not "just" ornamentation but ascribe a particular hierarchical status to the object in question. In this sense they have both a microcosmic function (as ornamentation) and a macrocosmic one, in that they remind us of the higher spiritual status of the soul.(15)

In the soul's monologue, Gumilev returns to the Sophia myth, but in doing so emphasizes elements that relativize her epistemological and eschatological importance - above all by playing up the story of her fall from grace and her "guilt" in the creation of the imperfect material world caused by her hubris and lack of true knowledge. In addition, he also ascribes to her attributes of his own mythopoeic concept of woman, who is invariably depicted as cold and unapproachable.(16)

The Body

Strictly speaking, the body's voice is not esoteric, although it does contain esoteric elements in its self-description. In general terms, the body corresponds in its sensuality and pathos to the lyrical persona used by Gumilev in his earlier love poems (compare, for example, the cycle "K sinej zvezde" as well as earlier poems such as "Dva Adama"). In a certain sense, in "Duša i telo" Gumilev seeks to overcome the mythopoeical antimony of sensuous man and indifferent woman that marked much of his earlier poetry.(17) This antinomy can be reconstructed schematically as follows:

Soul	Body
immortal	mortal
"cold"	"hot-blooded"
rejects love	loving
strives for knowledge	"simple"
passive, defensive	active, outgoing

There are also a number of more specific oppositions worth noting. Whereas the soul is associated with marble, which is traditionally the symbol of immortal art,(18) the body is linked to an alchemical (and once more catachretic)(19) metaphor: "The sunset of gold became as copper,/ The clouds were covered with a green rust." To understand the meaning of this complex catachretic trope, one must reconstruct it in two ways. The first would be to take the initial metaphor as a figural or representational construct: as a description of how the color of clouds changes. In this superficial sense we are dealing with a simile ("sunset of gold is like copper") with metonymical aspects ("copper" = copper color, "green rust" = green color). The catachresis results because there is little or no connotative overlap between "metal" and meteorological phenomena like the sunrise or clouds. The initial simile thus appears unmotivated and perhaps even "unsuccessful". To "understand" it we must turn to a second way of reading which might be called emblematic or allegorical. Here, we are not concerned with associating semes, but rather with relating elements of a complex (syntagmatically organized) trope to a higher or more abstract meaning. This process relies, of course, in part on the immanent message of the text, but also on extratextual codes which provide the missing key to the tropic enigma. In this particular case the code would seem to be that of alchemy. In alchemy, gold stands for perfection, oneness and unity - the ultimate goal of all alchemical striving - with all other metals representing various stages of impurity. What the metallurgical-meteorological simile is actually describing is a process of *debasement*: the transition from pure gold to impure copper stands for the transition from the immortality of the soul to the mortality of man. In addition, the verdigris, the "green rust" of the copper, is not only a physical sign of impurity or debasement but also stands for the love goddess Venus (both copper and green represent her in alchemical tradition). The trope functions not by the reader's associating two connotative semantic paradigms, but rather by his perceiving the emblematical or symbolic(20) status of the elements involved and by reconstructing the syntagmatic argument of the complex trope in which they are contained. The syntagmatic axis is projected on to the paradigmatic axis, and not the other way around.

By contrast with gnostic tradition, the problem posed by "debasement" does not result in a rejection of corporeality. While for Gumilev the ability to love erotically is positive or at least not negative, it would seem to conflict fundamentally with the search for knowledge of man's being: as the soul puts it, love is a sickness that "over and over again clouds the world" (a metonymical way of saying that love causes blindness, which is also expressed by the body in the phrase "When I kiss her clouded eyes"). Man is caught in a double bind: the soul is immortal but cannot love; the body loves but must die because of it. This is also why the body says: "But for everything that I took and that I want [...] I will pay with an irreversible, final death." Finding the solution to this dualist problem is of course the main problem behind "Duša i telo". In his speculative answer, Gumilev tries to "solve" this problem using a combination of both esoteric and orthodox Christian tradition.(21)

A few short observations are in order about the remaining imagery of the body's soliloquy, especially in the third and fourth stanzas. As noted above, these elements describe the body's sensuality and love of freedom in a straightforward way and are for the most part not suggestive of hermetic tradition. Some of these elements, however, are important leitmotifs in Gumilev's poetry as a whole. Thus it would seem that in the context of the late poetry the "falcon's cries" have distinctly eschatological connotations, especially if one considers the very frequent use of words like *kričat'*, *revet'*, *myčan'e*, etc. in other poems:

> Крикну я ... но разве кто поможет, —
> Чтоб моя душа не умерла?
> ("Память")

> Под скальпелем природы и искусства
> Кричит наш дух, изнемогает плоть
> ("Шестое чувство")

> Вот струны-быки и слева и справа
> Рога их — смерть, и мычанье — беда.
> ("У цыган")

These shrill, "natural" cries also represent a semantic counterpart to the heavenly music accompanying the soul's monologue.

Another important element is that of "drunkenness", or, in more abstract terms, of an artificially induced ecstatic state. The body's "drunkenness" is motivated not by alcohol but by love, by the "approach of danger" (here we have the *poet-voin* motif common to much of Gumilev's poetry) and finally (catachretically) by the body drinking "spring water", which connotes purity rather than intoxication. While we cannot deal with these thematic elements in detail here, it should perhaps be noted in passing that their individual motivations are also significant in terms of Gumilev's greater world view: ecstasy is motivated not by a Dionysian desire to flee from the self, to dissolve in the collective, but rather by the desire of the self to "potentiate" itself, to intensify its existing qualities with regard to an outside force: this can occur vis-à-vis woman in love, vis-à-vis the opponent in battle and, if we take the connotations of purity literally, vis-à-vis God in the visionary state.(22) Whereas the first two types of ecstasy can to a certain extent be subsumed under a mythopoeical rubric, the third situation - if we at all accept traditional Christian terminology - can only be described as mysticism, the attempt to know and experience God.

The Third Voice

The idea of a "third" that bridges the gap between two contradictions or oppositions is hardly a new idea: it exists as a literal phrase in the *tertio comparationis* of traditional rhetoric, it appears as the dynamic principle of the world in the Hegelian concept of synthesis, and it can be found as well in the Freudian concept of super-ego. This "third" always has a superior, regulating function in regard to the binary or dualist relations associated with it: in rhetoric it determines the "success" of a metaphor, in Hegelian philosophy it enables the world to develop dynamically and in Freudian psychology it acts as a "judge or censor"(23) for the ego. Since in spite of their archetypal similarity these "thirds" have very different functional implications, it is important to establish to which specific tradition the authoritative third voice of "Duša i telo" belongs.

Let us begin by examining the situation as depicted in the first two stanzas of Part III. In the preceding two sections, the "I" has addressed itself to the soul and body, who answer it but not each other directly; unlike the medieval poem, there is no real dispute or even dialogue between body and soul. In the third section the soul, as the speculative (heretical) faculty of man, turns on the "I" with the question, "Who, interlocutor, are you?" As noted earlier, the gist of the persona's answer is that he is a force suffused throughout the cosmos and time that is infinitely superior to the body and soul, whom he depicts as utterly insignificant. Thus unlike the medieval poem, it is the "I" - an immanent, internal principle rather than a dogmatic, external one - that here offers the solution to the dualist quandary.

Who is this cosmic voice which transcends both body and soul but which is nonetheless not God Himself? Once more, the most fitting - and I believe the only - explanation can be found in mystical or hermetic tradition:(24) Gumilev's answer is neither a psychological nor semantic construct, but the "astral body" originally formulated by Neoplatonic philosophy and indigenous to mystical and esoteric thinking since then.

The concept of the astral body was first developed by Neoplatonist thinkers to bridge the "dualist gulf" between spirit and matter; it represents a "mediating third party independent of soul and body"(25) and is composed of a very fine ethereal substance that envelops both. The astral (or sidereal) body is so named because in Neoplatonic myth

> the soul receives its envelope or vehicle (*ochema*) or "chariot" when passing downwards through the stars and returns it to the latter when after death it retraces its steps to achieve reunion with divinity. It belongs to the stars, it is truly an *astral body*.(26)

In later Western mysticism, the idea was primarily used as a means of explaining visionary states in which a temporary union with God is achieved during life:

> In a later state of "gnostic" development ... the external topology of the ascent through the spheres ... could be "internalized" and find its analogue in a pscyhological technique of inner transformations by which the self, while still in the body, might attain the Absolute as an immanent, if temporary, condition: an ascending scale of mental states replaces the stations of the mythical itinerary. [...] Thus could transcendence be turned into immanence, the whole process become spiritualized and put within the power and the orbit of the subject.(27)

By the same token, the astral body (or its Christian equivalent) also represents the "image of God in man";(28) it is the element that unifies the heterogeneous souls comprising human spirituality. Although the astral body in its mythical form is of course not a part of standard Christian theology, it is interesting to note that the Orthodox Church does acknowledge a trichotomous concept of the soul which is obviously based on the same tradition. As the Russian theologian Vladimir Losskij puts it:

> The difference between the partisans of trichotomy and of dichotomy is in effect simply one of terminology. The dichotomists regard the *nous* [i.e., the "third" element - R.E.] as a superior faculty of the reasonable soul, the faculty by which man enters into communion with God. The human person or hypostasis contains the parts of this natural complex, and finds expression in

the totality of the human being which
exists in it and through it.(29)

Thus, although Gumilev's trichotomous solution to the body and soul dispute is unusual in terms of traditional theology, it is not directly "heretical" in the sense that Symbolist doctrine was; it is, so to speak, on the borderline of the acceptable. This ambiguous balancing between dogma and heresy is something typical of Christian mysticism in general; the mystic attempts to introduce a certain tension into accepted doctrine, to make it more "alive" by "problematizing" it.

The suggestion that Gumilev is referring to the astral body can be substantiated by examining the concrete imagery of Part III of the poem.

It is first of all not accidental that the constellation *Ursa major* (*Bol'šaja medvedica*) is mentioned in the first stanza. In many mythological systems (for example in Greek myth) it is conceived of not as a bear, but as a wagon carrying souls to heaven (as is also the case in gnostic mythology). If we interpret its function symbolically, it could be said that the "word of God" has now taken over this role; Christianity usurps the original mythical function.

The next image of interest is that of the dog howling at the moon, which at first appears entirely unmotivated. Once more, however, if we are familiar with the esoteric code upon which it is based, it can be associated with a specific emblematical meaning, as depicted below:

The image of a dog barking at the moon is a common hermetic symbol of blasphemy and ignorance and can be found both on the Tarot card depicting the moon and in any number of emblem books (the example here is taken from Alciato's well-known work).(30) The dog barks at the moon because he sees his own reflection in it and ascribes himself a transcendent importance that he does not have or deserve - this of course being precisely what the soul (Sophia) does with its query.

By contrast with God, who is an indescribable acosmic principle, the astral body exists both within time (measured on a cosmic scale from the Creation to the Apocalypse) and has a physical "bottom" (across which the "weak reflection of a dream" runs). The same cosmic dimension applies to its eyes, for which the "earthly and sainted fields" are like a speck of dust. Here, the reference to the Nordic World Tree Yggdrasil is an example of Gumilev's mythopoeic eclecticism: Yggdrasil is in effect a natural counterpart of the astral persona.

The imagery of the last stanza is especially interesting because it brings the astral body into very close association with God, or, more properly speaking, with traditional appellations for God. (This is also marked by the shift from the "I" form to the third person singular in the last stanza.) Like God, the astral body is associated with "depth" (mystical tradition often refers to God as the "Abyss") and with namelessness (another Divine characteristic): as an anthropomorphic, suprapersonal cosmic consciousness, it is near to God but not identical with Him. The dualist controversy is thus not so much "resolved" as transcended by this cosmic consciousness, in which body and soul appear as "faint reflections of a dream", as entities which are insignificant from the cosmic perspective of the unifying astral subject. In a sense Gumilev gets to have his cake and eat it too: the dualist quandary is not really "solved" but is shown to be insignificant in the greater scheme of things; Gumilev inserts a quasi-immanent principle between the immanent problem of body and soul and the transcendent principle of God. This technique of mediating between immanence and transcendence is, it might be added, typical for mysticism as a whole, which has as its main goal making the transcendent and otherwise ineffable God of monotheism "knowable" or "experiencable".

Gumilev's technique - at least as exemplified in "Duša i telo" - uses not only mystical content but also assumes a typically mystical stance on the boundary between dogma and heresy. The one missing element - and this element is decisive for most modern secular readers - is that Gumilev does not call himself a "mystic" or use openly mystical terminology in his metalanguage. While this problem cannot be treated here in detail, it should suffice to mention two aspects that I believe kept him from doing so. First, as is well known, the use of "mysticism" as an appellation had been brought into extreme disrepute by the Symbolists, who, as Gumilev himself put it, "fraternized now with mysticism, now with theosophy, now with the occult".(31) Secondly, Gumilev and the Acmeists in general always made a principle out of *not* telling us what they were doing in programmatic terms (*mirooščuščenie* vs. *mirovozzrenie*). For this reason there is no explicit definition of "intertextuality" in Mandel'štam's work and for this reason there is – so I believe – no explicit definition of "mysticism" in Gumilev's. Nonetheless, the problem arises as to how we should read mystical poetry that does not identify itself as such and that demands of the reader an almost impossible erudition.

How is the Reader to Read "Duša i Telo"?

Up to now we have been concerned primarily with what the Germans would call *Produktionsästhetik* (the way that the author constructed the text) and not with the problem of reception, that is, the way that it should or can be read. Unlike Mandel'štam's infectious cultural ludism or Axmatova's intimate poetic snapshots, Gumilev's poem provides little that the reader can identify with culturally or emotionally. Its obscure details can be "understood" only by someone familiar with esoteric tradition, and its abstract, allegorical argumentation provides no room for identification with the author's biography (as is the case with the much more famous "Zabludivšijsja tramvaj", for example). Rather, "Duša i telo" follows in a tradition of didactic and allegorical poetry which, by confronting the reader with an enigma that he must solve, imposes on him a certain inescapable route of interpretation.(32) In other words, there develops a tension between the structuredness of the text, which suggests that there is a logical, unifying explanation behind the text's heterogeneous, enigmatic elements, and the obscurity of the text elements themselves. However, by contrast with allegorical tradition – which calls for a unified resolution – Gumilev is interested in letting this tension remain unresolved or at least in making its resolution extremely difficult (as is the case here). By juxtaposing esoteric obscurity and logical simplicity of construction Gumilev, so to speak, stylizes transcendence as such: a given argument is "understandable" on the basis of its superficial features (since we can understand the general premises of the arguments involved) but remains obscure in regard to its origins or underlying assumptions. As Angus Fletcher has pointed out, one effect of this allegorical type of poetry is to exert a kind of magical force upon the reader, who is entranced by the split between emphatically implied order and extreme, palpable obscurity.(33) This type of writing also demands that the reader subjugate himself entirely to the will of the author-master: since the allegorical solution is unitary, no reading is possible that goes "against the grain". This striving for authority is expressed even more clearly in Gumilev's essays on poetics. Whereas in his article "Čitatel'" Gumilev allows that poetry is a communicative process in which any manner of reader can participate, the only true reader remains the "čitatel'-drug" - a reader who in his disposition and knowledge is almost identical with the author himself. Gumilev's verse is thus deliberately anti-exegetical: because the origins of its imagery and argumentation are not meant to be immediately "understood", this in a certain sense evens out the difference between the simple, "emotional" reader and the more sophisticated (but still "unknowing") one.(34) This anti-exegetical stance runs parallel to a certain Christian attitude towards the Bible, that is, towards divine, transcendent words: they can be "understood" perfectly well at face value but their original divine meaning always remains ineffable.(35)

Summing up, we can say that although "Duša i telo" seems to represent an all-encompassing, definitive argument, its specific theme is not repeated in other poems. In fact, there is nothing at all resembling the solution to "Duša i telo" in Gumilev's other late poems: the argumentation of the poem represents a postulate, a speculative attempt to understand why the world is the way it is and to establish order in a catachretic cosmos; it is itself a monadic part of a greater, catachretically "organized" whole.

It is to be hoped that scholars researching the other aspects of Gumilev's world view will pay more attention to its speculative and mystical aspects as well as to the specific techniques and cultural assumptions that accompany them.

NOTES

1. The poems in *Ognennyj stolp*, which were all written in the period between Gumilev's return from Paris to Russia in 1918 and his death in 1921, are generally thought to mark a turn towards the mystical and the metaphysical not characteristic of Gumilev's previous Acmeist program or practice. For more on this see Gleb Struve's article "Tvorčeskij put' Gumileva" in *Sobranie sočinenij v četyrex tomax*, ed. Gleb Struve and Boris Filippov (1962-1968), II, pp.xxxiv-xxxviii.

2. This tradition, although ascetic and intent on developing inner spirituality, does not rule out acting in the world, and indeed formally demands of its practitioners that they do so. (The Christian tradition of the Middle Ages in fact speaks of a *via contemplativa*, mysticism as such, and an accompanying *via activa*). There is thus no "contradiction" between the outgoing active aspects of Gumilev's poetry and his speculative poetry. For more on Christian mysticism see Cuthbert Butler's *Western Mysticism. The Teaching of Augustine, Gregory and Bernard on Contemplation and the Contemplative Life* (New York, 1966; original 1926).

3. Since the theme was indigenous to medieval culture there is no telling which sources Gumilev might have been familiar with. One Russian study that he might have known is F.Batjuškov's *Spor duši s*

telom v pamjatnikax srednevekovoj literatury. Opyt istoriko-sravnitel'nogo issledovanija (St.Peterburg, 1891). (The specifically Russian folk tradition of body-and-soul disputes as outlined by Batjuškov does not appear to have been a source for Gumilev's poem.) "Visio Philiberti" may even have been familiar to Gumilev in the original, since as a graduate of the classical gymnasium at Carskoe Selo he could not help but know Latin.

4. The version used here is taken from *Poésies populaires latines antérieures au douzième siècle* (Paris, 1843), Edélstand du Méril's classic collection of Latin verse.

5. Among modern poets the body-and-soul tradition was also taken up by W.B.Yeats in his "Dialogue between the Soul and the Self" (1933).

6. "The Acmeist Conception of the Poetic World" in *Russian Language Journal*, Spring 1975 (Supplementary Issue), p.59.

7. One rather interesting aspect of Gumilev's poetry is his (of course, unwitting) anticipation and reversal of the structuralist method championed by Jakobson and Lotman: whereas structuralism of this sort assumes the existence of "hidden" or secondary binary structures within the text that must be analytically reconstructed, recombined and hierarchized to arrive at a thematic resolution (i.e., an interpretation), Gumilev - like all allegorically minded poets - presents this binary structure and its hierarchic resolution already on the text's "surface" or primary thematic level: he in effect does the structuralists' work for them. The poet thus "imposes" an interpretation on the reader - here as in other cases with an ethical or didactic intent.

8. F.I.Tjutčev, *Stixotvorenija. Pis'ma* (M., 1978), p.283.

9. The verb "plyvet" (flows) also implies the notion of a divine emanation approaching the poet (*emanatio* means "flow out of").

10. In A.Blok, *Stixotvorenija. Poemy* (M., 1978), p.14.

11. Gnostic myth could have been accessible to Gumilev either in the "original", i.e., in the anti-heretical writings of the Church Fathers (cf., for example, Irenaeus, *Adversus haeresos* 2, 1-6 or Hippolytus, *Refutatio omnium haeresium* 4, 21-37) or in any number of scholarly or popular writings on the subject. Contrary to its "esoteric" status in popular culture, gnosticism was by the end of the nineteenth century one of the best-researched aspects of early Christianity and Gumilev would have had little trouble finding information on it.

12. For more on the Symbolist version of Sophia see Samuel D.Cioran, *Vladimir Solov'ev and the Knighthood of the Divine Sophia* (Waterloo, 1977), especially the chapter "The Public Solov'ev".

13. The idea of a macrocosmic chaining can be found in a number of estoeric sources, among them the seventeenth-century Englishman Robert Fludd's depiction of the World Soul or *Anima mundi* (another name for Sophia). In this engraving, which is well known, the World Soul is depicted as a naked woman standing on the globe of the world; one hand is shown as being chained to a hand emerging from a cloud (God) and the other holds a monkey on a chain (man, the ape of God). While the imagery is not identical, it does suggest that Gumilev could have used sources similar to it. For more on the World Soul (as

well as for a reproduction of the engraving mentioned above) see Wayne Shumaker's *The Occult Sciences in the Renaissance. A Study in Intellectual Patterns* (Los Angeles, 1972), p.122.

14. For example, the Jewish gnostic Philo speaks of a "seven-stringed lyre corresponding to the choir of the Planets"; *Philo in Ten Volumes* (London, 1929 [Loeb Classical Library]), vol. 1, p.99.

15. Cf. Angus Fletcher, *Allegory. The Theory of a Symbolic Mode* (Ithaca and London, 1964), especially pp.108-120.

16. These attributes are not, as far as I can tell, typical of traditional Sophia myth. For more on Gumilev's own view of male-female relations see Elaine Rusinko, "'K sinej zvezde': Gumilev's Love Poems" in *Russian Language Journal*, 109 (1977), pp.155-66.

17. Cf. Elaine Rusinko's contribution to this volume, in which "Dva Adama" is treated in greater detail.

18. Compare for example typical lines from Gautier such as "Le marbre blanc, chair froide et pâle/ Où vivent les divinités" (in the poem "Symphonie en blanc majeur" in *Emaux et Camées*) or his Neoclassical depiction of statues as symbols of immortal art in the famous "L'art".

19. Catachresis as used here refers to a "defective" or internally contradictory trope, i.e., to one in which the substitution process does not produce the necessary "unity" or semantic overlap called for in traditional rhetoric. Catachresis has been characterized by I.P.Smirnov and I.R.Döring-Smirnov as a basic characteristic of Post-Structuralist consciousness and technique in

general. Cf. their *Očerki po istoričeskoj tipologii kul'tury* (Salzburg, 1982), in particular the chapter "Istoričeskij avangard kak podsistema postsimvolistskoj kul'tury", as well as I.P.Smirnov's article "Kataxreza" in *Russian Literature*, XIX-I, 1986, pp.57-65.

20. These terms are used here in the technical sense of semiotics, i.e., to refer to a fixed, conventional relationship between signifier and signified.

21. Normal Christian theology (and especially Orthodox theology) would in this instance point out that true love is not erotic, but spiritual, and that man's love of God - which is based on belief and not on knowledge - would be the necessary precondition for overcoming death. Gumilev poses the "wrong" question but answers it in the "right" way.

22. In his "P'janyj derviš" (also in *Ognennyj stolp*) Gumilev takes up the tradition of Sufi mysticism in which nearness to God is achieved in an intoxicated state.

23. *Das Vokabular der Psychoanalyse*, ed. J.Laplanche and J.-B.Pontalis (Frankfurt, 1977), p.540.

24. The third voice is not the "word of God" itself, which is carefully distinguished from body, soul and the "I" in stanza one of Part III. (It is, however, interesting to note that through the syntactical construction of the stanza it could appear at first that the "word of God" is posing the question - a situation that through the addition of a further syntagmatic element is revealed as false. This is an iconic depiction of the soul's [false] claim to possess spiritual truth.) Likewise, the persona is not the "unconscious", which even in a very free

interpretation of Freudian terminology cannot be said to be dispersed throughout the universe. Finally, it is not a semantic construct or synthesis: its semantic elements do not correspond in a systematic way to the utterances of body and soul and in fact, instead of reconciling or synthesizing them, it emphasizes their fundamental insignificance.

25. Gershom Scholem, *Von der mystischen Gestalt der Gottheit* (Frankfurt, 1977), p.250.

26. Walter Pagel, "Paracelsus and the Neoplatonic and Gnostic Tradition" in *Ambix*, 1960, vol. VIII, No.3, 128.

27. Hans Jonas, *The Gnostic Religion. The Message of the Alien God and the Beginnings of Christianity* (Boston, 1958), pp.165-66.

28. Vladimir Lossky, *The Mystical Theology of the Eastern Church* (London, 1957), p.127.

29. Losskij, *Mystical Theology*, p.201.

30. Alciato, *Emblemas*, 1549 (reprint Madrid, 1975), p.273. The text to the picture reads as follows: "The dog looks at the moon's globe at night as if if were a mirror/ And, seeing himself, believes that there is another dog in it/ And barks: but in vain, for his voice is dispersed by the winds/ And an unhearing Diana completes her rounds."

31. In his manifesto "Nasledie simvolizma i akmeizm" (1912), *Sobr. soč.*, IV, p.175.

32. This of course squarely contradicts the normative slant of Post-Structuralist criticism, which as a programmatic point calls for us to "read against the grain".

33. *Allegory*, pp.181ff.

34. This explains the contradiction between the simple readers of "Moi čitateli" (who appreciate the gesture and emotive intent of Gumilev's poetry without understanding its technical aspects) and the "Čitatel'-drug" (who, as noted above, is a kind of metonymical extension of the author himself).

35. The reconciliation of the sophisticated and the simple is of course one of the major problems of Christian Bible exegesis. Whereas the gnostics attempted to find the "origin" of words through unbounded, associative interpretation, orthodox Christianity of the Middle Ages developed an exegetical hierarchy (of literal, tropological, allegorical and analogical meaning) which regulated and structured the interpretatory process.

AN AGGRESSIVE IMPERIALIST?
THE CONTROVERSY OVER NIKOLAJ GUMILEV'S WAR POETRY

BEN HELLMAN

The tragic fate of Nikolaj Gumilev has complicated an objective approach to the man and his works. While his execution in 1921 for alleged involvement in an anti-Soviet conspiracy earned him a martyr's crown among Russian émigrés, he has been vilified in the Soviet Union. By the 1930s orthodox Soviet critics had turned him into the Trotsky of Russian literature, a demon figure to whom all possible vices could be attributed.(1)

In both camps special attention was paid to the war period, as Gumilev's activity and poetic output during the years 1914-1918 seemed to confirm the image of the poet that his death established. In émigré circles Gumilev's service at the front was seen as an expression of Russian patriotism, and the war poems were treated as reliable and esthetically valuable testimony of the inspired mood in Russia during the initial stage of the war. In an article with the revealing name "Poet-rycar'" ("The Poet-Knight"), the critic Jurij Nikolaevskij wrote shortly after Gumilev's death: "If our descendants want to learn from poems what the patriotic element of the Russian intelligentsia experienced, they have only to read this remarkable monument, the war poems of Gumilev..."(2) Nikolaevskij's feelings were shared by several other critics,(3) and as late as 1962, when the collected works of Gumilev were published, Professor Gleb Struve was prepared to class these poems among the best Russian poems about war.(4)

In the Soviet Union the official image of Gumilev was shaped in the late 1920s, as a dogmatic Marxist approach was gaining strength in literary criticism. As late as 1925 the minor poet Jurij Verxovskij could still write about Gumilev in a sympathetic tone,(5) but two articles in the RAPP journal *Na literaturnom postu* in 1927(6) and the young communist critic Vladimir Ermilov's book *Za živogo čeloveka v literature* (1928) set the standard for critics to come. It was made clear that Gumilev's ideological and moral position was not to be ignored. By this time the First World War had lost the epithet "The Patriotic War"(7) and was now called "The Imperialistic War" (or even "the imperialistic slaughter" [*bojnja*]), in accordance with the Leninist conception of it. Acceptance of and support for this particular war had been turned into a grave political error instead of an act of patriotism.

For O.Beskin, who wrote the article about Gumilev for *Literaturnaja enciklopedija* in 1930, Gumilev was "an aggressive nobleman", who in connection with the war became "a hundred-per-cent militarist-poet". Giving expression to pre-revolutionary Russian imperialism, Gumilev sang in praise of "the very spirit of the imperialistic slaughter". Beskin saw it as quite logical that the poet should end up among the active enemies of Soviet power.

An influential Soviet study was *Poezija russkogo imperializma* (1935), written by another young Marxist critic, Anatolij Volkov.(8) The conquistadors of Gumilev's early poems were here identified as imperialists. The poem "Turkestanskie generaly" (1912) was said to reveal the dreams the poet nurtured of spreading Russian dominance. During the war Gumilev idealized "the imperialistic slaughter". The critic singled out the poem "Oda d'Annuncio" (1915) for attack, implicitly linking Gumilev with nascent fascism. Volkov was also probably the first to draw attention to the notorious passage in *Zapiski kavalerista*, where Gumilev described his feelings about an unexpected encounter with two German soldiers in the woods. Summing up Gumilev's attitude to the war Volkov attributed to the Acmeist poet the thought that "killing Germans strengthens his bonds with the world";(9) in other words, Gumilev's Acmeist outlook was most fully realised in war.

Gumilev's public image in Soviet criticism was further denigrated by the Leningrad scholar Orest Cexnovicer in his book *Literatura i mirovaja vojna 1914-1918* (1938). Aggression was singled out as the dominant trait in Gumilev's works: "The whole of Gumilev's poetry, starting with the first book, is imbued by the idea of aggression."(10) The poem "Turkestanskie generaly" was duly quoted, as was the already mentioned passage from *Zapiski kavalerista*. Cexnovicer noted that Gumilev compared his feelings when faced with the enemy with the sensations he had experienced when hunting in Africa. Cexnovicer comments: "This is a cynical narrative ..., which in its heartlessness and cruelty is unique even in world-war literature, which has given us many examples of savage misanthropy."(11)

As the image of Gumilev fostered by such critics was so radically contradictory to the view of the outstanding humanity of Russian literature,(12) a natural tendency was to dismiss the writer as an alien in the Russian context. Aleksandr Blok was in this respect an important forerunner. In the article "Bez božestva, bez vdoxnoven'ja" ("Without divinity, without inspiration", 1921) Blok wrote: "In the poems of Gumilev there is something cold and foreign."(13) The statement clearly contained not only an objective description of Gumilev's love of the exotic milieu or his pronounced preference for modern French poetry, but also a moral accusation. A modern Soviet scholar developed Blok's thought: "The poetry of Gumilev ... was remote from national sources and tradition."(14) And this notion is most crudely expressed in the widely used textbook *Russkaja literatura XX veka*: "Hymns to the war and the poeticizing of the seizure of foreign soil have always been alien to great Russian poetry. Nobody in our literature has sung hymns to the war like Gumilev, and this makes him alien to our national culture."(15)

I have tried to show in another connection that this Soviet view of Gumilev and his poetry is greatly distorted.(16) But in Soviet literary criticism we can also discern another peculiar feature. It is not only Gumilev but the whole Acmeist movement which is accused of displaying attitudes foreign to the Russian literary tradition. Volkov's book was a fierce attack on Modernism, seen as an expression of the ideology of the Russian bourgeoisie. Until the war the Acmeists, according to Volkov, cunningly concealed their real aspirations, which, once the war started, turned out to coincide exactly with those of the Russian war ministry.(17) Cexnovicer in his turn asserted that the Acmeists were serving the aims of the Stolypin bloc,(18) and again the modern textbook *Russkaja literatura XX veka* completes the picture: Acmeist poetry, it says, is "an apologia for capitalist reality and the whole policy of Russian imperalism".(19)

The attack is sweeping, but it is not easy to see the connection between Russian early twentieth-century imperialism and writers like Anna Axmatova and Osip Mandel'štam. The *Cex poetov* journal *Giperborej* (1912-13) contains hardly any poetry that could be called nationalistic or even political. It is also curious that the Acmeists are criticized for a period when Acmeism in fact no longer existed as a movement. Its most important volume of poetry had already been published, *Cex poetov* was no longer functioning, and the writers involved were moving in different directions.

How then did the other Acmeists react to the war? First of all, the theme of war is almost non-existent in the poetry of the minor poets like Georgij Narbut, Mixail Zenkevič and Mixail Lozinskij. The war very seldom entered the poetic world of Anna Axmatova and Osip Mandel'štam. For Axmatova the war was a great tragedy that muted the voice of the individual.(20) Mandel'štam saw the world from a more detached point of view, fascinated by the grand-scale events, in poems like "Evropa" ("Europe"), but later clearly protested against the nationalistic fervour and the senseless killing in the poem "Zverinec" ("Menagerie").

That leaves us with a trio of Acmeist writers - Nikolaj Gumilev, Sergej Gorodeckij(21) and Georgij Ivanov. In a sense Gorodeckij and Ivanov can be seen as the cause of Acmeism's bad reputation in the Soviet Union, although criticism is most often focused on Gumilev. A comparison of these poets also helps us to see more clearly Gumilev's unique position in the war context.

In their critical writings of the period 1914-1916 Gorodeckij and Ivanov made a point of identifying Acmeist poetics and world view with the Russian war effort. In an article of 1916, "Poezija, kak iskusstvo" ("Poetry as Art") Gorodeckij described the split in Russian literature before the war, that is, the Acmeist revolt against Symbolism. The Acmeists wanted to replace Symbolist muddle, disorder and undisciplined thinking with clearness, order and craftmanship. While the Symbolists stood for egotism, nihilism and even satanism, the young generation of poets accepted the outer world in all its aspects. Gorodeckij explicitly connected the birth of the Acmeist movement with the forthcoming war: "This poetic mobilisation can boldly be seen as a pattern and a foreboding of the general Russian mobilisation of the year 1914."(22)

In his criticism Gorodeckij showed no indulgence to poets who did not join the joyous, patriotic choir of Russian writers. Much to his dismay young Petrograd poets like Mixail Lozinskij and Georgij Adamovič did not rise to the demands of the time. They wrote, to use Gorodeckij's expression, "poetry for oneself", talented and skilful but marred by estheticism, emptiness and pessimism. Such attitudes were not tolerated in the former *Cex poetov*, Gorodeckij reminded them, and were particularly inappropriate during the Great War. "The immense distances that our country is traversing, all this is a blank space for these clerk-versifiers [*kanceljaristy-stixoplety*]. Poor and blind, they do not see anything except their ink bottle."(23) As positive examples of war poetry Gorodeckij mentioned Georgij Ivanov's collection *Pamjatnik slavy*, and above all Gumilev's *Kolčan*. The theme of war had, according to Gorodeckij, given firmness to Gumilev's poetic voice: "Among the great number of war poems the poems of Gumilev are outstanding for their documentality and feeling of the importance of the actual event."(24)

A recurrent negative notion for both Gumilev and Gorodeckij was "neurasthenia" - nervousness, mental depression and disgust with life. We find it condemned in Gumilev's manifesto of 1913, where it was contrasted with the "forest animal" attitude, and later, in the poem "Moi čitateli", Gumilev took pride in having never offended his readers with "neurasthenia". Gorodeckij used the same word in his criticism as a description of an outmoded attitude to life, and it is also to be found as an important concept in his volume of short stories on the war theme, *Dal'nie molnii* (1916). Over and over again these stories affirm the war's positive influence on the individual, showing how the former neurasthenia and immorality were being replaced by an energetic belief in life and higher values.

As early as 1912 Georgij Ivanov had announced his preparedness for the forthcoming military feats. Deeply stirred by the centennial celebration of the war of 1812, he wrote in the poem "26 avgusta 1912 g.": "Verit serdce moe v grjaduščuju slavu otčizny!/ Znaju, poslednij geroj ne skoro umret na Rusi." ("My heart believes in the coming glory of my fatherland!/ I know it will be long before the last hero in Russia dies.")(25) His first reaction to the war was therefore joyful. In articles in *Apollon*, where Ivanov had taken Gumilev's place as the main poetry critic, Ivanov expressed thoughts similar to those of Gorodeckij. He confirmed the Acmeist principles and stressed the parallel between Acmeism and the psychological change that the war had brought about. The dominating feelings among poets should be "cheerfulness, soberness and joy".(26) Having got rid of their former narrow individualism and estheticism, poets could now become the voice of the people. As for poetics, Ivanov found a tendency in war poetry away from mysticism, obscurity and half-spoken words to "simple words, clear feelings".(27)

Both Gorodeckij and Ivanov wrote a great many short stories and poems about the war which reflect their theoretical statements. Here we find complete acceptance of the war, which is seen as a blessing both to individuals and the nation. Neither of them shuns the stereotypes and clichés of traditional war literature as far as motifs, characters and vocabulary are concerned. The picture of the enemy in their work is crude, and Gorodeckij especially excelled in outbursts of hatred towards the Germans.(28) To the imperialistic ambitions of the Russian government Gorodeckij and Ivanov gave their full support, anticipating the conquest of Galicia and Constantinople (or Červonnaja Rus' and Car'grad as they preferred to call them).

These two Acmeist writers made no secret of their right-wing political stance. They both published frequently in Suvorin's reactionary journal *Lukomor'e*, and their volumes of poetry, *Pamjatnik slavy* and *Četyrnadcatyj god*, were published by the *Lukomor'e* publishing house.(29) Ivanov himself confessed that he was "a monarchist to the marrow, further to the right of whom [...] there was 'only the wall'".(30) As for Gorodeckij, a notorious event was the publication of his poem "Streten'e carja" ("The Meeting of the Tsar") in the journal *Niva*.(31) The poem, which celebrated the meeting between the tsar and his subjects in Peterburg on the outbreak of the war, was met with extreme hostility. When he visited Moscow in the autumn of 1914, Gorodeckij was shown the door by the writer Vikentij Veresaev, with whom he had wanted to discuss participation in the respected Moscow almanac *Slovo*, because of "Sreten'e carja".(32)

In other words, we find that during the first two years of the war there was a strong feeling that certain important Acmeist principles had been established in literature as a result of the war. Like Majakovskij, who in "Kaplja degtja" in the Futurist anthology *Vzjal* (1915) began with the startling admission that Futurism was dead, but then went on to say that Futurism as a movement was no longer needed because its ideas had already conquered in Russian art, so the Acmeists could also have said that Acmeism "had taken" (*vzjal*) Russia.

The difference between Gumilev and his colleagues Ivanov and Gorodeckij is not hard to discover, but it has not, in my opinion, been adequately investigated. Gumilev was not the chauvinistic and imperialistic war poet, the ideal of Ivanov and Gorodeckij come true, that Soviet critics have made him out to be. Neither can he be accused of having participated in the lowering of the artistic level characteristic of the mainstream of patriotic literature. For Gumilev, as we can see both from his poems and the *Zapiski kavalerista*, the war was first and foremost a personal experience. It offered him the possibility to test himself, expose himself to danger, live on the edge between life and death — in short, to realize that "forest animal" side of his psyche. This enthusiasm for the war and the life of the soldier had no nationalist basis.

Seeing the war mainly as a personal challenge, Gumilev never seemed to perceive its tragic side. Occupied with registering his own feelings, he was not able to enter into the suffering of his fellow creatures. It was this callous attitude that already during the war met with disapproval on ethical grounds. The critic Nikolaj Vengrov in *Letopis'* reminded Gumilev that the war had also a tragic side,(33) while a minor Symbolist poet, Vladimir Pjast, wrote a parody on a poem by Gumilev, accusing him of romanticising a horrible reality.(34)

Recently a document in the same spirit was published for the first time. It is an article entitled "Poet-voin" ("The Soldier-Poet"), by the Symbolist Georgij Čulkov. The article was presumably written as a review of *Kolčan* and can thus be dated 1916-17.

As an epigraph for his article Čulkov chose two lines from a well-known poem by Gumilev: "Ja vežliv s žizn'ju sovremennoju,/ No meždu nami est' pregrada" (I am polite to modern life,/ But between us there is a barrier). The crucial conflict in the poem concerns the notions *pobeda*, *slava*, *podvig* (victory, honour, feat). For Gumilev these were lofty ideals, that had been abolished and forgotten by his contemporaries. While this insight gave Gumilev a feeling of superiority, Čulkov saw it as a sign of backwardness.

Gumilev's ideals are outmoded, Čulkov asserted, and to illustrate what the modern outlook was he quoted an entry from Lev Tolstoj's diary in which Tolstoj expressed his bewilderment over the fact that wars could still exist. At the time of the Napoleonic Wars or the Crimean War people could still honestly believe in what they were doing, but by the beginning of the twentieth century, when, according to Tolstoj, "every schoolboy knows that war is evil", war was something indefensible and deeply unnatural. According to Čulkov this pacifist standpoint was already shared by the majority of people.

There are many surprising things about this. Čulkov, for one thing, was not known as an opponent of the war; rather the contrary. Secondly, Tolstoj's moral authority was not generally felt during the war outside narrow Tolstoyan circles. Čulkov nevertheless touches upon a crucial issue when he says: "Only those who are not in harmony with the new life, the new culture, the new religious consciousness can sincerely accept war as a chivalrous and noble state, and not as an inevitable but always horrible evil."(35) According to Čulkov, Gumilev did not even suspect that the war could be a moral issue and thus he could be classified as a poet out of touch with the modern tragic spiritual experience.

Čulkov anticipated what was actually going to happen in war literature. The attitudes and the artistic manner that Gumilev displayed had indeed outlived themselves, and the prose and poetry of the First World War which is now generally accepted as being significant is the *anti*-war literature, written by men who, like Gumilev, fought at the front but who reflected more accurately the unprecedented nature of this particular war. An émigré critic, Nikolaj Curikov, who in 1931 wrote an article about Gumilev for a Paris journal, was more right than he probably realised in characterising Gumilev's war poems and letters from the front as the most effective antidote to "deceitful *remarkovščina*".(36) The parallel which has been drawn between Gumilev and the English poet Rupert Brooke is also significant.(37) Brooke's war poems were much admired on the home front during the war, but were later found inadequate and outdated, especially when compared to the poetry of the soldier poets David Jones, Isaac Rosenberg, Wilfred Owen and Siegfried Sassoon.(38)

A recent tendency has been to ignore the ideological and moral content of Gumilev's war poems and treat them simply as literary texts, evaluating them from a strictly literary point of view and commenting upon the vocabulary, the images and symbols. This attitude is most clearly expressed by Elaine Rusinko in her provocative article "The Theme of War in the Works of Gumilev" (1977):

> ... to emphasize the poet's spiritual approach to the war in his poetry is to stress speculative biographical and ideological content over artistic features, an approach which has persisted in Gumilev scholarship despite its generally recognized inadequacy. [...] his literature on the theme of war is best understood not as the direct expression of personal sentiments, but

as the distilled experience of a poet,
molded by literary tradition.(39)

This pronounced formalistic approach can be seen as partly evoked by a wish to improve the general image of Gumilev, whose reputation, as we have seen, has been harmed by his personal and artistic involvement in the war. But even though it is possible to show Gumilev's conscious use of a literary tradition, we still can ask: why did Gumilev follow the rhetorical, romantic literary tradition and not, for instance, the Garšin tradition? And even though there is, of course, a danger in reading poems as personal statements, the problem with Gumilev is that all the other texts and statements point in the same direction.

Gumilev's position is, of course, not unique in the European context. Parallels have been drawn with poets of Gumilev's own generation like Charles Péguy(40) and the already mentioned Rupert Brooke, but we can also go back to the ancient Greeks like Tyrtaeus and Archilochus. It was the timeless aspects of the soldier's profession that inspired Gumilev. But this was a tradition that had come to an end even before the First World War and Čulkov was right to stress the inappropriateness of Gumilev's poems in connection with modern war. In contemporary Russian poetry a more suitable tone was struck by a group of Futurist soldier-poets: Sergej Tret'jakov, Vadim Šeršenevič and Konstantin Bol'šakov. These were writers who felt that the modern experience of war demanded a new poetic language.

As for Gumilev, his merits must be looked for in other poems and other connections. And here it is important to question the deeply rooted, one-dimensional view of him as the "warrior-poet" and the adventurer. The attention that has recently been paid to Gumilev's love poems and the religious, mystical poetry of the last years helps us to get a richer and a more comprehensive image of Gumilev as poet and man.

NOTES

1. The differing responses have been pointed out by, for example, Elaine Rusinko in "The Theme of War in the Works of Gumilev", *Slavic and East European Journal*, 21 (1977), 212, note 1.

2. Jurij Nikolaevskij, "Poet-rycar' (O Nikolae Stepanoviče Gumileve)", *Obščee delo* (Paris), 26.9.1921, No.436.

3. See, for example, Georgij Ivanov, "Voennye stikhi", *Apollon* 4-5 (1915), 84; V.Žirmunskij, "Preodolenie simvolizma", *Russkaja mysl'*, 12:II (1916), 51; Jurij Ajxenval'd, *Poety i poetessy* (M., 1922), p.38; N.Curikov, "Gumilev i ego zavety", *Rossija i slavjanstvo* (Paris), 29.8.1931, No.144: Leonid Strakhovsky, *Craftsmen of the Word. Three Poets of Modern Russia. Gumilyov, Akhmatova, Mandelstam* (Cambridge, Mass., 1949), p.37, and Nikolaij Ocup, "N.S.Gumilev", in N.Gumilev, *Izbrannoe* (Paris, 1959), p.24.

4. Nikolaj Gumilev, *Sobranie sočinenij v četyrex tomax*, (Washington, 1962-68), II, p.xxiii.

5. Jurij Verxovskij, "Put' poeta. O poezii N.S.Gumileva", in *Sovremennaja literatura. Sbornik statej* (L., 1925). In 1908 and 1910 Gumilev had written reviews of Verxovskij's two collections of poetry, *Raznye stixotvorenija* and *Idillii i elegii*.

6. "O poezii vojny", *Na literaturnom postu*, 10 (1927); "K voprosu o sud'bax akmeizma", *Na literaturnom postu*, 17-18 (1927).

7. The expression "the Patriotic War" (*Otčestvennaja vojna*) linked the world war with the war of 1812. In an article about Gumilev it was used in Soviet Russia as late as 1920:

E.Gollerbax, "N.S.Gumilev. (K 15-letiju literaturnoj dejatel'nosti)", *Vestnik literatury*, 11 (1920), 17.

8. The book had been preceded by an article by Volkov, "Akmeizm i imperialističeskaja vojna", *Znamja*, 7 (1933).

9. A.A.Volkov, *Poezija russkogo imperializma* (M. 1935), p.190. Volkov also wrote the article about Acmeism for the monumental *Istorija russkoj literatury* in the 1950s. Here he repeated what he had said twenty years earlier: "The aggressive imperialistic substance (*suščnost'*) of the bourgeois ideology of these years found a distinct expression in the works of N.Gumilev. It is hardly possible to find another Russian poet who so challengingly, with frank cynicism, reflected the ideas of imperialistic expansion on the eve of and during the first imperialistic war." (*Istorija russkoj literatury*, t.X. *Literatura 1890-1917 godov* (M.-L., 1954), p.776.

10. O.L.Cexnovicer, *Literatura i mirovaja vojna 1914-1918* (M., 1938), p.45.

11. Cexnovicer, p.156.

12. In a recent textbook it is said that Gumilev "broke with the humanistic traditions of Russian literature" (*Istorija russkoj literatury XIX-XX vekov. Kratkij očerk* [ed. A.S.Kurilov], M., 1983, p.428).

13. A.Blok, *Sobranie sočinenij v šesti tomax*, (L., 1982, IV, p.427.

14. A.G.Sokolov, *Istorija russkoj literatury konca XIX-načala XX veka* (M., 1979), p.342.

15. *Russkaja literatura XX veka. Dooktjabr'skij period* (Kiev, 1977), p.268.

16. Ben Hellman, "A Houri in Paradise. Nikolaj Gumilev and the War", *Studia Slavica Finlandensia*, 1 (1984), 22-37.

17. Volkov, p.197.

18. Cexnovicer, p.44.

19. *Russkaja literatura XX veka*, p.267.

20. See, for example, "Ijul' 1914", "Molitva" (1915) and "Pamjati 19 ijulja 1914" (1916).

21. Gorodeckij's position as an Acmeist after 1914 has been questioned, but, as his literary criticism from the war years indicates, he was still as late as 1916 affirming some elementary Acmeist principles like "beautiful clarity" and a life-affirming attitude.

22. Sergej Gorodeckij, "Poezija kak iskusstvo", *Lukomor'e*, 18 (30.4.1916).

23. Sergej Gorodeckij, "Poezija dlja sebja", *Lukomor'e*, 6 (6.2.1916).

24. Ibid.

25. *Giperborej*, 2 (1912).

26. Georgij Ivanov, "Ispytanie ognem", *Apollon*, 8 (1914), 52.

27. Ibid.

28. See, for example, Gorodeckij's article "Germanija i kul'tura" (*Birževye vedomosti*,

14308 [13.8.1914]) and "Ljubov' k nemcu (Počti ne paradoksy)", *Golos žizni*, 2 (1914).

29. Gumilev's name appeared only once in *Lukomor'e*, but he could not have chosen a worse time. The poem "Konkvistador" was published in December 1915, just a short time after a large number of *Lukomor'e* writers had publicly announced that they were leaving the journal, because of its reactionary attitude. Gorodeckij and Ivanov do not seem to have been very much shaken by this event but went on publishing. Shortly afterwards they were joined by Gumilev.

30. K.Pomerancev, "Georgij Ivanov - ego poezija", in Georgij Ivanov, *Izbrannye stixi* (Paris 1980), p.8.

31. *Niva*, 35 (1914).

32. Vikentij Veresaev, *Sobranie sočinenij* (M. 1961), V, p.454.

33. N.Vengrov, "N.Gumilev. *Kolčan*. Stixi", *Letopis'*, 1 (1916), 416.

34. Quoted in Gumilev, *Sobranie sočinenij*, II, pp.311-13.

35. G.I.Čulkov, "Poet-voin", in Nikolaj Gumilev, *Neizdannoe i nesobrannoe* (Paris, 1986), p.206.

36. *Rossija i slavjanstvo*, 144 (29.8.1931). The word *remarkovščina* is derived from the name Remarque and expresses a hostile attitude to the pacifism of Remarque's novel, *Im Westen nichts Neues*.

37. Elaine Rusinko, op.cit., 212, note 1.

38. See, for example, Ifor Evans, *A Short History of English Literature* (Harmondsworth, 1969): "Brooke saw war as a purifying, romantic experience, and death as heroic. A generation living to experience the sordid reality of trench warfare turned against him " (p.78).

39. Rusinko, op.cit., 211.

40. Nikolaj Ocup, "N.S.Gumilev", in N.Gumilev, *Izbrannoe* (Paris, 1959), p.24.

APPENDIX

A biographical poem by Vadim Gardner about a sea voyage from England to Murmansk in 1918, with a commentary by Ben Hellman.

Among the great number of minor poets who were reviewed by Nikolaj Gumilev in *Apollon* we can find the name of Vadim Gardner. Gumilev wrote a few lines about Gardner's volume of poetry, *Ot žizni k žizni*, which had been published by the renowned Symbolist publishing house *Al'ciona* in 1912. He called it "a charming book of light verse", but at the same time he criticised Gardner's style for being insipid and sickly sweet and expressed the fear that Gardner might forever remain a dilettante.(1)

In Gumilev's *Sobranie sočinenij* 1880 is given as Gardner's year of birth; it is also stated that he emigrated to Finland after the Revolution.(2) What is not widely known is that Gumilev's and Gardner's ways crossed not only in 1913 but also in 1918, an event described by Gardner in a poem which was never published.

Vadim D.Gardner was born in 1880 in the town of Viborg, Finland.(3) His father was an American engineer, and his mother, Ekaterina Dyxova, a minor Russian writer and businesswoman. Gardner studied law at St.Petersburg University, but did not complete his studies as he was expelled because of his involvement in the 1905 revolution. He spent two months in prison before he was eventually released (partly thanks to his American passport). Gardner completed his university studies in Dorpat.

Gardner's first book of poetry, *Stixotvorenija*, was published in Petersburg in 1908 at the writer's own expense. It was reviewed by Aleksandr Blok, who found it more interesting than most of the works by new poets that year, but still not very promising.(4) Blok nevertheless gave Gardner one of his books with the inscription "Vadimu Gardneru, poetu".

Stixotvorenija gave Gardner an entrée into the literary life of Petersburg. He became acquainted with Vjačeslav Ivanov and visited his famous "Tower". Ivanov is even supposed to have been willing to write an introduction for Gardner's second book, conditional on being given freedom to select the poems. This condition was, however, not accepted by Gardner.

When the young generation of Petersburg poets formed the Acmeist movement in the early 1910s Gardner became one of the active participants. After his second book of verse, *Ot žizni k žizni*, had been published, Gardner was accepted in February 1913 as a new member of the Acmeist-dominated poetry circle *Cex poetov*.(5) In the same year he published a few poems in the circle's journal *Giperborej*(6) and in the respected literary journal *Russkaja mysl'*.(7) *Ot žizni k žizni* was favourably reviewed in *Giperborej* by the minor poet Mikhail Lozinskij, who called it a book "which leaves no one cold". The best poems combined, according to Lozinskij, "concreteness with a winged fantasy".(8) Sergej Gorodeckij displayed a more negative attitude to the book in his review in *Reč'*.(9)

During the First World War, in 1916, Gardner applied for Russian citizenship, spurred by patriotism. As a Russian citizen he was immediately drafted. Because of his knowledge of English (Gardner was bilingual), he was sent to London to work under General Gedrojc in the *Komitet po snabženiju sojuznikov oružiem*. Gardner stayed in England two years, visiting, as his poem tells us, at least Woolwich, Barrow and Manchester. In 1918 he met Gumilev, who had come from Paris at the beginning of that year. In a letter to Axmatova Gumilev mentions a meeting with Gardner.(10) The two poets returned to Russia in the spring of 1918 on the same ship. Four years later Gardner wrote down his memoirs in the form of a poem about the trip.

From the poem we can see that the ship was a Russian military transport. A huge number of Russian soldiers were being transported away from the western front to Russia. Because of German submarines and mines the trip was dangerous and for the first three days the ship was escorted by British destroyers. According to the poem, the trip lasted twelve days in all.

Unfortunately, Gardner does not give very much attention to Gumilev in the poem, although they shared the same cabin and read poems to each other. For some reason he is more interested in the third person in the cabin, a Russian railway engineer, Lavrov, who had also been serving in England during the war. It is Lavrov's wide interests and his kindness that Gardner praises.

The Russian soldiers on the ship were rebellious and thus gave a foretaste of what was happening in Russia. Gardner relates an interesting scene, a hot-tempered discussion between an artillery captain and a soldier. While Gardner, the former revolutionary, defended the October Revolution at this time, Gumilev is supposed to have been very upset by the scenes he witnessed on the boat.

Upon arriving at Murmansk the travellers showed documents signed by the political representative of Soviet Russia in England, Maksim Litvinov. Only after this could they travel on to Petrograd. About Gardner's later fate it can be said that he stayed in Petrograd until 1921, working mainly as a teacher. In that year he fled to Finland, where the rest of his family was already living in the village of Vammelsuu on the Carelian Isthmus. In the late twenties Gardner published a third volume of poetry, *Pod dalekimi zvezdami* (Paris, 1929). This volume was to be his last, but he was nevertheless writing poetry until his death in Helsinki in 1956.

NOTES

1. *Apollon*, 3 (1913), 75. Also in Nikolaj Gumilev, *Sobranie sočinenij v četyrex tomax* (Washington, 1962-68), IV, p.315.

2. Gumilev, *Sobranie sočinenij*, IV, p.615, p.643.

3. I received the poem and the information about Vadim Gardner from the poet's widow, Maria Gardner.

4. *Russkaja mysl'* 1:III (1909), 3. Also in A.Blok, *Sobranie sočinenij v šesti tomax*, (M.-L., 1962), V, p.648.

5. R.D.Timenčik, "Zametki ob akmeizme", *Russian Literature*, 7/8: Special Issue devoted to Acmeism (1974), 37.

6. *Giperborej*, 6 (1913).

7. *Russkaja mysl'*, 2 and 10 (1913).

8. *Giperborej*, 6 (1913), 27.

9. *Reč'*, 18.2.1913, No.48.

10. Timenčik, *Russian Literature*, 37, note 48.

Из дневника поэта Вадима Гарднера

Воспоминания 10 декабря
записаны 27 ноября 1922г.

В последний раз был в Dartnell парке
Я в восемнадцатом году.
Мне жить велели злые Парки
В коммунистическом аду.

Я, в настроеньи безотрадном,
Отдавшись воле моряков,
Отплыл на транспорте громадном
От дымных английских брегов.

Тогда моя молчала лира.
Неслись мы вдаль к полярным льдам.
Три миноносца-конвоира
Три дня сопутствовали нам.

До Мурманска двенадцать суток
Мы шли под страхом субмарин –
Предательских подводных "уток",
Злокозненных плавучих мин.

Хотя ужасней смерть на "дыбе",
Лязг кандалов во мгле тюрьмы,
Но что кошмарней мертвой зыби
И качки с борта и кормы?

Лимоном в тяжкую минуту
Смягчал мне муки Гумилев.
Со мной он занимал каюту,
Деля и штиль и шторма рев.

Лежал еще на третьей койке
Лавров – (он родственник Петра),
Уютно было нашей тройке
Болтали часто до утра.

Стихи читали мы друг другу.
То слушал милый инженер,
Отдавшись сладкому досугу,
То усыплял его размер.

Быки, пролеты арок, сметы,
Длина и ширина мостов —
Ах, вам ли до того поэты?
А в этом мире жил Лавров.

Но многогранен ум российский.
Чего путеец наш не знал.
Он к клинописи ассирийской
Пристрастье смолоду питал.

Его душа не уставала
Давать и помощь и совет.
Добряк, бежит чуть свет, бывало,
Он вниз к солдатам в лазарет.

Заботливости полн и ласки,
За ближних вечно хлопоча,
Лечил и делал перевязки,
Будил храпевшего врача.

Могу-ль о славном капитане-
Артиллеристе позабыть?
И с ним в полярном океане
Пришлось при снежном шторме плыть.

Он в Комитете по снабженью
Работал в Лондоне у нас.
Но ставя грань воображенью,
Укорочу я свой рассказ.

Скажу, что мы друзьями были
И скорбь и радость пополам
По-братски целый год делили.
То мчались в Вульич по делам,

То в Барроу, то в Манчестер дождливый
На полигоны, в арсенал;
Но больше Лондон хлопотливый
Друзей в стенах своих держал.

Так вот, хоть и в каютах разных,
Мы возвращались вместе в Русь.
Бывало, при звездах алмазных
На палубу я поднимусь.

Смотрю, там офицер наш бродит,
На пену гулких волн глядит,
Солдат-бунтарь с ним речь заводит.
Я вижу, капитан сердит.

Готов на рядовом досаду
И справедливый гнев сорвать.
Кто родину привел к распаду?
Вождей кто вздумал предвавать?

Кто Мать-Россию опозорил?
Расстроил фронт? В своих стрелял?
С бунтовщиком так друг мой спорил.
А серп луны меж тем сиял.

Но вот добравшись до Мурмана,
На берег высадились мы.
То было, помню, утром рано.
Кругом белел ковер зимы.

С Литвиновской пометкой виды
Представив двум большевикам,
По воле роковой планиды
Помчались к Невским берегам.

Провел три злополучных года
Я в красном Ленинском раю.
Но муки русского народа
В другой я песне воспою.

FUNCTIONING POETICS AND POETIC FUNCTIONS.
GUMILEV'S POEM "PERED NOČ'JU SEVERNOJ, KOROTKOJ..."

DENIS MICKIEWICZ

INTRODUCTION

From the moment Nikolaj Gumilev took charge of the poetry section in the prestigious journal *Apollon* in 1909, throughout his leadership of the First and Second Guild of Poets, the Acmeist School and his studio teaching in "Zvučaščaja rakovina", he displayed a remarkably constant and, one can safely affirm, successful theoretical and critical position on the art of making poetry.[1] This position is not modeled after any one else's; the debates of the time show that his senior peers were, or would have been, hostile to his doctrine, and there was little theory to be gleaned from his followers. Although Gumilev's essays attest to close cognizance of, and discrimination among, the real and potential strengths of his Modernist contemporaries and their Russian and French forebears, an eclectic dependence on the ever shifting work of others would not explain the initial stability and steady development of his poetics.

Nor did Gumilev arrive at his poetics by abstracting the more fruitful precepts from his own creative practices. Gumilev's psychological and technical gains developed in the wake of his established poetics. It is also paradoxical that all his accurate, pithy and far-reaching pronouncements emanated from a mind that by most, even friendly, accounts (Makovskij:1962: 199-200; Ocup:1953:135) was neither learned nor intellectual; and, although the pronouncements were couched in rational, even didactic terms, one must conclude that his theory sprang from a deep-seated, remarkably secure intuition. However, to be fully effective in one's own poetic creativity, such a judgmental intuition must combine with appropriate levels of experience, not yet available to the young Gumilev. Not being a Mozart, it took him a decade and a half of steady work to begin to realize his potential. He admitted to his mentors, Annenskij and Ivanov, his lack of creative assurance and expressed gratitude "for all the efforts you made in helping me to understand my creativity" (Timenčik:1981:183). And even after withdrawing from Ivanov's Academy of Verse to form his own Guild of Poets, he still signed his letter of 3 June 1911, asking the maître for an appraisal of four of his "experimental" poems, as "your eternally wavering, but always devoted pupil" (Ibid:175).

Powerful diction was always one of Gumilev's strongest assets. The effect of the striking utterances of his early poetry on his reputation was, however, also paradoxical. As recently observed, "they entered one's memory like nails, from the first stroke of a strong, exact word" (Pospelov:1986). Similarly, Innokentij Annenskij observed in a review of *Romantičeskie cvety* (*Reč*:1908:308) that after reading these verses one feels as though one had "swallowed a strong gulp of Chartreuse". However, despite (or because of) the frequently very felicitous diction, Gumilev's earlier poems were perceived by experts as having a content that was too weak to sustain its powerful expression.[2] Similar judgements, not unreasonable for juvenilia, have been rather uncritically and damagingly applied by experts to Gumilev's entire oeuvre.[3] Despite all critics' admission that, with each collection, Gumilev reached higher levels of accomplishment, there remained a reserve, if not condescension, based on Gumilev's alleged "posing" and "formalism". In Georgij Adamovič's words, "Undoubtedly, Gumilev's verses have many virtues: articulateness and purity of style, energy of rhythm, constancy in the development of design and composition. No less indubitable, however, is the fact that they lack the mysterious 'something', which justifies the very existence of poetry." (Adamovič:1971) (That "something" remains to be explained).

A penetrating attack was leveled in *Apollon* at Gumilev's "first fully mature" collection, *Kolčan* (1916), by Margarita Tumpovskaja (1917:6-7:58-66). She observes how that work evokes the expectation of formal perfection with all the sonorous, chiseled verses, rich in plastic images and virile themes. Such is the demand of the "large canvas" or decorative mode of Gumilev's art. But this expectation is frustrated by the too noticeable abundance of devices. Gumilev reveals not only himself in his work, but also the mechanism, the "progression of his creative process". Since there is no "classical" divorce between the process of construction and the finished work, the latter is not a perfect separate object. In the visual arts the sketch allows the public to delight mentally in the development of each feature of the painting, or to follow that feature back to its source. But Gumilev's rare gift of reaching "that ineffable moment of combining stillness and motion" and his tone are the equivalent of a painting, not a sketch. Thus the various parts of his poems are left to their own devices to seduce the reader. They do this fully, but they do not satisfy, because Gumilev mixes the two basically alien genres, painting and sketch. Architectonically, this means that the poems cannot hold their own weight, they contain too many isolated effects. In Gumilev's art creative action predominates over creative reflection; this makes his art "neither totally simple nor enigmatically unreachable".

However, the poem under consideration (*SS*, II:332; see Appendix I,II) may well refute these fundamental charges. In this work most of the terms are semantically interconnected by multiple and therefore subtle relations. At the same time, the semantic span of their connotations provides a content rich enough to sustain the tone of Gumilev's diction. Since those "certain norms that let his talents grow and strengthen" (as Gumilev said about Gorodeckij, *SS*, IV:333) are acknowledged, in Gumilev's case, as rather demanding, and his relentless pursuit of *prekrasnaja trudnost'* (magnificent difficulty)[4] constituted a major part of his norms, his poetry was bound eventually to catch up with them. Ultra close reading of this poem may illustrate a critical point in Gumilev's two creative curricula: an intersection of the axis of his ascending practice with that of his high-ranking theoretical acumen.

1. *ENSTEHUNGSGESCHICHTE*

The morphogenetic story of "Pered noč'ju severnoj, korotkoj..." is important for our examination; it brings to the fore some of Gumilev's thinking about poetics during his creative process. Gumilev was known to be a methodical writer, who painstakingly reedited and repaired the various aspects of his work. A glance at facsimiles of his drafts confirms this. (According to his pupil Irina Odoevceva [1973], he wrote only one piece, "Zabludivšijsja tramvaj", in a single impulse.) Regrettably, not having access to draft manuscripts and other relevant documents, I am unable to report fully on the *Entstehungsgeschichte* of this poem. The version to be examined must have been written some time after the Revolution, possibly as late as his last year, 1921. According to Gleb Struve's annotations (*SS*, II:317-18), the earliest version (consisting of five stanzas) was dated, in a posthumous volume edited by Georgij Ivanov, "1916". The poem was first published in that form in 1917, in the almanac *Tvorčestvo*. In that year Gumilev included the poem in his unpublished Parisian *Al'bom*, with an additional title, "Ljubov' vesnoj" ("Love in the Spring"), an added sixth stanza, and changes in lines 8, 15 and 18. Gumilev evidently sought to improve the piece and Struve consequently published the newer reading as the main version in the collected works. The version we shall discuss appeared for the first time posthumously, undated, in the almanac

Literaturnaja mysl', No.1. The year on the cover is given as 1923, and as 1922 on the title page, presumably when the issue was being assembled.

In this latest version, one half of the poem – the last three stanzas of the *Al'bom* version – are replaced by three entirely new ones, the title is removed, and the change in line 8 is retained, suggesting that the 1922-23 version is newer than that published in 1917. I do not know how many times Gumilev re-worked this poem and whether this, apparently last, draft was finished in Paris in 1917, in London in 1918, soon after his return to Petrograd, or shortly before his execution in August 1921.

It is evident that Gumilev attached a lot of importance to the idea of this poem, and that he valued its first twelve lines, rewriting the rest several times after the work had already been "finished" and published. It is also evident that in the process Gumilev exhibited a conscious coming to grips with his own general as well as technical imperatives. Creative consciousness itself, so highly esteemed by him, obviously took part in this process, making it easier for us to relate his creation to his proclaimed norms.

2.0. URGE TO REWORK

Although space does not allow us to compare the extant versions formally, we can readily appreciate why Gumilev saw the need to return to and revise the piece. To my mind, each later version represents a major improvement, all changes are clearly motivated, and the last effort marks a quantum leap in the significance of the work. Gumilev must have come to realize that stanzas four and five of the original version emerged merely out of the momentum of the rhythmical, emotional and imagerial energies of the preceding, stronger, verses. The fourth and fifth stanzas add little to the development of the content, or, as he would call it, 'composition'.

To recapture the thematic drive of stanzas one and two, a sixth, final, stanza is added to the second,

Al'bom, version. It foregrounds the motif of the ominousness of love conceived in the spring; hence the added title "Love in the Spring". The confessional adverbs *bol'no* and *gor'ko* (painfully and bitterly, line 24) add immediacy to the superstition. However, this strengthened ending renders the preceding two stanzas even more lightweight. Reminiscent of the fin-de-siècle, decadent, early phase of Modernism (and Gumilev), with their "unconquerable" aesthetic pose, stanzas four and five of this draft do not sustain the initial tragic potential. Nor can an overwhelming "aestheticising" motivate (an imperative in Gumilev's criticism) the peril of being "scorched" (12) or even the notions "painfully" and "bitterly", which the author, as will be shown, genuinely needed in this poem. And a simple omission of the two static stanzas would have caused a stylistic as well as motivational abruptness, placing the last stanza out of synchrony with the established discourse. Hence, Gumilev composed an entirely new second half (stanzas four, five, six) for the third version.

2.1. AN OPENING FOR THEMATIC RAMIFICATION

The two adverbs "painfully" and "bitterly" of the earlier closing line, amplified by their psychological near-synonymity, are the only notion to survive from the latter half of the second draft. Converted into direct objects, the terms serve, in the opening line (13) of the new version's second half, as departure points for a new, competing theme of overcoming the disaster, and breed a series of subthemes. The content of this line serves as a denominator for the wide-ranging acts expressed or connoted in the other lines: agony (5-6), oblivion (14,24), incantation ("will - it will - they will" [14-15], including the grammatic switch into future tense [14-15,17,21]), summoning by storms (16), communication (17,21,4-5,16), consent (17,21,6), conspiracy (19), departure (6,17,13), precariousness (12,22) and condition for survival (10,12,22). The content of the coda thus acquires its formidable dynamics; and the action does not end, because the connotations of the key terms retain the potency to ramify even beyond the text.[5]

3.0. MULTITIEREDNESS

Semantic resonance of the above kind unifies the whole work and adds depth to each echo-bearing image and sound element. It also creates a *mnogoplannost'* (multitieredness) of the content. Such simultaneity of planes is characteristic of Modernism; the relationship between experience and expression advances, in Marcel Raymond's terms, from one of equivalence to one of polyvalence. Authors manage to capture and convey in their expressions, as Nabokov says in *Dar*, "the multifarious awareness" of disparate, simultaneously occurring realities, mental or physical. The same can be said about "multitieredness" in poetic composition. In Russia, such polyvalence found a fertile soil in Symbolist and post-Symbolist poetry and, as these poets said, in all good poetry.

3.1. The *mnogoplannost'* of the poem becomes apparent with line 13 of the last version: "Tixij sneg zasyplet grust' i gore" ("Quiet snow will cover grief and woe"). That line and its stanza stand out in the poem in many basic ways, mental as well as physical:
a) Rhythmically, that stanza has the greatest number of possible accents (seventeen, compared with fourteen possible accents per average stanza). Its opening line (13) is the only one in the poem that can have all five feet accented, as opposed to an average maximum of 3.35 accented feet.
b) Phonetically, beginning with *grust'* (13), this is the only stanza in which the "dark" vowel u is dominant (six times accented, and one unaccented); in other stanzas the average use of u is only 0.5 stressed, and 0.55 unstressed.
c) Grammatically, from line 13 on, the mind of the poet-persona advances from the perfective past (stanzas one and two) and rhetorical present (three) into the future tense, ending with the anaphoric, oblique jussive mood ("If only..., If only...", 23, 24).

And the subject of the narration switches from the third person (3-6) to first (9). Further on, that "I" becomes objectified, in turn, as a third person, the "friend" who is being called by the storm (16), enabling the persona to merge with the apostrophe in a first person plural (17, 19).

d) Dramatically, the introduction of the syntagm-image "tixij sneg" (quiet snow) expands the affair to all four seasons. Its direct lyrical function is to carve a distinction vis-à-vis "summer", "enchantment of May" and the "lightness of Fall", but chiefly to create thematic oppositions between *tixij* and the "fiery" act of "reducing to ashes" and the magic call by the storms.

e) Psychologically, the "snowy quietness" looms as an essential intermittent stage (21, 22) between actuality and norm.

f) Semantically, 13 is the first line to force attention on what will be discussed below as "referential indeterminacy" between literal and metaphoric terms.

g) Lexically, this stanza introduces a greater volume of words. The last three stanzas average twenty-one words per stanza, whereas the preceding stanzas, and all stanzas of the previous drafts, average eighteen. It is revealing, in this connection, that the added sixth stanza of the *Al'bom* version also has an increase, to twenty-two words.

h) Rhetorically, line 13 offers the persona's answer to his own questions of the preceding stanza, about survival.

3.2. The *vypadanie* (standing out) of this stanza in so many basic respects makes it apparent that Gumilev at this point took a fresh approach to the poem. And the very freshness indicates that, possibly due to a significant lapse of time, a distancing took place between the event and its original poeticization and the retroactive remodeling of the experience. The poem has assumed its own systematic life, *beyond* retelling the original events. It is at this point in the poem that the connection between the artist and his work becomes demonstrably "polysemious and indirect, rather than spontaneous" (see Rusinko's essay in this volume). In such cases there is no algorithmic procedure for discovering, in any text, all the interrelations of elements that cause this "coming to life". But a number of semiotic functions of the substantial and relational features can always be isolated for observation.

4. REFERENTIAL INDETERMINACY between literal and metaphoric uses forces the decoder's thought from a single way of viewing a given reality. Part of the semantic depth of this poem stems from the many examples of this type of apparent ambiguity. Physical "quiet" might, but "snow" cannot "cover sadness and woe" (13) literally. Which, then, are the metaphors: the subject and predicate or the two objects? In a way, "zasyplet" + "grust' i gore" (will pour over + sadness and woe) is not a purely metaphoric utterance. In the imperfective mode, the verbs *zasypat'* (to cover by pouring) and *zasypat'* (to fall asleep) become interchangeable homonyms; and *zasypljat'* (to put to sleep), formed after *usypljat'* (to put to death, i.e., to sleep, metaphorically), can be heard as a direct reference to sorrow, and not as a metaphor. In that case, only the subject "snow" remains metaphorical. Thus it can cover the (also metaphoric) mental road to paradise (24), and what is on the road, "sadness and woe" (13). But "snow" is also a literal index of the concrete passage of time between the events in May and the following winter. Life will take its course, whether or not the persona survives to witness that snow. And as in most of life's journeys, there is literal regret, remorse and burning sorrow that beg to be quietly cooled and forgotten. The literalness of that psychological sensation escalates the semiotic (rather than the semantic or denotational) role of "snow" as an image (see section 8).

And the "road" becomes a *peregrinatio vitae* (cf. Eulalia Papla's essay in this volume). Gumilev was grappling with that Dantean concept at the time; he intended to entitle his last collection (*Ognennyj stolp*, 1921) "In the Middle of my Life's Journey". The journey to bliss may be long, and that destination may not even be reachable without the torment being gently covered and cooled. Bliss itself can be a number of heterogeneous things: a mere oblivion, a social union with the apostrophe, a promise of a *vita nuova* in a transcendental or, literally, "paradisiac" union. The synonym of the predicative prerequisite "zasyplet" (will have poured over, 13), namely "zametet" (will have swept over, obliterated, 24) implies oblivion; but the first of the synonyms, "zasyplet", relates explicitly to the undesirables "sadness and woe", and not to the road's metaphorical ascent to paradise. The explicit rejection of the local white skies, in favor of the distant azure, tilts my interpretation toward the Dantean paradise rather than toward oblivion. "Love", the component of paradise and main subject of this poem, is another object that is now abstract, now personalized, and now ethereal, capable of acting in social, psychological and transcendental dimensions. We shall discuss the hypostases of this love in our section on mythopoesis (12.0).

"Indeterminacies" of the above kind show how poetic arrangement or context can loosen what are conventionally stable and mentally static equations between signifiers and signifieds. This loosening stimulates the reader's efforts to impose his own equations, which has been the goal of certain Symbolist schools. Words so used can be likened to "poetic symbols" as interpreted by V.Ivanov and Annenskij.[6] But these "symbols" are by no means vague signs. They serve a greater precision of psychological nuances and mental movements between categories by the "contaminating force of 'context'". "Snow" conveys the desired state more clearly than if Gumilev had named a specific brand of tranquilizer. The opposition of the mundane "neighbors" (19) to a fairy-tale "king's daughter" (20) evokes several literal and metaphoric connotations of both terms, due to contextual juxtaposition. A king's daughter does not have "neighbors" in the social or "rooming" sense. Neither does a sea voyager. But the stylistically odd term "neighbors" points out the *others*, who restrict one's choices, although one is bound to those meddlers only by surface obligations, which can be overridden by not explaining. "Tsarevna", on the other hand, is quite literally the sovereign of one's thoughts, wishes, and fate, and is qualified to give or to deny her supreme consent. The historical apostrophe, therefore, need not be literally of royal blood.

5.0. INTRATEXTUAL RESONANCES: Structural, Semantic, Sensorial.

Works of art, generally speaking, are known to resound with inner echoes or "contrapuntal" imitations. Such palpable and mental echoes lend cohesion, depth and incandescence to artistic texts. With the advance of Modernism, artists and theorists became conscious of more subtle and more varied sets of "balances" than those traditionally extolled. Thus, Osip Brik discovered in 1916 the principle of sound patterning (*zvukovye povtory*) marking thereby the founding of the Formalist School, and Roman Jakobson began to explore the symmetries of grammatical tropes. Parallelisms became for Jakobson the constituent element of poetic diction. Thus, he defined "poetic function", in his famous formula (1960:357), as "the projection of equivalences from the axis of selection upon the axis of combination". Taken usually for granted as subsidiary "service devices", or as ornaments, elements that create the various equivalences are seldom credited by readers with structuring the "context" of poetic works (cf. Fn.7 below ; also 11.1). Some even see Jakobson's findings as irrelevant, ingeniously found coincidences of semi-subliminal equivalences, because he alludes to, but does not expound upon, their effect on the content, and because it seems to critics that he stacks his cards by selecting a few examples that happen to reward his method. Indeed, it will take massive research to sort out the varieties of realized and potential equivalences in all poetry; so one must begin with representative samples.

Gumilev demonstrates the principle of equivalences on several levels, symmetrically and asymmetrically (cf.9.0-9.9). He selects and combines the traditional "equivalences" with ostentatious simplicity. The rhyming lexemes are, by modern standards, quite banal, and so is their plain, alternating (*perekrestnyj*) order. The metric equivalences form an uninterrupted trochaic pentameter. The syntax is, on the level of clauses, symmetrical, and features no "poetic violations". The four-line strophic arrangement, too, promotes a very regular progression from thought to thought, neatly contained in each stanza and/or distich. Complexities in this poem arise *within* the various types of equivalences (cf. 9.0-9.9). And semantic resonance forms its own type of equivalence: the balancing of concepts. In this poem the semantic equivalences or echoes occur in pairs.

5.1. SEMANTIC ECHOES (Among Key Terms).

Diverse concepts may recall each other, progressively and regressively, in such a way that corresponding terms contaminate and explain each other directly or through their immediate contexts. "Paradise" (23) clarifies the meaning of the two skies (18). It defines the Petersburgian, Maytime "white" as the nebulous "here and now" *realia*, and "blue" is the metaphor for the transcendent *realiora*. "Snow" (13) expands the concept "Northern" (1) from being only geographical to that of season and climate. Its tautological repetition links the meanings of lines 13 and 24, and explains why a "road to paradise" should be covered (cf. 4.0, 5.2.1). "Sorrow and woe" (13) recall "blood" (2) and turn the mere simile of color into a "gutsy" affair with a tragic portent. "Nothing will be regretted" (14) switches the focus from the third person (3, 4, 5, 6,) to the first (7, 17). "Wind" (15) renders the bewitching "breath" (5, 6) ephemeral. "Sweeter than roses" (6) anticipates Eden (24), and makes a whiff of her breath its palpable token. From the echoing waters of the Neva and the Black Sea rises the crucial switch from the static mirrors to the dynamic storms. "We shall move away" (17) now recalls "she left" (6) as both partners' desire to escape. Stanza 5 (with its five negatives) is devoted to the dramatization of that motive. Synonymia among the substantives, predicates, adjectives and adverbs has already been mentioned. The anaphoras "if only" (22, 23) link the perils of "summer" with those of the "road". The internally rhyming parallelism "ni tvoim - ni moim" (19) links the princess with the poet-persona by parallel conditions, as "I shall ask - You will not refuse" links them by parallel acts. Conquering "love" becomes *tsarevna*, and vice versa. Echoes wedge the information from a corresponding source into a new context and multiply the content while enhancing its cohesion.

5.2. SEMANTIC CONTAMINATION: The Dominance of Key Terms.

Returning to the syntagm *tixij sneg* (quiet snow), we can see that the adjective "quiet" is redundant as a qualitative attribute of "snow"; but as a descriptive epithet "tixij" is a metonym for a (withheld) adverbial clause (< *tixo padajuščij, ležaščij*: quietly falling, lying). The meaning of such a metonym spreads psychologically, that is (ultimately), semantically, over the entire distich. That meaning conditions the act of *zasyplet* (will pour over). (The insertion of the optional liquid consonant *l* acts as a phonological analogue of a prolongation of that act). In the following line "tixij" conditions, further, the very quality of "grust' i gore" (grief or sadness and woe) and the way in which all the regrets will cease. Beyond that, the adjective opposes the "calling by the storm" and determines the dynamics of the tone of the direct speech of the next stanza; it also forms a synonymy of means of expression with "neslyšnoju poxodkoj" (inaudible gait, 3).

A good example of the subtle but important opposition between "semantic" and "expressive" functions of diction, the term *tixij* works here in two ways. As an "expresseme" (a sign regarded as an articulatory-euphonic gesture), *tixij* contrasts with the dynamism of *ognennoe* (fiery, 11), and sharpens the sudden change between 12 and 13, and their respective stanzas four and five. Due to this semiotic contrast, the phonemes of that "quiet" denotation dominate the tone, above the other more accented vowels of that line. At the same time, that epithet cushions or intervenes, predicatively, before the sudden appearance of "snow". Apart from reducing the abruptness, *tixij* is a substitution of an action metonym for the usual attribute of visual perception *belyj* (white), and for the later (24) attitudinal attribute *milyj* (dear) and the combined attitudinal-qualitative *xrupkij* (delicate).

5.2.1. The key word *sneg* (snow) motivates in its own line the substitution of the more abstract object *grust'* (sadness) for the more sensuous *bol'* (pain). *Grust'* captures the crunch (*xrust*, cf. *xrupkij*, 24) and alliterates with *gore* (woe) and with the other key words of the stanza: *buri* (storms), *druga* (friend), and resonates with the evocatively thrice-repeated impersonal link word *bud'et* (it will be). The evolution of the second object from *gor'ko* to *gore*, (a particularizing truncation of the nominalization *goreč'*), simplifies the diction and rhymes with *more* (sea). The etymon thus becomes widened on several levels. The effect of "strengthening" terms by placing adjacent tautologies was pointed out by Gumilev in his review of Axmatova's collection *Večera* in 1914. The two pseudo-synonyms *grust' i gore* reach, through connotation, the concretizing simile *krov'* (blood, 2), its rhyme *ljubov'* (love - the feeling, not apostrophe), and its deadly attributes (3, 4, 5, 6), as well as the "bitter", scorching nascent of summer (11, 12, 13). And the much craved for "dear snow" and its synonymous perfective predicates - "will have poured over" and "will have swept over" - connect "sadness and woe" with the penultimate line's "road to paradise" (23). By terminating all regrets (14), "snow" marks the turning point of the plot. As an opposition to summer, snow is but a metonym for winter; and, in opposition to events associated with other colors, it is a metonym of whiteness. In turn, the familiarity of this metonym is chosen to distinguish its specificity against the intangible whiteness of May and blind mirrors.

6.0 MATERIALITY OF WORDS (Of Signifiers and of Signifieds).
It has long been established that the phonological, dynamic, graphic and motor-articulatory elements of language are substances by which verbal signs are formed and recognized. Social discourse mobilizes, amasses, foregrounds or dampens these material elements for purposes of greater expressiveness, and poetry employs these devices more consciously than other types of speech, creating such functions as rhyming, alliteration, meter and so forth. Modernist poets discovered that the Kantean "three characters of communication" - word, gesture, and tone - that correspond to the division of the arts into, respectively, *Redende Künste*, *Bildende Künste* and *Künste des schönen Spiels der Empfindungen* are all at once engaged, as substances, in poetic speech. (G.F.Lessing relegated "gesture" and "tone" to a separate art form, as they serve to raise the arbitrary lingual signs [of poetry] to the higher level of natural signs, whereby drama becomes a higher medium than poetry.) The aggregate of these features in poetry is generally, and somewhat amorphously, regarded as "style". But Formalist scholars opened the way to a solid empirical scrutiny of the linguistic attributes of the word, and semioticians may, as predicted by Gumilev's fellow critic in *Apollon*, Valerian Čudovskij (1915: #4:55-94), commence with an objective study of the other two "characters of communication", "gesture" and "tone". So far, the formal cataloging of verbal

and articulatory substances has proved to be relatively easy, but describing the semantics and expressivity of their various relational functions is still a very difficult part of such analyses. Meanwhile, poetic schools like Cubo-Futurists, Dadaists and so on claimed that speech particles can be interrelated so as to communicate artistic messages "over the head" of conventional linguistic rules or common sense. *Zaum'*, or nonsense poetry, provides vivid examples of such uses. Gumilev was highly conscious of the "dramatic" potential of material verbal elements, and this poem reveals his own, more subtle, method of employing them.

6.1 RAYONISM. The color scheme: red, white, black, blue and again white, assumes a deeper function than that of a set of adjectives or qualitative attributes attached to certain object nouns. Colors, by themselves, do not automatically generate a thematic dialectic. To do that, they must be a part of a special context. Through Gumilev's association with Larionov and Goncharova in Paris in 1917, that is to say, during the writing or rewriting of this poem, Gumilev became acquainted with their theory of Rayonism, and we may recognize the use of certain peculiarly "rayonist" devices here. According to Larionov's theory, the colors of objects emanate reflections, and such rays fill the spaces between and penetrate the boundaries of all things, within a given environment. In this case, such "filling" takes place within the semantic jurisdiction of the competing colors in our text. Thus, "red", the color of dawns (2), reified by "blood", colors all events, spectacularly and tragically, until all gets covered by "snow". But "white", the color of northern, Petersburgian May (4), is not that of fragrant blossoms; its "charm" is negative in a twofold way. The original term *mutnye* (turbid) and, even more so, the retained one, *slepye* (blind), describing the quality of the White Nights as a severe impairment, can penetrate the consciousness with their agonizing, irreal, bewitching and, hence, poisoning (5) effect. This "white" effect is, of course, distinct from the white of the snow-covered oblivion which, incidentally, will manifest a "quiet" (13), "dear" and "fragile" (or "delicate", 24) extension of the concurrent storminess in the south, over the Black Sea. The idea of the "black" toponym, amplified by the or-or echoing of "v Č'ornom more" (cf. 3.1.b, 6.4, 6.5), touches, with its romantic "calling of its friend" (16), all the other "future" events of the poem.

The target "blue" is an entirely new plane, that of concord. It either lies further south, or in a different dimension altogether. That dimension is outside our seasons and our red and white reality; it is even beyond oblivion; it is a celestial *realiora* (cf.#380,6. "The new world was blue and starless"). As Vjačeslav Ivanov insists, all good poetry guides one's psyche *a realia ad realiora*. Blue lends, as a norm, conviction and orientation to the persona but, not being part of the *realia*, it does not color, semantically or otherwise, the events within the "context"[7] of the poem; it remains an external, conditionally victorious, symbol of a norm.

6.2 "TRAVELS IN HYPERREALITY" Another analogy with Rayonism is Gumilev's lingual response to the "transparency and fourth-dimension vision" theory, advocated by Larionov and Goncharova from 1913.[8] Their notion of "realističeskij lučism" (Realist Rayism) seems to be especially relevant here. The painters argued that it is the *sensation* that arises from beholding the "slippery" and "difficult to penetrate" appearances of the "intangible forms" and "immaterial objects", produced in paintings by the "intersection of the sum of refracted rays from the visible physical objects", that causes the sensation of an extra dimension. It also lies "outside our experience of time".[9] In this poem we are dealing, then, with a transition from tangible substances and forms of signifiers to their implications, their mental content, that is, to the signifieds (cf., below, 8.0 and 12.0).

6.2.1 In our "picture", within a wide "realistic" frame of "dawns", "Neva" and "Black Sea" (stanzas one, two and four) "love" vanishes into a strange dimension of "white May" and "blind mirrors". Apparently that dimension is inaccessible to the persona, but it is within earshot, as we learn from stanza five, where the apostrophe is being invited to move, in secrecy, neither to the eery local "white", nor to the bewitching alien "white", but toward yet another dimension, the unspecified "skies of blue" (generally associated with Paradise in Gumilev's poetics of that time). Under that condition the persona is certain to receive the apostrophe's consent. That possibility, indicated by the conditional adverb "then" (21), arises from the regeneration the persona will gain through a contact with *his* element, the sea storms, which have in the past reliably endowed him with the wings of the "tenth Muse", the Muse of Travel. Instead of, or above and beyond, the stormy skies there shall be the transcendental azure.

6.3 ALLEGORY OF REFLECTION. The entire narrative is conducted on the level of "the refracted rays from visible physical objects". The action is presented as a reflection of reified colors in the sky. There is the "bloody" encounter with love (dawns), its turbid-white disappearance (May), the ensuing "fiery" suffering (scorching summer sun), the snow-white oblivion (from heaven), the beckoning "black" (toponym) storms and, finally, the transfigurative, stormless blue.

Gumilev did not need to become an adept of the Fourth Dimension theory or of the occultism popular then among international Modernists. He could avail himself of this notion simply as an artist. His poetry often invokes his Christian beliefs, and he is said to have been acquainted with Bergson's theory of escaping "scientific" time (see footnote 9). The likelihood that the escape here took the route of the Rayonist notion of the two painters seems to be confirmed by Gumilev's poem entitled "Gončarova i Larionov" (#354), also written in 1917. To call attention to its Malayan form, the poem is subtitled "Pantoum". It is remarkable for its virtuoso form and its ambitious content. Each of its sixteen lines (repetons) finds itself repeated, in its entirety, in a different semantic context, reversing its rhyming position and conducting the message of the opposite artistic essences of the two painters and uniting them in a single, greater truth: that each of the essences contains the other. The *sensation* produced by the sixteen phraseological and phonological mirror reflections is, again, that of inter-penetrating sememes which, like rays, fill the poem with semantic resonances. It is noteworthy that in this poem Gumilev twice uses the term *snopy lučej* (bundles of rays). A remote hint at Rayonism can also be found in a dedication written as early as 15 December 1915 (#322), in which Gumilev contends that his diverse works, throughout his career, have a unity that is akin to that which embraces the very diverse buildings of Rome. He predicts, however, that the hour will come when a new edifice, one of (pure) sounds and rays, will emerge.

6.4 SOUND AMPLIFICATION. Phonemes or vowels, like forms or colors, or any artistic element, taken separately, are semantically inherently neutral substances, but they can form alliterative "nests" or clusters around a semantic key word that features the same sound. The clustering amplifies the expressiveness of the key term, by extending the concept into the context. The phonetic domination of u in stanza four has been pointed out above (3.1.b). If expressiveness stems, normally, from an alliterative amplification of a key word, here the alliteration is, first of all, set in a deeper, "low" tonality. It comes from varied groups of phonemes, and not from a single phoneme: *gru*, *gor*, *čor*, *bur*, *dru* and *bud*, *bud*, *bud*, *ut*, *ut*. These clusters tie together at least four key concepts: a) sorrow (*grust'*, *gore*), b) the tripled auxiliary verb of future tense (*bud.ut*), c) sea (*č'ornom*, *more*, *buri*), and d) friend (*druga*). The dialectic role of this phonetic clustering emerges by contrast with dominant sounds or "tonalities" of other stanzas: the "epical narrative" first stanza features short accented o's with such key words as *nočju*, *korotkoj*, *zori*, *krov'*, *ljubov'* (plus twelve unaccented o's or *schwas*: cf. 9.7).

The narrator-persona's psychological reaction to "love's breath" (stanza two) modulates conspicuously to the "bright" tonality of eight long accented a's: *vzgljadom*, *dyxan'em*, *slašče*, *dyxan'em*, *ušla*, *maj*, *očarovan'em*, *zerkala* (plus two unaccented a's). We can begin to associate such clustering of sounds with a mimetic set of analogues established between semantic and phonetic "nests". Gumilev must be given credit for the unobtrusive naturalness with which each stanza receives its tonal key. In that respect, his phonology compares favorably with that of the pioneer sound specialist Bal'mont, whose ostentatious alliterations often appear without sufficient semantic motivation. (Compare his "čuzdyj čaram černyj čeln".)

Again, it is certain that Gumilev was fully conscious of the semantic role of the alliterative device. In the third stanza of the poem "Na dalekoj zvezde Venere" (*SS*, II:#378), written in July 1921, the angels on Venus are said to speak only in the language of vowels, and the following stanza demonstrates it in "algebraic" and alliterative *zaum'* terms akin to those of the Futurists Xlebnikov and Kručenyx:

> Если скажут *еа* и *аи*,
> Это - радостное обещанье,
> *Уо*, *ао* - о древнем рае
> Золотое воспоминанье

(If they say *ea* and *ai* / It [will be] a joyous promise. / *Uo*, *ao* [is] of an ancient paradise / A golden remembrance.)

6.5 SOUND GESTURES. Rhymes, of course, call attention to the rhyming elements' euphonic equivalences, but also to semantic discriminations among the rhyming members and, beyond that, to the discriminations among their respective lines. Jurij Lotman (1971:150-3, 158) finds that the degree of "sonority" or "musicality" of the rhyme depends on the degree of its semantic span; tautological rhymes, therefore, "ring" only if their placement in different formal and semantic contexts prevents them from being truly tautological. The same goes for homophonic rhymes. One can also deduce the reverse: the degree of sonority of rhymes affects the semiotic structure of its members and, ultimately, their semantic load. For example, in stanza two the rhyming words *ušla* and *zerkala* ("she left" and "mirrors") display many obvious differences. In terms of "gesture", attention should be called to the shift in what linguists call the "dynamic equivalent". In these words there is a difference of ratios between the articulatory effort that the rhyming words demand and their lexical load. The backward, hushed sibilant s̲, following the dark, unaccented u̲, together with the semantic and psychological load of this verb of "disheartening" departure, differentiate between the two dynamically and durationally identical rhyming elements la̲. Its enunciation in *ušla* begins from the back and proceeds through protruding and opening lips "stunned by the departure"; whereas that of *zerkala*, pertaining to glossy, hard, cold surfaces, has a bright, frontal, almost dental articulation with the tightened lips of one facing, perhaps, an impenetrable shield. The effect of these two contrasting "dynamic equivalents" extends to their respective lines. Compare the prolonged a̲, o̲, a̲, alternation (6) with the short e̲'s and their surrounding consonantal clusters (8). Similarly, in stanza three the rhyming words *dožit'* - *ispepelit'* (to live to - to reduce to ashes) even have differing accented vowels (y ≠ i). Of the numerous words that could have occupied its valuable slot, *ispepelit'* was chosen as a *Lautgebärde* (Wundt) - an analogue to experience not by way of denotation, connotation or sound imitation (onomatopoeia), but by the articulatory-motor effort that parallels the described act mimetically. Here, too, the phonetic and the semiotic character of the entire rhyming lines is counterposed: the long (four o's) vowels of the "open", semi-dark line 10 versus the four short, unaccented e's and two i's of the labial, bright and "tight" line 12. The "dependence of rhyme on the momentum of the whole line" was observed by Gumilev in the verses of Blok who "shed the yoke of precise rhymes by finding [that] dependence ... his assonances always achieve some particularly refined effect". If his words are like musical notes, the phrases are like chords. Klujev, too, is said to have "realized that the center of gravity is not in the rhymes but in words that stand within the line". In this poem the effect of rhymes is also determined by the *razbeg* (run-up) of their respective lines.

6.5.1. Writing in his 1910 essay about phraseological gestures engaging the reader's imaginatory and articulatory faculties, Gumilev extended the views of Wilhelm von Humboldt, Darwin, Wilhelm Wundt and, in Russia, of A.Potebnja, A.Veselovskij and A.Belyj.[10] In Gumilev's terms, the choice of phonetic and rhythmic devices causes the reader to assume, involuntarily, the pose and histrionics of the persona. The reader, by "the suggestive means of his own body, experiences the same [impulses] as the poet so that 'the uttered thought' becomes no longer a lie, but truth". Like Tjutchev and the Symbolists, Gumilev knew that lyrical communication requires more than merely lexical means. Only he put his faith, almost like the Futurists, in the sub-lexical, physical stratum of articulatory factors, rather than in the supra-lexical network of "corresponding ideas". Gumilev found the Symbolist Ellis's (L.Kobylinskij's) "profound verses with important themes surprisingly boring" because his otherworldly symbols became, due to the lack of gesture, mere allegories. Gumilev anticipated the Formalist notion of "context" by regarding the objective, quantifiable factors of poetic language not in terms of traditional lists of rhetorical and linguistic elements, but in terms of their combinations, or "chordal" arrangements and progressions. He advocates employing verbal gesture even if it might become theatrical in order to create a stronger analogical link between verse and reality. By stressing the "bodily" vividness of verse, Gumilev defends not only his "exotic" predilection for vivid images and "a forest animal's" response to the depicted objects; he extols the predilection for "native" words perceived as deeply familiar, sensory objects. (Compare Mandel'štam's notion of poetic words as *utvar'* [household items]. See also 7, 8.0).

6.6 DIVERGENCE OF GUMILEV'S SCHOOL. It is on the grounds of bodily or histrionic engagement that Gumilev insisted, in 1911, on the widening gulf between him and his group and Vjačeslav Ivanov, whose aloof verbalism is, indeed, objective but does not treat words as everyday objects. His "powerful, virtuoso language is more like that of a philologist than a poet"; to Ivanov

> words, like images, are only covers for ideas.... To him all words are equal... for him there is no secret classification into words which are "one's own" and "not one's very own", [he has] no profound, often inexplicable sympathies and antipathies [for certain words]. He does not care about their origin.... But his always intense thinking, his exact knowledge of what he

> wishes to say make his selection of
> words so amazingly diverse.... so
> distinct from the language of other
> poets... It seems that there is not a
> single complicated device which Ivanov
> would not know. But for him device is
> not a friendly aid, a golden joy, but
> only a means. This is why Ivanov likes
> to write in difficult, ambitious, but
> already available [*gotovye*] forms (*SS*,
> IV:267-8).

(Gumilev may have had in mind his own group's "newly rethought" meter/rhythm relationships, such as the *dol'niki* forms with omitted syllables in stress groups, as one example of wrestling with new forms.)

It is noteworthy that in 1912 Ivanov began to argue, chiefly in response to Gumilev's attacks, that "true Symbolism does not tear itself from the earth; it wants to combine the roots and the stars and grows like a stellar flower from its nearby, native roots. It does not substitute things and, in speaking of the sea, it means the earthly sea, and in speaking of snowy heights... it means the tops of mountains" (1974:II:612). Having no trouble in accepting this approach, Gumilev insists on his "unwillingness to sacrifice all other means of expressiveness to the [ostentatiously 'Symbolist'] symbol", seeking rather their "full correlation" (1913/*SS*, IV:173).

Beyond modes of expression, the incompatibility between Gumilev's and Ivanov's poetics lies in the difference of their perceptions of *realia* (*Weltempfindungen* or *mirooščuščenija*). Ivanov maintained that items from the author's environment, which enter the arsenal of a poem, should be seen as transparent phenomena (*prozračnosti*), beyond which lie deeper or higher psychological and spiritual realities. The names of these items to be incorporated into poetic texts are chosen as symbols precisely for their capacity to encompass that intellectual penetration, beyond the physicality of the named objects. This approach presupposes a contextual way of viewing things, a mental continuum, and the use of extensive semantic energy in expression (1912/1974:612). Gumilev, on the other hand, looks upon the world as a "discrete quantity" (in the mathematical sense), made up of separate parts, so that even the poetic thought is perceived as a series of discontinuous states, that is, combinations of impulses acting on the sensory system (see 8.1). Hence the abundance of phraseological leaps between, and within, stanzas in this poem.

7. TONE OF SPEECH.

The conception and production of tone is always the ultimate and most refined stage of interpreting literary as well as musical texts. Recitation makes each translation of all the semantic and sensory signs of a text into the audio-oral medium irrevocable. It demands a finite weighing and calibrating of all those signs and parts of signs in order to decide on tempo, volume, pauses, accentuation and intonation on both the level of an overall standard and of the individual deviations from it. It is not possible, of course, to decree the definitive tone in which a poem is to be delivered; the reader imposes his own notion of that; this fact, however, does not prevent the author from planting in the text tokens of his own version of the tone. And the sensitive reader adapts his attitude in response to the recognized tokens, and communes, as Gumilev hoped, physically with the resultant modes. If literary themes express the intellectual assignment of the work, the speaker's tone mirrors the volume and progression of his emotions. Since the emotional state may motivate the very theme of lyric poetry, the tone carries a double assignment. In this poem, it is the changes in tone that provide the story. Conceivably, many lyrical poems are written for the sake of capturing and releasing a given tone. In this poem, coping with the disaster of being forsaken by the beloved is composed into a plot of changes in tone.

Clichés like "slašče roz", "milym snegom" or informalities like "oprošu soveta", "xočeš' ... uedem", "nikomu ne skažem", "tol'ko b poskorej" simulate the spontaneous intimacy of speech, and provide examples of what Vinogradov (1925:149) calls "grimaces of dialogue" (cf. 5.2, 6.5, 6.5.1). These tonal grimaces and gestures form oppositions with those of other stanzas and hemistichs, and modulate the (respectively) dramatic, despondent, and hortatory phases of the experience, that is, the "psychological" or lyrical plot of the poem. Seamless coinciding of tonal and imagerial expressiveness is what produces poetic vividness of diction and "that ineffable moment of combining motion and stillness", a moving sound and a still image.

8.0 MATERIALITY OF IMAGES.

Detailed study of imagery, eidolology – a prominent subject in Gumilev's later theory – warrants a transition from linguistic to semiotic categories. Images satisfy the linguistically oriented literary inquiry only to the extent that they are treated as words, i.e., as signifiers; the other functions of images, produced by the sensorial (pictorial, acoustic, etc.) perception of the imagined "thing", fall outside such investigation. It seems counterproductive, however, to dismiss the rich aesthetic, emotional and thematic effect produced in poetry by the signifieds upon the content. Again, the effect of the imaginary objects may be suprasegmental, subliminal, or fully conscious, and it may extend to unlimited segments of the text. Such is the effect of "dawns like blood", "white May", "quiet snow", "Black Sea storms calling", etc. Objects of this sort contaminate portions of the text not as abstract semantic bits, but as real things, through the properties of their substances and behavior, as they evoke, through memory, the appropriate sensory responses.

A poetic image, as distinct from the same sign's function as a word or symbol, may then be defined semiologically as "the imagined materiality of the signified".

As with the tone of a poem, each reader "sees" the physicality of image-objects in his own way; here, too, the author can implant tokens of his own perception with semantically contiguous predicates and epithets. For example, in stanza one the strong simile "blood" reifies not only night and its dawns; it helps the adjective and instrumental agent "inaudible gait" and the perfective "glanced at" to reify "love", backgrounding temporarily its "fourth dimension". The image-object is made more palpable by the materiality of its surrounding lingual elements, which align themselves to serve as reinforcing analogues for the term. Onomatopoeia, sound gestures and alliterative echoes (15, 16) are the obvious devices of such reinforcement (cf. 6.4., 6.5). But the onomastic act itself, the "naming of things", whether spontaneous as with Adam, or engrained in us as a cultural habit, can evoke private associations between words and "things", vivifying the images, and dictating the "preferred" words (see 6.6). And good technique, as Gumilev wrote about Kuzmin, "never obscures an image, it only endows it with wings".

8.1. POWER OF IMAGES. Whereas word-concepts require, for communicability, a degree of logical alignment, imaginary objects need only syntax to determine their relations. The specific presence of the image-object may be conjured up by metonymic or synecdochal selection among its attributes, or predicates. (A "tree" may be imagined first by its rustling, its shadow or transparencies, its greenness, wetness, thickness, etc.) In speech, the flexible, mentally reflected multifariousness of images tolerates logical and even semantic imprecision, as well as irrational or oxymoronic combinations of word-images. It does so by engaging the reader's own reflexes. Thus, the "unmotivated" switch from "dawns" to "love" can be "accepted" due to the polyfunctional ties between the multiple concrete features of "dawns" and the abstract polysemia of "love". The same applies to all the "unmotivated" image+image combinations (5-6), or "she went away into white May" (6-7, also 16) and the image *versus* concept juxtapositions (13, 17-18). Thus, the materiality of images can effectively exploit "referential indeterminacy", cast a manifold "sensory contamination" on surrounding portions of the text, and be better "felt" than concepts and better remembered than the material elements of the signifi*ers* (graphics, sounds, rhythms, etc.). Finally, the materiality of images may guide the tone, and gravitate the phatic balance towards anywhere in the line, apart from the rhyming ending. In line 13 it falls on the beginning. The emphasis here is not dynamic but agogic, due to the semantics of the key word "quiet" and, even more so, because of the physicality of the attached image, "snow".

9.0 BALANCING ASYMMETRIES.

According to Jakobson, symmetries stabilize the content of works of art, by structuring their "context" (cf. 5.0) and help, in W.B.Yeats's words, "express better what I thought and felt when I was a very young man", because "pattern and rhythm are the road to open symbolism" and provide "a more appropriate simplicity (quoted in Jakobson and Rudy: 1981: 601, 600, 604). It is beneficial, then, to note how the various elements are increasingly balanced in our parallel case. Gumilev refrains, on the whole, from "specializing in one or a few aspects of poetic diction" (1913/*SS*, IV:173), from "generally Modernist clichés" (which Gumilev regretted to find in Gorodeckij's *Cvetuščij posox*; *SS*, IV:336), from "blurring of the senses" and from neologisms; there is no preeminence of euphony, no syntactic violation or complication, which "carefully obscures the meaning of the phrase" (as he saw in Ivanov's *Cor ardens*; cf. *SS*, IV:297), no *obnaženie priemov* (devices made bare), no *ostranenie* (de-familiarization), no effacement of reality. At the same time, Gumilev does not return to pre-Modernist methods. This work illustrates well the distinction between "simple symmetry" and "complex balances" of poetic functions. Whereas the former features ostentatious equivalences within the same prosodic species (anaphoras, rhymes, syntactic parallelisms, tautologies, etc.) or parallel oppositions (I *versus* You; referents *versus* allegories; nature *versus* psychic phenomena, etc.), the "complex balances" present substitutions or compensations for equivalences derived from mixed levels of speech and prosody (changing semantic loads within syntactic parallels, stressing rhythmic prominences over metric regularity, alliterations instead of rhymes, etc.). Gumilev manages to combine both approaches; the traditional equivalents are boldly displayed and subtly subverted. With astonishing consistency there is in virtually every instance, on every level of prosody and design, a progression from simple to complex functions.

9.1. The composition is centered around the simple theme of being together with "love". That togetherness is seen as possible under three conditions, which oppose each other by the degrees of independence they allow "her" and, conversely, allow "him" to have his say. These three conditions exist in four realms which are like concentric circles, distinctly apart from each other. Seen in terms of the plot, the first circle is the most narrow; it is that of private waking during the dawns (visitation). The second extends along the banks of Neva (disappearance). The third expands to the Black Sea (proposal), and the fourth to the azure (consent). Lines 9-12 (rhetorical questions) form a buffer zone between circles one, two and the much wider three, as lines 13-14 and, retroactively, 23-24 (snow coverage) separate the action from the widest and most distant, fourth realm.

9.2. The time of action is indicated by the tenses of the verbs. But, as with the places of action, the heterogeneity of tenses produces a complex overall frame. The verbless lines 1 and 2 suggest a generic time, a gnomic present tense of consciousness. The behavior of "love" is given as a background to awareness in the perfective past (3-6). The anterior future of the interrogative stanza three returns the mind to the current wondering about survival. Along that line, stanza four combines perfective (13), imperfective (14, 15), simple (15) and compound (15-16) future. Stanzas five and six have a different type of combination: in five the first person singular and plural act in the simple perfective future, and the second person in the present tense; whereas in six the roles are reversed. The verb of cognizance, *znaju* (21), governs with its present tense the hypothetical future and the jussive mood of the ending of the poem. The state of anxiety is intensified by the repeated anaphora with the repeated simile *skorej* (sooner, 22, 23). Such a mixture of tenses and aspects effects a shift from historical and dramatic narration to state of consciousness. Facts of the past, present and future merge in its synchronous dimension.

9.2.1. Time is also marked by (the weather of) the four seasons. The moment of narration is set at the end of spring ("departed [perfective past] into... May"). The narrator must face the summer, is not certain of surviving till fall; if he does, he will be healed in winter; he will travel through storms to reach the cloudless azure. The psychological nadir is summer. It appears twice; first, when facing the immediate aftermath of having had love (11-12), second, in the finale, *after* this mental recovery, by arriving at the hypothetical reunification with love (23). Both times, summer is followed directly by winter (mental opposition). But nadir is not easily counterbalanced. In addition to the phase of oblivion, there must be the phases of the storms and of the consent to join in a New Spring of the distant, fabulous azure.

9.3. The vocabulary is rather simple. Of the twenty-nine nouns only one is an abstraction ("enchantment", 7), but the "things" rapidly unfold the expanded view. There are no repeated verbs or adjectives, and only three repeated nouns: "breath" (a prepositionless object, which forms a tautological rhyme between line 5 and the following caesura), "summer", and the metonym of its opposite, "snow" - a subject (13) that becomes an instrumental functive (24). There is one logically redundant synonymity (13). In each of the three instances of coupled heterogeneous adjectives (1, 8, 24) entirely different realities are specified. And the summarizing totalizer "nothing" (14) acts as a subject roomy enough to "swallow" all signifieds of regret.

9.4. The narrative pace is deliberately ordinary, almost casual. It is quite lively due to the simplicity of syntax and the relatively high count of twenty-one verbs, all (with the exception of "reducing to ashes", 1.12) quite simple. But the text is of high semantic density. Of the 117 words, 89 turn out to be polysemic key words. Only twenty-one have purely formal (prepositional, conjunctive and pronominal) duties.

9.5. We have a perfect syntactic and logical clarity of diction, but at the same time an abundance of what was called (5.0) "referential indeterminacy" between literal and figurative meanings in more than half of the lines: 2, 4, 5, 6-7-8, 11-12, 13, 16, 17-18, 23-24 (for details, see 4.0, 5.0, 6.2, 6.2.1, 8.0, 9.4). Asymmetries among syntactic and semantic hierarchies abound on the lexical level, but elements which make perceptible a symmetric norm, or its violation, within a line *mark* themselves as distinctive signs. And the signs so marked - "night" (1), "dawns" (2), "love" (4) - thus gain in semantic weight due to their positioning; the repeat of "by breath" (5,6) eliminates "weak" terms like a correlative pronoun and auxiliary verb, emphasizes the upward (superior) comparison ("sweeter than roses" (6). Bracing the "rose", the repeated "breaths" fuse with the genitive plural attribute (*roz*), omitting the comparative conjunction *čem*. In many such cases, the poet gains more than economy by eliminating "service words" without losing precision. Words, then, receive greater semantic and semiotic roles, their context becomes more densely saturated, and the text gains in expressivity or "muscle".

9.6. The coinciding of the strophic and syntactic mechanisms can be readily seen from the punctuation. Each stanza ends with a period mark; therefore, stanza = period. Three other punctuation marks delimit the clauses within each stanza: 4 lines = 4 clauses. Thematically, all adjacent lines are coupled into pairs: 12 ideas = 12 distichs. But they differ strongly in their internal formation, and the linking words are always varied in form. The first distich, a verbless anapodoton, has two subjects, two prepositions, two instrumentals of time; and it has the two verses joined by a copulative conjunction (*i*); the second - by a subject, placed at the end (*ljubov'*); the third by inverse symmetry: verb-copula-adverbial instrumental, same adverbial instrumental-copula-verb (*otravila... - i - dyxane'em, dyxan'em - i - ušla*). The fourth distich (exceptionally, without verb and subject) is linked by the anaphoric preposition of direction, etc., etc. We also have syntactic coupling of distichs: the third and fourth are connected by a common verb and indicative mood: *ušla*; in the following stanza, distichs 4 and 5 are linked by the verb *dožit'*, but in the infinitive mood. Distichs 6 and 7 are joined by the auxiliary verb *budet* (holding a triple opposition [negative-positive, adverb-noun, two semantic fields]: *ne budet žalko - budet veter*); 8 and 9 by parallel predicative negations: *ne skažem - ne belym*; and the concluding two by the extended anaphoras: *tol'ko b (po)skorej - tol'ko b(y) skorej* plus the two verbs in the non-realized, exhortative mood.

9.7. The meter, a five-foot trochee, with its alternating masculine and feminine endings, is highly uniform, but the rhythm is varied. In Russian poetry, as in English, the trochee is a rare choice, compared to the iamb, the other binary meter. Marie Maline (1964:303) has counted only sixty poems in Gumilev's oeuvre that employ this meter.[11] For Gumilev, meter served as an analogue to an emotional experience, and he spoke of the trochee as "violins" (presumably due to a down-and-up bowing effect). But he stressed the necessity of rhythmic elasticity. And he announced, in his Acmeist manifesto (1913/*SS*, IV:172), that his group had recently rethought the relationships between meter and rhythm. (Cf. Sampson:1975:21-41 and R.D.B.Thomson:1975:42-58.) Here we have flexible rhythmicity superimposed on a uniform meter which, to the dismay of statisticians, eliminates the possibility of simple charting. We have, in fact, three kinds of accents: obligatory, possible, and actual, as created by a given interpretation of whoever recites.[12] Despite the consistent trochaic pentameter with a typical accent on second, third and fifth foot, the number of optional, semantically determinable accents illustrates the insufficiency of a straight count of accents according to lexemes as they are accented in dictionaries. There are, within the total of 120 places, fifty-six obligatory accents, eighty-seven possible accents, and a flexible in-between number of "real" accents as chosen by the individual reader who, each time, becomes the final arbiter of the poem's melodics. My own last reading called for seventy accents. The caesura ambulates irregularly between the third and fourth syllables, falling on eleven masculine, twelve feminine, and one dactylic endings. The rhythmic cohesion of the poem is increased by occasional equality of caesuras among lines with feminine and masculine endings. The exceptional fifth-syllable caesura occurs in line 21 (coinciding with the turning point in the plot). The shorter, left-hand hemistichs become highly distinctive by reason of the optional (6,7,10,13,15,22,23) and obligatory (8, 16, 24) accents on the first foot.

9.8. Each of the twelve rhyming pairs is perfectly matched, but they feature twelve different vocalic properties, and the twenty-four constituent words display a remarkable syntactic, not to mention semantic, heterogeneity. The accented rhyming vowels echo the "drone" characteristic of each stanza: I = o̲; II = a̲; III = e̲ and i̲: IV = o̲; V = e̲ and y̲; VI = a̲ and o̲. This order, too, displays a complexity of symmetry.

9.9. The aggregate phonology, in keeping with the phraseology, syntax, and vocabulary, is quite ordinary; but the melodicity of the verses is highly varied due to semantic distinctions, which lead to intonational as well as rhythmic distinctions among the verses. The frequency of individual vowels is roughly equivalent to that used in regular speech; of the 83 accentable and 156 non-accentable vowels, respectively: 18 and 19 are a̲'s, 18 and 38 e̲'s, 8 and 12 i̲'s, 26 and 43 o̲'s, 9 and 12 u̲'s and 4 and 9 y̲'s. But the clustering of the vowels is conspicuous. Each stanza has its own dominant vowel that highlights the corresponding key concept (cf. 6.4). In stanza one, relative to other vowels, o̲ predominates, being 7 times accented = 53.8% (+ 8 unaccented *schwas* = 40% of total vowels). In that stanza, e̲ is next most frequently accented = 30.1%. In stanza two a̲ = 57.1% and e̲ = 14.2%. In stanza three o̲ = 42%, e̲ = 21.4%. In stanza four u̲ = 37.5%, o̲ = 25%. In stanza five e̲ = 30.8%, a̲ = 23%. In stanza six, o̲ = 35.7%, a̲ = 28.6%

Against the dominant "drone" sound of each stanza or distich, the melody of each verse features its independent design of accented and unaccented vowels and individual consonantal admixtures. Line 13 stands out, again, with its varied palate of vowels (i̲ i e̲ a̲ y̲ e̲ u̲ i o̲ e̲), its sibilants, made more prominent by strong palatalization of six consonants, starting with those in the first word, *tixij*, and extending through the two negations in the following line, 14.

As seen in 9.0-9.9, every complex function is made to look simple at first glance. Most Futurists, Dadaists and so on chose not to appear simple, and to stupefy the reader from the start. Their strategies, too, have merits; but Gumilev's advance "along the line of greatest resistance", as proclaimed in his 1913 manifesto, consistently involves greater care, as seen here. Despite all the internal *zatrudnenija formy* (making form difficult), no "careful obliteration of the meaning of sentences" (as Gumilev observes in V.Ivanov's verses) or outright obfuscation, as in *zaum'*, takes place. Kuzmin's ideal *prekrasnaja jasnost'* (magnificent clarity) remains unimpeded because the signifieds always *appear* to be equal to their signifiers. The reader is never semantically overwhelmed. But in actuality most signifiers in this poem represent *several* signifieds.

10.0 POLYSEMIA.

Certain apparent ambiguities have been pointed out above (4 and 5.2) on the lexical level. But the poet's ear, and attentive reading, can discern semantic distinctions that emanate from parts of words and from relations between these parts. Although complex, the distinctions on this micro-level serve to resolve whatever lexical ambiguities occur in texts; they tilt the total of the perceived meanings in a specific direction. These mini-functions, called sememes or semes, may be expressed by various means: by morphemes, sub-morphemes, by interrelations of adjacent or non-adjacent phonemes; they may also spring from associations of such particles with their denotative, grammatical, imagerial or connotative contexts. It is the semes that influence the author in his specific word choices, for example, among synonyms, rhymes, etc. Even the selection of meter, and its violations, may frequently be attributed to this process of choice. These particles may also trigger inter-contextual associations. In short, semes are produced by the substances of expression, but their functions operate on the level of "content", in the mind of the beholder. As causes, semes are not always visible to the naked eye but, like viruses, their effects can sometimes be isolated, tested, explained, and traced to the physical verbal substances that produce them.

A simple example of polysemia, in this poem, comes with the word *otravila* (she poisoned, line 5). Besides the grammatical markings of the preposition-based prefix o (about, surrounding, enveloping the parameters of a phenomenon) and the suffixes il + a, (active voice, imperfective past, singular, feminine), the word form abounds with additional lexical meanings, all of which relate to the content of this poem: *travila* (she hounded, *also* laid a design, [as acid does in metal etchings]; *also* damaged, extinguished, devastated, wasted); and the desinence *vila* (pitchfork, weapon) is commonly used as a metaphor for threatening hostility. The nominal root of the verb is very rich in uses: *trava* (grass, any annual weed, herb, medicine [*travu pit'* - to drink medicine]); also, it is the archaic word for ornaments in illuminated manuscripts, and *traven'* is the archaic name of the month of May.

10.1. Perceived etymology always wedges a new semantic series into an expression, each comprising another tier, including a mythological one. *Trava* prefixed by o implies here an all-around inebriation, as by a witch's toxin (cf. 8.1). Hence the effectiveness of her (no longer metaphorical) instruments: *vzgljadom* (by a look, glance, stare, 5) and *dyxan'em* (breath, 5, 6) which remind us, as a metonym, of the stupefying Medusa, or Gorgon, and of the Dragon, respectively. The polysemia of "snow" stems from its numerous functions as an endearing object, a stuff that covers the ground, an image, an index of time, a metonym of winter and color, an index of time span and a metaphor for oblivion (cf. 4.1, 5.0).

11.0. POLYFUNCTIONS

Sections 2.1, 4.0, 6.2, 6.5, etc. dealt with certain poetic "echoes" on the traditional level of univerbations and their content. Lexical interactions are traceable in linear fashion in texts, because words follow each other in an order determined by syntax and versification. Semes, on the other hand, are distributed randomly in a text; their etymological, extra- and sublexical presence is, more often than not, accidental and, as mentioned in 10.0, their function is realized in the mind. The lines, therefore, that connect the individual semes crisscross within the text and often intersect outside the text. Each such instance represents a nexus of functions, and the multilinear progressions of such clusters will henceforth be called here "polyfunctions". Such a method is effective when one seeks to preserve the paradigmatic nature of a quality or object (for example, a complex mood or gesture) in the process of sequential transmission. The medium of compound signs (words) may be made subject to this kind of transmission. For example, the various connotations of the concrete object "blood" can be linked with those of the nebulous "love", of the polyseme *otravila* (she poisoned) and of "snow" and "storms", etc. *above* the line of syntax; and the connections along the multiple tracks may proceed in any order or direction. Bypassing the syntagmatic dictates of "practical" speech, poetic semes need not be semantically subordinated to a dominant seme. Yet, when presented in word formations, polysemic structures relate to each other syntactically, in a linear-sequential progression, as does normal speech. With close reading semes may emancipate themselves, and their patterned relation allows them to interrelate as semantic co-equals and establish simultaneous relations with other relevant concepts within, and even outside, the text. Semantic threads, thus extended throughout the communication, are multilinear, as are the semiotic functions of the progressions from one polysemic structure to the next.

"Polyfunctions" have been defined as semiotic relations among progressing polysemic structures.[13] Gumilev here chose most of the key concepts that partake in the various metamorphoses for their capacity to conduct polyfunctional progressions. I would generalize that any poem "comes to life", that is, receives its extra charge of semantic energy, through its semic activity, whereby the simultaneous sets of mobile ideas spring up, as we have seen, in crisscross fashion.

11.1. POETIC FUNCTION. In my opinion, then, it is the increment of semantic energy, caused by the various equivalences, that makes these functions "poetic". Jakobson's definition (6.1) may be expanded by adding that the "projected equivalences" must generate an additional semic activity, since the recognition of equivalences involves the superimposition of those elements' semantic distinctions, which are juxtaposed above the ordinary, syntactic alignments. Jakobson is correct in saying that "poetic functions" are not confined to poetry alone. Nor does all, especially modern, poetry feature straight equivalences. But poems do seek an economy of expression by projecting maximal information on a minimal terrain. Mandel'štam rightly called a poem "a monstrously condensed reality". Gumilev's poem, too, presents a content whose whole is greater than the sum of the parts, because its multilinear, poetically connected terms create additional extra-lexical and extra-grammatical semic relations that may be termed "contextual" or "secondary" semantics. Symmetries draw attention to such relations and become the major factor in structuring the context, that is to say, the supra-lexical meaning in poetry.

Readers and critics oriented toward finding the informational and phatic expressiveness primarily in the lexical load of texts usually take the services of grammatical categories and phonological features for granted. They tend to dismiss the equivalents among such elements as non-essential coincidents. Occurrences of rhyme and meter are too striking to be missed, but these factors are rarely discussed in terms of their contribution to the "poetization" and semantics of the text, let alone how "poetization" can also take place without these factors, and without an ostentatious observance of "rules". Poetic functions can emerge from an infinite gradation within equivalences, as well as from a vast variety of species. The "equivalent" elements need not always be analogous; they can be chosen from a gamut of substitutions for analogies, including oppositions. For example, a member of a rhyming pair may be replaced by increasingly approximate phonemes, forming "rhymoids", "dissonant rhymes", "left rhymes", "semantic rhymes" and "absent rhymes".

Furthermore, even such purely cognitive, linguistic phenomena as negations are capable of forming positive pairs with their oppositions, the withheld positive entities. Michael Shapiro defines negation, semiotically, as a species of metonymy and, by the nature of the minimal paradigm (the binary opposition), "the negative term of such an opposition necessarily and overtly makes reference to the positive". (1979:111). Thus, "I ne budet žalko ničego" (And there will be no regret for anything, 14) is not a mere rewording of "Quiet snow will cover grief and woe" (13). The totalizer *ničego* (nothing) summons *all* the preceding denotative and connotative data, pairing line 14 with the entity of all experiences, including ones not given in the text.

The structure of Gumilev's poem points to the inexhaustible variety of equivalences and their substitutions that make up poetic functions. This type of economy of selection and ingenuity in combining them may help, some day, to put to rest the "means and ends" controversy of aesthetic functions. Whether one views the constituents upwards, from the smallest substances of expression toward the dynamics of the formal constellations, and toward their mental effect (the multi-layered complexion of content), or whether one starts from the feeling of a perceived message and then appreciates its implications and constituent functions and their building blocks, one learns about the medium, about the author and about oneself.

12.0. MYTHOPOESIS.

Poetic symbols (as defined in Footnote 6) may be expressive as univerbations and also by their polysemic connotations. In concert, the connections within one of their semantic strata can comprise a mythopoetic work and vivify fundamental historic forces that are at the same time basic, "primitive" parts of the collective human psyche. According to Ivanov (1974:554-5), when endowed with predicative action symbols take on the functions of myths. Their curriculum, given in super-human characters, conforms to cycles of struggle, death and rebirth. These cycles reveal, in their various manifestations, the same underlying mythical structure. The hypostases of "love", in this poem, are a case of mythopoesis. The semes combining to produce the notion of the witch (10.1), not lexically denoted in the text, are operative, first of all, during the supernatural appearance and disappearance of the subject "love". It is during the unspecified duration of, and in connection with, the eery dawns that the bewitching "love" makes its "inaudible" entrance. It becomes embodied in order to confront the narrator-persona by means of the three caesarian acts (the specific act *veneno necavit* pertains to her "witchness"). It is during the eery dawns that the reified, unholy being makes its appearance, and damaging disappearance, into the enchanting, "hyperreal" dimension (7, 8; cf. 6.2.1). It is only after the persona connects with his own elemental forces, emanating from the stormy Black Sea, that the sorceress turns into a social apostrophe or, rather, into a mythical princess ("tsarevna", 20), to be redeemed, or seduced, as in the ancient Russian tales (*byliny*), by a super-effort of a super-knight (*čudo-bogatyr'*). The diction here becomes reminiscent of Aleksej Tolstoj's stylization of the myth of Aleša

Popovič, who seduces his tsarevna through his Orphic song. The persona's dependence on natural forces such as the seasons, the sea storms and quiet snow, as hers was on dawns, on May, and on the reflecting river, is in keeping with folk mythology.

The "witch's" weapons, her "stare" and "breath" (5-6), evoke Medusa, or the Gorgon, and the Dragon. In "Poet" (*SS*, II:292) Gumilev associates dragons with primeval "sacred poets of the seas" (cf. also 225, 226, and 396: 12 songs of the extant Book One of *Poema Načala*, entitled "Drakon"). Here, the dragon's first effect is the searing fieriness of the summer (11, 12), targeted at the persona (12). It comes with incredible sweetness, also directed exclusively (4) at the persona. If the apostrophe combines the opposing principles of love, witch, dragon (combination of annihilation and poetic vision), tsarevna and paradise, it is, indeed, a potent symbol of profound psychological dimensions.

13.0 "HERE AND NOW" REALITY.

Psychological time, even if complex, is not indicated vaguely here. The two prepositions (both of time and space: lines 1, 2) extend their function beyond the syntactic limits of the first distich; their effect is to make the entire utterance "before the short... night and after it" define, adverbially, the actions of "love" as being simultaneous with the "dawns".[14] The dawns dwarf the northern short night, by the two bracketing prepositional adverbs of location. They also syphon the attention away from "night" toward what happens "before" and "after" it, by their vivid and ominous simile "blood". "Night" is further deemphasized by the change in the last version's punctuation. But the splitting of "dawns" by the intervening night, and the punctative forms of the actions of "love" indicate that her visitations must have been repetitive. The fact that the narrator-persona notices the color of the dawns shows that those were waking hours, and the "shortness" of the night reminds us that these were, respectively, very late and very early hours. These are the intimate times of privacy, during which the persona is, naturally, most sensitive to the impact of the "sorceress". There is a number of poems in which "dawns" are associated with creativity (cf. Fn.13).

By substituting the denominalization *nevskie* (pertaining to the Neva, 8) for *mutnye* (turbid), Gumilev avoided the redundancy with "blind", while presenting a concrete topos. Linking the name of the river with the metaphor "blind" and the possibly real "mirrors", suggests the reflections of the water in the agonizing light of the White Nights. More literally, these plural "mirrors" could be windows, in that light, on Petrograd's main street, the Nevskij Prospekt - popularly referred to as "Nevskij". The plural adjective "nevskie" would, then, pertain to properties on that street. The Eliseev Shop, a big department store on it, with its large windows, suggests itself as a possible real place into which the apostrophe disappeared.[15]

13.1. THE PERSON BEHIND THE APOSTROPHE. There are too few documents and too many hints to allow a good biographical guess. The apostrophe could be a historical person, a mythological borrowing, a real psychological tribulation, an archetypal figure, or a composite person of several experiences. Within the formative period of this poem (1916-21) Gumilev dedicated and re-dedicated many poems (cf.##248, 332, 333, 361, 362, 377, 380-2, 383), especially to "Those women who prove to me/ The immortality of my soul" (#317, 23-24). Names within texts are more reliable; lines 21-22 of this last poem say, "And I know that about distant me / Rings Axmatova's siren verse". But, even more indelibly, her name is etched in three undated acrostichs. Possibly written before our poem, the images and context are conspicuously reminiscent: "A rozy dušny, rozy krasny /..../ Tam smotrit v dušu čej-to vzgljad, / Otravy polnyj i obmanov" (And the roses [are] stifling, roses [are] red/..../ There stares into the soul someone's glance/ Full of poison and deceits. #380.3, 5, 6, cf stanza two of our poem).

"Novyj mir byl *sinij* i bezzvezdnyj/..../ Aloj krovi robkoe bien'e,/ Xrupkix ruk ..." (The new world was blue and starless/..../ The red blood's timid pounding,/ The delicate hands ... #381:3, 5, 6, cf. stanza five, 17, 18; stanza one, 2; stanza six, 24).

"Though details of the Axmatova-Gumilev relationship are yet to be clarified, there is little doubt that it was a major emotional involvement in Gumilev's [and Axmatova's] life and might naturally play a central role in his poetic reconstruction of his biography" (Rusinko:1982:395). Sergej Makovskij, a mutual friend and colleague, was convinced that Axmatova remained "his only real love" (1962:210). And their contemporary Julij Ajxenval'd (1923:III) even constructed a whole dramatic novel by juxtaposing verses of Axmatova and Gumilev in which they may, or may not, have addressed each other. Much more cautiously, Rusinko constructs through intertextual scrutiny an argument for regarding Axmatova as the heroine and apostrophe "Mashenka" in "Zabludivšijsja tramvaj" (ibid., 392-5, 401, 402 [Fns]). Earl Sampson (1972:289) comes to a similar general conclusion that the failure of Gumilev's relationship with Axmatova may have been the turning point of his inner development and "in spite of the vicissitudes of their relationship, each poet was conscious of his presence in the other's verses".

13.2. Our poem, too, has intertextual links with Axmatova's verses. Her "Anno Domini" (1921, 1-8) reads:

>   Заплаканная осень, как вдова
>   В одеждах черных, все сердца туманит.
>   Перебирая мужнины слова,
>   Она рыдать не перестанет.
>   И будет так, пока *тишайший* снег
>   Не *сжалится* над *скорбной* и усталой...
>   *Забвенье боли и забвенье* нег -
>   За это жизнь отдать не мало.

(Tear-stained autumn, like a widow, / In black clothes clouds all hearts. / Going through husband's words, / She will not cease weeping. // And it will be so, until the *quietest snow* / Will take *pity* on the *grieving* and tired; / *Oblivion* of *pain and oblivion* of langours, / For that to give up life is not too little.)

The last stanza speaks of the "*white threshold* of *paradise*". Ever since the early, 1911, poem "Iz logova zmieva" (*SS*, I:#132) one of Gumilev's epithets, *koldun'ja* (sorceress), entered the multifarious stream of Gumilev's notions about Axmatova. "Whiteness" is repeatedly linked to his image of Axmatova, and so is *xrupkost'* (delicacy, fragility). (Cf. "O samoj strojnoj, samoj beloj /... O samoj beloj, samoj nežnoj / Poet moe vospominan'e" [About the slimmest, the whitest /... / About the whitest, the most tender / Sings my memory] #242, 7, 11-12. Compare, too, the title of her collection *Belaja staja* [White Flock]). Compare also:

> Тихо, тихо, нежно, как во сне,
> Иногда приходишь ты ко мне.
>
> Надо лбом твоим густая прядь,
> Мне нельзя ее поцеловать...
>
> Нежный друг мой, беспощадный враг...

(Softly, softly, tender as in sleep, / Sometimes you come up to me. // On your forehead is a thick lock / I may not kiss it /.../ Tender friend of mine, mercyless enemy, #243:3-6). "Tvoix volos ne smel pocelovat' ja" (Your hair I did not dare to kiss) is line 33 of the first, *Apollon* version of "Pjatistopnye jamby", a biographical poem dating from 1912 which definitely refers to the break with Axmatova. Lines 35-6 of that poem read "I ty ušla...// Poxožaja na drevnee raspjat'e" (And you went away... // Looking like an ancient Crucifix; cf. our lines 4-5). Also, lines 15-20 of the *Al'bom* version of our poem recall stanza nine of "Pjatistopnye jamby". According to Gleb

Struve (*SS*, II:291), lines 5-10 of "Ezbekie" (#246) are also probably related to Axmatova, referring to a time ten years earlier, in 1907, when he contemplated suicide because she refused his proposal of marriage. Gumilev was said to have returned from Western Europe in 1918 because of his intention to reunite with Axmatova. Since both she and he had other associations, it may be that Gumilev is referring to those two people as "Your and my neighbors to whom we [simply] shall say nothing" (19, 20).

13.3. Whether our poem stems from a single or from a composite experience, it responds to one sensibility's search for an adequate expression of his preoccupation. This fact explains the intertextualities among numerous poems of Gumilev of the 1916-21 period. Besides the poems just quoted (## 317, 380, 381 and 242, 243) and the poems cited earlier, ## 322, 354 and 378, concept-images belonging to the same "context" are also used in ## 233, 234, 236-8, 343, 345, 348, 349, 357, 362, 363, 368, 369, 377, 379, 382 and, more distantly, in many others. Taking the poems together, this shared context reflects a recurring state of mind, and represents a substantial and characteristic part of Gumilev's psychobiography. By subconsicous or partly conscious trajectories of symbols, or by strategies of design, lyrical searching becomes part of the author's *Lebensweise*. Poetic symbols with their "referential indeterminacy" and, even more so, the hovering poetic "context", penetrate whatever areas are being concentrated on. Overarching the strata of events that are put into focus, symbols and the work's context relate to more distant, subliminally lurking realities, such as mythological or archetypal configurations, artistic reflexes and impulses, values, memories, notions of the future, and plain objective circumstances that reside on the periphery of consciousness. The arbitrary order in which these areas may be probed places the experience of a poet outside concepts of fixed time, "which calls for psychological research" (Gumilev, 1914, quoted in

Rusinko:1982:383). For example, the mythical term
"tsarevna", enforced by "azure", symbolizes a
Wonderland that opposes more than the dragon and his
sea or the dimension into which the sorceress has
vanished. The symbol "tsarevna" is counterposed to an
increasingly grim biographical and cultural reality
(#356). As Gumilev wrote in the first of the poems
entitled "Sčast'e" ("Happiness", #186), "The sick
believe in May roses / And tender are the fairy tales
of paupers./ Falling asleep in jail, paradise visions
/ You are certain to see." Gumilev's "I", "who could
have been the best of poems/ ... [but] in this world
became a nobody" (#356), was facing a reentry into
"The Runaway Streetcar" of the historical developments
in Russia; he saw her culture and its goals, in the
realization of which he had played an undeniable role,
irrevocably collapse. Coping with his real and
superstitious (##327, 228) forebodings, he, as a poet,
summoned his faith in the Beyond. The borrowing of
A.Tolstoj's "tsarevna" mingles, in Sheelagh Graham's
words (1985:75-76), "...in one symbol the longing of a
religious mystic, the desire for harmonious One-ness
of his exalted soul, and Romantic yearning for
unattainable Beauty" and her "wonderland". At that
point in Gumilev's career, such summoning was probably
a greater necessity than for Tolstoj, and it was a far
cry from youthful romantic reveries.

The corpus of the above-mentioned poems, related to
each other by context, represents what Mandel'štam
calls "psychological constructivism" or, as Samuel
Schwarzband notes in this volume (speaking about
Kolčan), "a polythematic structure with recurrent, but
not cyclic, thematic strains, strongly felt, firmly
perceived and relentlessly pursued". Our poem
expresses one such strain which by that time had
become one of the dominant strains.

14.0. From the outset of his career Gumilev pursued
Théophile Gautier's ideal: "L'Art robuste /Seul a
l'éternité." Reviewing Gorodeckij's collection
Cvetuščij posox in 1914, Gumilev argued that

"pročnost) i krasota, (durability and beauty) are not merely the result of felicitious formal arrangement and nice thoughts. The "best words in the best order" must come from "a combination of three conditions: a deep unconscious surge, its strict apperception, and a powerful will in its embodiment." Through the felicitous employment of the various poetic functions (see 11.1), especially through the subtlety with which the progression is effected in every prosodic instance, from simplicity to complexity (9.0-9.9), the last version of this poem comes close to meeting the above goals. The level of simplicities accounts for the direct communicability of the "apperceived unconscious surge", whereas complexities create cohesion in the deep strata of the work. Even though many avenues of our discussion can and should be extended and new ones added, it seems safe to conclude that Gumilev was fortunate to live to see his poetry catch up with his own demanding poetics.

We can also observe a new lyrical gain in this particular work: as Gumilev said early in his career, "... the poet gives himself [in his creation], but it is a mysterious, unknown to himself [person which] he allows his readers to surmise". That discovery is given, here, through the poet's tone. In it there is at least one well orchestrated note which neither his Russian readers, familiar with his more brassy diction and bearing, nor he himself, would have anticipated:

"...Tixij sneg zasyplet grust' i gore..."
(Quiet snow will cover grief and woe).

NOTES

Footnote numbers are given throughout the text in square brackets to distinguish them from poem line numbers which are between curved brackets.

1. A younger peer, Georgij Ivanov, summarized his preface to his 1923 edition of Gumilev's criticism quite aptly: "... Russian poets and Russian critics will, for a long time to come, study their difficult 'sacred craft' from these diverse 'Letters'". And an older maître, Valerij Brjusov, echoed this sentiment in his review of that collection: "... N.Gumilev had the intuition of a genuine critic, and his evaluations express - in short formulas - the very essence of the [given] poet....most of N.Gumilev's judgements about individual poets have been vindicated by their future development and, most importantly, N.Gumilev maintains proportion in his judgements." (N.Gumilev, *Sobranie sočinenij v 4-x tomax* [Washington, 1962-68], IV, pp.605-6. All references hereafter are to this edition, indicated as *SS* followed by volume and page number.) After Modernism had long ended, Nikolaj Ocup (1953:135) continues this idea: "... in the enormous household of Russian poetry which had arrived at a chaotic state, it was precisely he [Gumilev the critic] who created order." And Georgij Adamovič (1971) says: "no other master had ... such an infallible, purely formal incisiveness". About Gumilev's impartiality see Vladimir Markov (1962:34) and Simon Karlinsky (166:34). Gumilev's well known imperatives concerning *Weltanschauung*, the technique of verse-making, and the "perfect balance" between these two realms are articulated in the series "Pis'ma o russkoj poezii", "Žizn' stixa", "Nasledie simvolizma i akmeizm", "Čitatel'", "Anatomija stixa" etc.; they are all reprinted in Volume IV of *Sobranie sočinenij*. Many of these

writings appeared in English (Nikolai Gumilev, *On Russian Poetry*, transl. David Lapeza, Ann Arbor, 1976).

2. Vjačeslav Ivanov (1911) speculated from his Symbolist position that "... the real experience of the soul, obtainable through suffering and love, that will tear the veils which conceal from the poet's eyes the true reality..." was yet to be acquired by Gumilev.

3. Some of the facile characterizations by peers that linger in textbooks and anthology introductions are compiled by Marie Maline (1964:101): "formalism without soul" (Blok); "a poet-chevalier, victim of his political and religious convictions" (G.Ivanov - standard for émigré opinion); "imperialist and aristocratic, condemned to solitude" (*Soviet Encyclopedia*); "a poet of picturesque exoticism" (Mirsky); "a poet of forms and colors" (Ajxenval'd); "a neoclassicist" (Gleb Struve); "a Romantic, despite his reserve" (L'vov); "an epigone of Brjusov, and nothing else" (Xodasevič, Pil'skij); "a technician above all" (Brjusov); "a manly poet, in love with life" (G.Struve, Strakhovsky), etc., etc.

4. This concept, reminiscent of Kuzmin's famous 1910 formula *prekrasnaja jasnost'* (magnificent clarity), stems from Annenskij's article "The world of antiquity in contemporary French poetry"; Gumilev uses this term in his 1914 review of Annenskij's "Famira Kifared", referring to the attempt to capture "natural" speech by combining the diction of antiquity with contemporary speech (*SS*, IV:330). Cf. also "prekrasnaja prostota" (magnificent simplicity), in Gumilev's 1913 review of Vjačeslav Ivanov's collection *Nežnaja tajna*, with reference to this work's highly complex content (*ibid.*:315). Cf. also Blok's title "Prekrasnaja dama" ("The Most Beautiful Lady").

The escalated use of the super-term prompts me to translate the attribute *prekrasnaja* as "magnificent" rather than, etymologically, as "most beautiful".

5. For a discussion of expanding poetic diction through "extensive", "intensive" and "fission" semantic energies see Mickiewicz:1975:59-83.

6. V.Ivanov's conception of a poetic symbol may be summarized as a concept whose semantic energy penetrates various levels of consciousness, and functions on each level in a specific, semantically relevant way. (Cf. 1908, 1909, 1910, all reprinted in 1974:II). Annenskij contends that "all the force, value and beauty lie outside of [denotations]", i.e., in the indeterminacy between their literal and figurative meaning. Accordingly, "it is a crude mistake to confuse poetic words with denotations related to the so-called real world or even to logical, moral and aesthetic relationships in the world of ideals" (1909:23; see also 1911:52-53).

7. In the literary medium, the parallel phenomenon to Rayonism has been described as "context" - "a kind of contagion of meaning in poetry". Elaine Rusinko (1979:214) summarizes Jurij Tynjanov's notion of context (1924): "As the verse is read, a new meaning arises which is not that of any single word but rather each word throws light on every other word, creating a kind of general semantic tonality." And Jurij Lotman (1971:155) sees such "context" in a relation of opposition to "text" - "a graphically fixed artistic whole".

8. For a concise description of this theory and its background see Anthony Parton:1983.

9. Professor Rusinko (1982) discusses Gumilev's "escape from time" in his "Zabludivšijsja tramvaj"

in the light of Henry Bergson's views on employing memory for that end. However, much of Gumilev's manipulating of time, in that poem as well as in our poem, entails also the forecasting of events by placing different forms of future into the present. Imagination, or intersections of lines of discrete awarenesses and perceptions, provides a more immediate subject for Gumilev's composition than the abstraction "time".

10. For a concise survey of the notion of primeval oral mimesis see Gerald Janecek (1985).

11. Maline found only seven of Gumilev's five-foot trochee poems, all with exclusively feminine endings (304); she overlooked our piece, which has strict feminine/masculine alternation.

12. For example, accents in line 13 can vary between the obligatory minimum of two feet (on 1 *or* 2 and 4 *or* 5) and the possible maximum five (stressing each foot). Within that range, no fixed number can be stipulated, and any variation would be correct in terms of the grammar, logic, expressivity and naturalness of diction. Most reciters would presumably settle on a median number for their *actual* choice; at the moment, I would make three accents (1st foot agogically, 2nd and 4th dynamically), omitting the two other possible accents. Throughout the poem, half the lines (1, 2, 3, 4, 5, 9, 11, 12, 14, 18, 19, 21) have a mandatory omission of accent on the 1st foot (prepositions, conjunctions and unaccentable syllables in polysyllabic words), allowing only four stresses as a maximum. On the stanzaic level, the clustering of mandatory patterns may cause dramatic intonational and semiotic effects, but within admissible ranges, a canonic number can

hardly be set in view of the variable vocal, acoustic and emotional factors and the interpretative whims that bring the verse to life.

13. The term "polyfunctions" originated among music theorists in the mid-1950s at Yale University, in reference to Modernist telescoping of tonalities into complex clusters and creating multilinear resolutions between them. For applications to Modernist poetry, see Alexis Rannit's introductory article to *Anna Axmatova, Sočinenija*, 1968, II, esp. pp.17-23, and Mickiewicz:1984:15.0.

14. At the beginning of this century, the plural noun *zori* (dawns) was the avant-garde's favorite symbol of anticipation of great changes in personal awareness and in Russian culture at large (cf. Andrej Belyj:1922:10-12). Whether Gumilev's favorite time was the morning twilight ("In this hour I was born/ In this hour I shall die" [#251.13,14; Odoevceva: 1973]), or the evening twilight, "very often associated with the hour of death" (Nikita Struve, 1973), the term *zori* captures both times. "Budet veter" (15) may come from Gumilev's possible acquaintance with the saying "Bagrovaja zarja k vetram". In #382 he compared the dawns to bloody lips, and in #255 he compared the perception of dawn to that of immortal verses and the "sixth sense". Cf. also #231:I-II.

15. I am indebted to Dr Samuel Schwarzband for suggesting this possibility to me.

REFERENCES

Adamovič, Georgij, 1971 — "Gumilev (1921-1971)", *Novoe Russkoe Slovo*, 5 Sep.

Ajxenval'd, Julij, 1923 — *Siluety russkix pisatelej*, III (Berlin).

Annenskij, Innokentij, 1908/1965 — "O romantičeskix cvetax", Repr. *Novyj Žurnal*, 78, 285-7.

1909 — "O sovremennom lirizme", *Apollon*, 1, 12-42; 2, 3-29; 3, 5-29.

1911 — "Čto takoe poezija?", *Apollon*, 6, 51-57.

Belyj, Andrej, 1922 — "Epoxa do pervoj vstreči", *Zapiski mečtatelej*, 6:10,12.

Graham, Sheelagh Duffin, 1985 — *The Lyric Poetry of A.K. Tolstoi* (The Hague), p.75.

Gumilev, Nikolaj, 1962-68 — *Sobranie sočinenij v četyrex tomax (SS)* ed. G.P.Struve and B.A.Filippov (Washington).

Ivanov, Vjačeslav, 1974 — *Sobranie sočinenij*, II, ed. D.Ivanov and O.Deschart (Brussels).

Jakobson, Roman, 1960 — "Linguistics and Poetics", *Style and Language*, ed. Thomas Sebeck, pp.351-367.

1981 — "Yeats's 'Sorrow of Love' Through the Years", (with Rudy Stephen), *Selected Writings*, III (The Hague), pp.600-638.

Janecek, Gerald
1985
"Zaum' as the recollection of primeval oral mimesis", *Wiener Slawistischer Almanach*, 16, 165-86.

Karlinsky, Simon,
1966
Marina Tsvetaeva: Her Life and Art (Berkeley).

Lotman, Jurij,
1971
Struktura xudožestvennogo teksta (Providence).

Maline, Marie,
1964
Nicolas Gumilev (Brussels).

Makovskij, Sergej,
1962
Na parnase serebrjanogo veka (Munich).

Markov, Vladimir,
1962
The Longer Poems of Velimir Xlebnikov (Berkeley).

Mickiewicz, Denis,
1975
"The Acmeist Conception of the Poetic Word", *Toward a Definition of Acmeism*, (Supplementary Issue) *Russian Language Journal*, 39-83.

1984
"Semantic Functions in *Zaum'*", *Russian Literature*, XV-4 (Special Issue), 363-464.

Odoevceva, Irina,
1973
"V zaščitu Gumileva", *Novoe Russkoe Slovo*, 28 Aug.

Parton, Anthony,
1983
"Russian Rayonism", *Leonardo*, XVI-4, 298-305.

Rannit, Alexis,
1968
"Anna Akhmatova Considered in a Context of Art Nouveau", *Anna Axmatova. Sočinenija*, II, eds. G.P.Struve and B.Filippov (Washington), pp.5-38.

Rusinko, Elaine, 1979	"Soviet Intertextuality", *Dispositio* (Essays), IV-11, 12, 213-215.
1982	"Lost in Space and Time: Gumilev's 'Zabludivšijsja tramvaj'", *SEEJ*, XXVI-4, 383-402.
Sampson, Earl, 1970	"Nikolaj Gumilev: Toward a Reevaluation", *Russian Review*, XXIX-2, 301-313.
1975	"Dol'niks in Gumilev's Poetry", *Toward a Definition of Acmeism*, 21-41.
1979	*Nikolay Gumilev* (Boston).
Shapiro, Michael, 1979	"Pushkin's Modus Significandi: A Semiotic Exploration", *Russian Romanticism: Studies in the Poetic Codes*, ed. Nils A. Nilsson (Stockholm, *Studies in Russian Literature*, 10, pp. 110-134).
1980	"Poetry and Language, 'Considered as Semeiotic'", *Transactions of the Charles S. Pierce Society*, 16, 97-117.
Struve, Gleb 1964	"Tvorčeskij put' Gumileva", *SS* II, v-xl.
Struve, Nikita, 1973	"O predsmertnom stixotvorenii Gumileva", *Novoe Russkoe Slovo*, 28 Aug.

Thomson, R.D.B.,
1975

"The Anapaestic Dol'nik in the Poetry of Axmatova and Gumilev", *Toward a Definition of Acmeism*, 42-58.

Timenčik, R.D.,
1981

"Zametki ob akmeizme, III", *Russian Literature*, 1981, IX-2 (Special Issue), 175-89.

Vinogradov, V.V.,
1925

Poezija Anny Axmatovoj (Leningrad).

APPENDIX I

Перед ночью северной, короткой,
И за нею зори - словно кровь,
Подошла неслышною походкой,
Посмотрела на меня любовь;

5   Отравила взглядом и дыханьем,
Слаще роз дыханьем и ушла
В белый май с его очарованьем,
В мутные, слепые зеркала.

У кого я попрошу совета,
10 Как до легкой осени дожить,
Чтобы это огненное лето
Не могло меня испепелить.

Как теперь молиться буду Богу,
Плача, замирая и горя,
15 Если я забыл мою дорогу
К каменным стенам монастыря.

Если взоры девушки любимой
Слаще взора жителей высот,
Краше горнего Ерусалима
20 Летний Сад и зелень сонных вод.

1916 год (?)
Альманах "Творчество", 1917.

APPENDIX II

Любовь весной

Перед ночью северной, короткой,
И за нею зори - словно кровь,
Подошла неслышною походкой,
Посмотрела на меня любовь;

5 Отравила взглядом и дыханьем,
Слаще роз дыханьем, и ушла
В белый май с его очарованьем,
В невские, слепые зеркала.

У кого я попрошу совета,
10 Как до легкой осени дожить,
Чтобы это огненное лето
Не могло меня испепелить.

Как теперь молиться буду Богу,
Плача, замирая и горя,
15 Если я забыл свою дорогу
К каменным стенам монастыря.

Если взоры девушки любимой
Слаще взора ангела высот,
Краше горнего Ерусалима
20 Летний Сад и зелень сонных вод.

День за днем пылает надо мною,
Их терпеть не станет скоро сил.
Правда, тот, кто полюбил весною,
Больно тот и горько полюбил.

                    Парижский Альбом, 1917.

APPENDIX III: FINAL VERSION

Перед ночью северной, короткой -
И за нею зори, словно кровь -
Подошла неслышною походкой,
Посмотрела на меня любовь.

5   Отравила взглядом и дыханьем,
Слаще роз дыханьем - и ушла
В белый май с его очарованьем,
В невские слепые зеркала.

У кого я попрошу совета,
10   Как до легкой осени дожить,
Чтобы это огненное лето
Не могло меня испепелить?

Тихий снег засыплет грусть и горе,
И не будет жалко ничего,
15   Будет ветер, будут в Черном море
Бури кликать друга своего.

Я скажу ей: "Хочешь, мы уедем
К небесам, не белым, к голубым,
Ничего не скажем мы соседям,
20   Ни твоим, царевна, ни моим."

Не откажешься тогда, я знаю...
Только б лето поскорей прошло,
Только бы скорей дорогу к раю
Милым, хрупким снегом замело.

               Альманах "Литературная мысль"
                    Петроград, 1922 г.

FINAL VERSION

    Before the night, northern, short -
    And after it, dawns, like blood -
    Came up to me with inaudible gait,
    Looked at me, love.

5 Poisoned with glance and breath,
    Sweeter than roses' breath - and walked away
    Into white May with its charm,
    Into Neva's blind mirrors.

    Whom shall I ask for advice,
10 How until light fall to survive
    So that this fiery summer
    Should not reduce me to ashes?

    Quiet snow will cover sadness and woe
    And there will be regretted nothing
15 There will be wind, there will, in the Black Sea,
    Be storms calling their friend.

    I shall say to her, "D'you want, we will ride away
    To the skies, not white, to the blue,
    Nothing let us say to our neighbors,
20 Neither to yours, king's daughter, nor to mine."

    You shall not refuse, then, I know...
    If only the summer would sooner pass,
    If only sooner the road to paradise
    Were with dear, delicate snow swept over.

(Literal translation of #324 [*SS* II, 143], the last, 1922-3 version, by D.M.)

HOMO PEREGRINANS В ЛИРИКЕ НИКОЛАЯ ГУМИЛЕВА

ЭУЛЯЛИЯ ПАПЛЯ

> Апостол Петр, бери свои ключи,
> Достойный рая в дверь его стучит.

> ... Всегда помнить о непознаваемом, но не оскорблять своей мысли о нем более или менее вероятными догадками, - вот принцип акмеизма. Это не значит, чтобы он отвергал для себя право изображать душу в те моменты, когда она дрожит, приближаясь к иному; но тогда она должна только содрогаться. Разумеется, познание Бога, прекрасная Дама Теология останется на своем престоле, но ни ее возводить до степени литературы, ни литературу поднимать в ее алмазный холод акмеисты не хотят.(I)

После таких категорических заявлений Гумилева-акмеиста не странно ли говорить о *sacrum* в его творчестве? Но ценители стихов автора "Памяти" (1921) знают, что Бог и вера не только один из характернейших мотивов, но и наглядный критерий *эволюции* его поэзии. Религиозные мотивы показывают путь, совершенный художником от единичных библейских образов по идущую извне лирической структуры сакральную насыщенность зрелых стихов. Словом - это путь от внешнего ко внутреннему, от оболочки к сути.

В этой статье мне хотелось бы проследить этот процесс, его источники и художественно выраженные формы.

В условно-декоративном мире раннего Гумилева библейские истории, например о Каине и Авеле или о Блудном сыне, применяются ради их, так сказать, фабульных достоинств. И они остаются только фабулой, пусть аллегорической, но не глубокой ни по мысли, ни по эмоции. Заключенный же в них образ Бога представдяет собой нечто промежуточное между строгим и далеким человеку Богом Ветхого завета и жестоким языческим богом.

Юного поэта - что вполне естественно - привлекает прежде всего земное в чувственном и несколько поверхностном его восприятии. Но так же естественным кажется, что именно ощущение красок и форм, любовный взгляд Адама на *созданный* мир становится первым импульсом к рефлексии о *Создателе*.

Исследователями уже отмечалось неожиданное для дерзкого конквистадора предпочтение смиренного художества Фра Беато Анджелико, прозвучавшее в одноименном стихотворении (около 1913 г.):

> Есть Бог, есть мир, они живут вовек,
> А жизнь людей мгновенна и убога,
> Но все в себе вмещает человек,
> Который любит мир и верит в Бога.(2)

Восторг и *смирение* перед творением Божьим является несомненно переходным моментом к настоящему постижению *sacrum*. Чувство особого согласия с природой, с миром внешним, но проникающим внутрь как часть того же родословия, характерно для зрелой лирики Гумилева. "Канцона вторая" или "Детство", стихотворения (оба с 1916 г.), где сенсуальное и духовное начало гармонически сопряжены, - пример того, что Пруст назвал однажды "содействием религиозного духа и любви вещей":

> [. . . . .]
> И я верил, что я умру
>
> Не один, - с моими друзьями,
> С мать-и-мачехой, с лопухом.
> И за дальними небесами
> Догадаюсь вдруг обо всем.
>
> Я за то и люблю затеи
> Грозовых военных забав,

> Что людская кровь не святее
> Изумрудного сока трав.   (II, 6)

"Грозовые военные забавы" можно считать вторым источником гумилевского "богоискательства". Стихи о войне 1914 года, несмотря на их рыцарскую атрибутику и патриотическую экзальтацию, - свидетельство нового опыта. Непосредственное прикосновение смерти, уже не книжной, но реальной, не могло не сказаться на миропонимании художника. Прежнюю гедонистическую и в том смысле одностороннюю, одноцветную перспективу обогощает эсхатологический момент. Как ни прелестным казался маркиз де Карабас, он должен уступить место психологически более сложному герою.

Но одновременно следует подчеркнуть, что эсхатологическая рефлексия имеет у Гумилева довольно оптимистический оттенок. Это связано с основной чертой миросозерцания Гумилева-художника, а именно с принятием определенного порядка бытия, в основе которого лежит принцип *иерархии* и особое чувство "равновесия обязанностей": поэт воспевает земной мир Божий, - тот же, в свою очередь, вознаграждает его вечной жизнью.

Понятно, что этот своеобразный договор приводит к заметной трансформации образа Бога: сейчас он - как "договорщик" - становится ближе герою, доверявшему ему свои поступки для справедливой оценки. Герой, следовавший законам этики - те же, как известно, у Гумилева связаны прежде всего с традиционными мужскими добродетелями, с "рыцарским этосом" - может расчитывать на толерантность. Такая позиция, не лишенная дозы кокетства, заметна в стихотворении "Рай" (1916), шуточной полу-биографии, полу-исповеди. Однако доверие и надежда на милость не нарушают иерархии: все мы, смертные, рано или поздно должны явиться перед лицом праведного Судьи.

В последнем Гумилевском сборнике, *Огненный столп* (1921), доминируют произведения, представляющие собой отчет о пройденном жизненном пути. "Память", "Слово", "Душа и тело", "Мои читатели" - результат развития и углубения самой важной и самой личной темы любого лирика: авторефлексии, раздумья о сути и цели бытия. И на них, конечно, надо смотреть как на итог определенного процесса.

После первоначального спонтанного принятия жизни как ошеломляющего приключения, более серьезная рефлексия появляется впервые в третьей части поэми "Открытие Америки" (1910), вершины акмеистического, "розового" периода творчества. По сравнению с бравурным строем поэмы, диссонансной нотой звучит монолог-молитва свершившего подвиг Колумба:

> Вместо славы и великолепий
> Дай позор мне, Вышний, дай мне цели! (I, 207)

Горечь и сомнения передаются образами внутреннего опустошения, метафорами пустой формы: "жалкий (т.е., пустой) ком", "раковина без жемчужины", "спущенный поток" (I, 208). Депрессия, конечно, психологически оправдана как реакция на сильное напряжение, тем более, что Колумб Гумилева - персонаж, несомненно с романтической генеалогией. Но вопрос не ограничивается одним Колумбом. Разочарование, по выражению самого поэта: "...то, что прежде было непонятно,/ Презрение к миру и усталость снов" (I, 222) - ностальгическим лейтмотивом проходит через сборники *Колчан* (1916) и *Костер* (1918).(3) Приведу несколько цитат:

> Я не прожил, я протомился
> Половину жизни земной. ...   (I, 245)

> И вот вся жизнь! Круженье, пенье,
> Моря, пустыни, города ...   (II, 21)

> . . . . хмурый странник,
> Я снова должен ехать, должен видеть
> Моря и тучи, и чужие лица,
> Все, что меня уже не обольщает ... (II, 31)

Автобиографические "Пятистопные ямбы" заканчиваются внушительным образом жизненного убежища:

> Есть на море пустынном монастырь
> Из камня белого, золотоглавый,
> Он озарен немеркнущею славой.
> Туда б уйти, покинув мир лукавый,
> Смотреть на ширь воды и неба ширь...
> В тот золотой и белый монастырь! (I,225)

Чувству усталости сопутствует отчуждение и тоска по настоящей родине:

> Я знаю, что деревьям, а не нам,
> Дано величье совершенной жизни,
> На ласковой земле, сестре звездам,
> Мы - на чужбине, а они - в отчизне.
> . . . .
> О, если бы и мне найти страну,
> В которой мог не плакать и не петь я ...(II,3)

> И понял, что я заблудился навеки
> В слепых переходах пространств и времен,
> А где-то струятся родимые реки ... (II,19)

Строки эти как будто не нарушают общей светло-гармонической интонации гумилевской лирики. Тем не менее они знаменательны. Они симптомы последовательного процесса в поэтическом сознании художника.

Весьма показательно, что депрессивные чувства, как правило, сопряжены с основным гумилевским мотивом, темой путешествия. Путешествия реального, так сказать, в топографическом смысле или же в смысле метафорическом, то есть жизненного пути.

Как известно, путешествие - тема, связанная с литературой чуть ли не со дня ее возникновения. Среди различных форм реализации этой темы мне хочется обратить внимание на тот вариант, который получил название *паломничества* (лат. *peregrinatio*). Характерный для литературы ХVI и ХVII веков, он обозначал не только паломничество в точном смысле (в том числе крестовый поход), но и любое странствие, в инвариантном же виде стремление к изоляции (например, уход в монастырь).

С точки зрения семантики термин "паломничество" содержит в себе некую двойственность. С античной традицей связано то его значение, которое подчеркивает скитальчество, путешествие по чужой стране.(4) Здесь кроется терминологический источник одного из основных тезисов христианской антропологии: из-за первородного греха человек на земле только скиталец, его настоящая родина - небеса. Возникает вечный мотив христианской культуры - *peregrinatio vitae*, ставший также литературным топосом. Но в литературе средневековья рядом с пессимистическим представлением жизни как томительного и бесцельного скитания (символ замкнутого круга, в частности образ *danse macabre*), возможно и оптимистическое понимание земного пути. "Ежели желаешь заслужить награду и отдых, считай себя избранником и пилигримом на земле" - учил св. Фома Кемпийский, намекая на путь совершенный на земле самим Христом. Так осмысленная жизнь теряет скитальческий характер, становится целеустремленным путем, возвращением на небесную родину. И вот читаем у Гумилева:

> Когда же смерть, грустя немного,
> Скользя по роковой меже,
> Войдет и станет у порога, -
> Мы скажем смерти: "Как, уже?"
> И не тоскуя, не мечтая,
> Пойдем в высокий Божий *рай*,
> С улыбкой ясной узнавая
> Повсюду нам *знакомый край*.
>
>   (II, 176. Курсив мой-Э.П.)

"Высокий Божий рай" и "знакомый край" - не только созвучны как рифма, но и как синонимы. Цитированное "Приглашение в путешествие" (1918) и другие произведения поэта передают нам привлекательный по своей простоте образец человеческой жизни. Образец в сущности - христьянский: жизнь как путешествие-паломничество, путь кончавшийся входом "в высокий Божий рай". Поэтическая иконография рая у Гумилева заслуживает, несомненно, большего внимания; здесь заметим только, что вряд ли найдутся в литературе многие столь "безоблачные" картины конечного этапа человеческого пути.

"Приглашение в путешествие" не только выразительный пример реализации мотива жизни-паломничества, но и ключ к интерпретации ностальгического лейтмотива: он звено эволюции темы путешествия. В свете христианского образца человеческой жизни можно указать на следующие этапы художественной конкретизации этой темы в лирике Гумилева:

1. путешествие-*приключение*: путешествие реальное, с экзотическим привкусом, вдохновляемое Музой Дальних Странствий,

2. путешествие-*скитание*, передающее чувтсва разочарования в одних светских целях странствования и тоски по настоящей родине,

3. путешествие-*паломничество*: к буквальному значению понятия прибавляется метафорическое, позволяющее найти определенную модель бытия.

Притом следует обязательно подчеркнуть, что эта модель у Гумилева никогда не принимает аскетического характера. Наоборот, его герой – активный, любящий рисковать – остался верен земным радостям. Гумилевский *homo religiosus* гармонически сочетает в себе идеалы св. Франциска Ассизского с идеалами рыцарского этоса. "Приглашение в путешетсвие" хорошо показывает, как светское согласуется с духовным, что передается композицией стихотворения: оно начинается с приглашения в земное путешествие, кончается же входом в рай.(5) Другим примером столь же наглядного синтеза двух начал является "Вступление" к циклу *Шатер* (1921); Африка – обетованная земля, где герой может реализовать и земные и духовные цели:

> Дай за это дорогу мне торную,
> Там, где нету пути человеку,
> Дай назвать моим именем черную,
> До сих пор неоткрытую реку.

> И последняя милость, с которою
> Отойду я в селенья святые,
> Дай скончаться под той сикоморою,
> Где с Христом отдыхала Мария.   (II, 72)

Разумеется, такой идиллический образец может показаться наивным и упрощенным или просто анахроническим. В этом, пожалуй, отдавал себе отчет и сам поэт, предвещая в визионерских стихах последнего периода темные картины "звездного ужаса". Но они скорее были вызваны резким "чувством истории",(6) чем сомнениями трансцентдентного порядка. В том смысле Гумилев остался верен акмеистической декларации сохранить Даму Теологию на ее алмазном престоле. В отличие от своих предшественников он предпочитал не познавать непознаваемое, благодаря чему, быть может, и избежал синдрома "пустого неба", терзавшего художников XX века. Вопрос бытия был для него скорее вопросом этики, нежели онтологии. Читателей он на самом деле "неврастенией не оскорблял", но учил принимать "всю жестокую, милую жизнь" и, как подобает мужчине, "ждать спокойно Божьего суда". Это и есть вера, вера-доверие, недаром они этимологически родственны.

Гумилевскому герою незачем было отправляться в потусторонние миры в поисках *sacrum*. Господь говорил с ним на доступном каждому смертному языке своего Творения, не пугая ни демонами, ни адскими муками. Характерно, что в зрелой лирике Гумилева не появляется диавол,(7) зато ангелы тихо парят над весенними полями, а серафимы участвуют едва ли не в каждом сражении; вспомним тоже светлую фигуру Христа-младенца в свадебной "Балладе" или странствующего Христа-рыбаря.(8) Обыкновенный пейзаж полон знаков Божьего присутствия:

> Храм Твой, Господи, в небесах,
> Но земля тоже Твой приют.
> Расцветают липы в лесах
> И на липах птицы поют.

>   Точно благовест Твой, весна
>   По веселым идет полям,
>   А весною на крыльях сна
>   Прилетают ангелы к нам. ...   (II, 23)

Потому и нам хочется верить, что когда поэт, сопровождаемый возлюбленным серафимом на свое последнее сражение, постучался в рай, врата были ему открыты настежь.

ПРИМЕЧАНИЯ

1. Цитирую по кн. *Русская литература XX века. Хрестоматия.* Сост. Н.А.Трифонов, Москва, 1962, с.428.

2. Н.С.Гумилев. *Собрание сочинений в 4 томах.* Под ред. Г.Струве и Б.Филиппова, Вашингтон, 1962-1968, т.I, с.218. В дальнейшем рядом с цитированным текстом указывается том и стр. того же издания.

3. В частности имею в виду следующие стихотворения: "Пятистопные ямбы", "На острове", "Я не прожил, я протомился...", "Деревья", "Стокгольм", "Прапамять", "Эзбекие".

4. В римском законодательстве *peregrinus* - в противовес "гражданину" - это чужой, чужеземец. Соответствующие греческие термины: *xenos* - гость, тот, кто пребывает на чужой стране, *xenitea* - странствование по чужбине.

5. Аналогично по направлению "фабульной линии" одно из лучших ранних стихов, "Путешествие в Китай" (1910); красочные образы путешествия под покровительством "мэтра Раблэ" кончаются неожиданным *memento mori*.

6. Выражение М.Цветаевой по поводу стихотворения "Мужик".

7. Исключением подтверждающим правило является Асмодей из самого "темного", пожалуй, произведения, "У цыган" (1921), но тут он впрочем, персонаж совершенно другого порядка.

8. При полном отсутствии образа Христа страдающего.

"GONČAROVA AND LARIONOV" - GUMILEV'S PANTUM TO ART

ANTHONY PARTON

The first recorded meeting between the poet Nikolaj Gumilev (1886-1921) and the two artists Mixail Larionov (1881-1964) and Natalija Gončarova (1881-1962) took place in Paris in July 1917. They had known of each other's work in Russia and may have met there before the First World War, as they had several colleagues and acquaintances in common. Moreover, their interests had frequently overlapped. Gumilev was deeply interested in painting. He had written three reviews of art exhibitions(1) and had based some of his poems upon painterly subjects, such as "Fra Beato Angelico" in *The Quiver* (*Kolčan*), "Portrait of a Man" ("Portret mužčiny"), after a painting in the Louvre, in *Pearls* (*Žemčuga*), "Perseus", after a sculpture by Canova, in *Romantic Flowers* (*Romantičeskie cvety*) and "Andrej Rublev" in *The Pyre* (*Koster*). Furthermore he knew the artistic fraternity in St.Petersburg well - painters such as Rerix, Sudejkin, Boris Anrep and Stelletskij - all artists with whom Larionov and Gončarova had collaborated. More specifically, Larionov's and Gončarova's work was reproduced and discussed in both *Vesy* and *Apollon*, for which Gumilev worked. Gumilev had also favourably reviewed the almanach of poetry *A Hatchery of Judges II* (*Sadok sudej II*), which Larionov and Gončarova had illustrated, in 1913.(2)
Larionov and Gončarova, on the other hand, maintained strong links with the literary world in Moscow. They knew and collaborated with Russian Futurist poets of various persuasions including Xlebnikov, Kručenyx, Bol'šakov, Sergej Bobrov, Majakovskij and Il'ja Zdanevič. They appeared in "shocking" cabaret performances with the poets, in which they painted their faces and abused their audience in all manner of ways, and by 1915 they had

illustrated twelve books of Russian Futurist poems written by some of the leading avant-garde poets of the time, books such as the experimental *World Backwards* (*Mir s konca*, 1912), by Xlebnikov and Kručenyx. The cover of this particular edition was decorated with collage flowers individually cut out of various textured and coloured papers by Gončarova and with the poems crudely printed, using a variety of methods. Larionov and Gončarova had even published their own avant-garde poems in the style of Vasilij Kamenskij, Apollinaire and Marinetti, with the words broken up and spread across the page in visual patterns. Several examples were reproduced in Larionov's almanach *The Donkey's Tail and Target* (*Oslinij xvost i mišen'*, 1913).

The two artists would have been fascinated by the development of Acmeism. They both subscribed to *Apollon* in which Gumilev's poems appeared and in which the first official manifestos of the Acmeist group were published in January 1913. The ancient and exotic themes of Gumilev's poetry in *Pearls* of 1910 and *Foreign Skies* (*Čužoe nebo*) of 1912 mirrored the ancient and exotic subjects of Larionov's and Gončarova's paintings, such as Larionov's "Imaginary Voyage to Turkey" (collection of Mme. A.Larionov, Paris) of 1912. Exotic subjects such as these fostered an enthusiasm for ethnography, another common interest. We know that during the spring and summer of 1913 Gumilev led an ethnographical expedition to Abyssinia and Somaliland, whilst Larionov and Gončarova were fascinated by the life and culture of Eastern peoples as well as by the life, religion and art forms of the many primitive tribes living in Siberia.(3)

Before the First World War Larionov and Gončarova had been the two leaders of the Russian artistic avant-garde, bold and polemical painters who had more than once scandalised the public with their modernist styles and outrageous behaviour. However, following Larionov's injury in the First World War and his subsequent hospitalization during the winter of 1914-1915, they had abdicated this role, moved to the

West and had established themselves as two of the major theatrical designers for Diaghilev's "Ballets Russes" and were working in this capacity in Paris when they met Gumilev.

Like Larionov, Gumilev had joined the army on the declaration of war and had fought on the East Prussian front. In 1915 he won the St.George Cross twice and in April 1916 was promoted and transferred to another regiment. During these years Gumilev continued to write and it is possible that a knowledge of Gončarova's series of patriotic lithographs *War: Mystical Images of War* (*Vojna: mističeskie obrazy vojny*, 1914) informed Gumilev's choice of imagery in some of his poems which dealt with the conflagration.(4) His vision of angels hovering over the Russian army as it goes into battle in the poem "War" ("Vojna"), for example, is an exact transcription of one of Gončarova's "mystical images". In the spring of 1917 Gumilev was again transferred and ordered to join the Russian brigades in Salonika. He left Russia in May and travelled via Scandinavia and England (stopping in London briefly) to Paris where he arrived in July. Here his orders were changed and he was temporarily attached to the Provisional Government's Military Commissariat.

During the next six months, before Gumilev was posted to London, the two painters struck up a close relationship with the poet which has been charmingly described in Larionov's letters to Gleb Struve.(5) Gumilev and the two artists saw each other nearly every day; Gumilev was living at the Hôtel Galilée in the Rue Galilée which was a stone's throw from Larionov's and Gončarova's quarters in the Hotel Castille in the Rue Cambon. They frequently visited the Tuileries together, where Gumilev had an odd habit of sitting on a bronze lion and where he saw the statue of a woman whose intertwined hands held a star, which inspired the title of the cycle of poems "To the Blue Star" ("K sinej zvezde"). They would walk together talking about Annenskij and Nerval. Larionov introduced Gumilev to Russians in social and military circles who could help and advise him during his stay and the two artists took him to the "Ballets Russes" performances at the Théâtre du Châtelet.

This close personal relationship which developed between the two artists and Gumilev naturally fostered a fruitful creative relationship in which cross-fertilisation took place between the art of Larionov and Gončarova and the poetry of Gumilev. In particular the two painters, attracted by Gumilev's bold and uncompromising facial features, were inspired to draw a series of portraits of the poet. Three of these have already been published and will be familiar.(6) They rely on a few strong and expressive lines to capture something of both the inner and outer character of the elusive Gumilev. But there are many more drawings by both Larionov and Gončarova which are still unpublished and which reveal Gumilev in different poses and attitudes. There is a fine series of pencil portraits by Gončarova, now in the Print Room of the Victoria and Albert Museum, one of which depicts the poet dressed in his uniform and wearing one of his St.George Crosses - a drawing which compares with the many photographs of the poet in military uniform which still exist. Other drawings by the artist in the same collection depict more informal poses and are perhaps more spontaneous in style. They include a powerful profile view and a three-quarter view, both of which, in boldly drawn lines, attempt not only a representational but also a psychological approach to the poet.

Other portraits of Gumilev dating from this time exist in private collections. There is, for example, a magnificent watercolour in the collection of Mr John Stuart (London) in which Gončarova, with her characteristic finesse and imaginative flair, depicts the poet against a gorgeous oriental backdrop. Here Gumilev appears seated at a writing desk, composing the first verse of "The Chinese Maiden" ("Kitajskaja devuška"). Behind him is an exotic wall hanging which features the metallic bird with the resplendent golden tail which is referred to in stanza four of the poem, and a Japanese screen which recalls characters such as the legendary samurai Ikyu from Japanese "kabuki" theatre. In his letters to Gleb Struve, Larionov also refers to a series of drawings depicting Gumilev in the company of Diaghilev and Apollinaire, but none of these has come to light. In return the poet responded with his own literary portrait of the two artists, a poem which he dedicated to them and which was simply entitled "Gončarova and Larionov":

ГОНЧАРОВА И ЛАРИОНОВ
ПАНТУМ

Восток и нежный и блестящий
В себе открыла Гончарова,
Величье жизни настоящей
У Ларионова сурово.

В себе открыла Гончарова
Павлиньих красок бред и пенье,
У Ларионова сурово
Железного огня круженье.

Павлиньих красок бред и пенье
От Индии до Византии,
Железного огня круженье—
Вой покоряемой стихии.

От Иднии до Византии
Кто дремлет, если не Россия?
Вой покоряемой стихии—
Не обновленная ль стихия?

Кто дремлет, если не Россия?
Кто видит сон Христа и Будды?
Не обновленная ль стихия—
Снопы лучей и камней груды?

Кто видит сон Христа и Будды,
Тот стал на сказочные тропы.
Снопы лучей и камней груды—
О, как хохочут рудокопы!

Тот встал на сказочные тропы
В переидских, милых миньятюрах.
О, как хохочут рудокопы
Везде, в полях и шахтах хмурых.

В персидских, милых миньятюрах
Величье жизни настоящей.
Везде, в полях и шахтах хмурых
Восток и нежный, и блестящий.

       Париж [1917]

The tender and splendid East
Gončarova discovered within herself,
The grandeur of real life
Larionov sternly possesses.

Gončarova discovered within herself
The delirium and singing of peacock colours,
Larionov sternly possesses
The spinning of ferrous fire.

The delirium and singing of peacock colours
From India to Byzantium,
The spinning of ferrous fire—
The wailing of the subdued element.

From India to Byzantium
Who sleeps, if not Russia?
The wailing of the subdued element—
Is this not the element renewed?

Who is sleeping if not Russia?
Who has a dream of Christ and Buddha?
Is this not the element renewed—
Sheaves of light rays and piles of stones?

He who dreams of Christ and Buddha,
Has set forth on fabulous paths.
Sheaves of light rays and piles of stones—
Oh, how the miners roar with laughter!

> He sets forth on fabulous paths
> In sweet Persian miniatures.
> Oh, how the miners roar with laughter
> Everywhere, in the fields and the gloomy pits.
>
> In sweet Persian miniatures [is]
> The grandeur of real life.
> Everywhere, in the fields and the gloomy pits
> The tender and splendid East.(7)

The poem was modelled upon a Malaysian form of poetry known as the pantum, which was one of several eastern poetic forms with which Gumilev was experimenting at the time and for which, Larionov tells us, he had developed a passion. However it was also an eminently suitable form for a poem concerning Larionov and Gončarova, who themselves had a high regard for and had been influenced by Eastern art forms. Moreover, the structure of the poem, in which the second and fourth lines of a stanza are repeated as the first and third lines of the following stanza, is perhaps an iconic representation of Larionov's and Gončarova's cubo-futurist style of painting, in which an image is fragmented and its parts are reproduced a number of times in different positions across the canvas.(8)

Apart from its literary qualities, the pantum to the two artists is an interesting and important poem demonstrating Gumilev's deep insight into and interest in the art of Larionov and Gončarova. Throughout the pantum Gumilev intertwines what at first sight appear to be two disparate themes: a characterisation of the bases of Larionov's and Gončarova's aesthetic ideologies. In the concluding stanza, however, the two themes are finally resolved and are shown to be complementary.

The first theme occurs in the first two lines of each verse and refers to the paintings of Gončarova.

Gumilev begins by saying: "The tender and splendid East Gončarova discovered within herself." For a number of years Gončarova had been enthusiastic about

Eastern art. She had written polemical manifestos in which she denigrated the art of Western countries and claimed that the source of all arts lay in the East:

> My path is toward the source of all arts, the East. The art of my country is incomparably more profound and important than anything that I know in the West.... I am opening up the East again, and I am certain that many will follow me along this path.(9)

In her artistic researches Gončarova was trying to discover the influence of Eastern artistic traditions in the history and culture of her own country and hence, in a sense, within herself.

A feature of Eastern art is the use of bright colours applied in a flat and decorative manner, and Gumilev refers to this in stanza two when he speaks of "the delirium and singing of peacock colours". But the phrase "peacock colours" is not used simply for poetic effect, to suggest the wealth and richness of Eastern colour which Gončarova has discovered. It also refers to her series of flamboyant and exotic paintings "Artistic Possibilities à Propos a Peacock", first shown at "The Donkey's Tail" ("Oslinij xvost") exhibition in Moscow in 1912, for which Gončarova had become famous. Moreover, later works such as "The Peacocks" (coll. Mme. A.Larionov, Paris), executed about the time Gumilev was in Paris, echoed not only the clarity of outline and the simple yet expressive shapes of Eastern art forms, but also the rich colour experience which they offer and which had evidently impressed Gumilev as being characteristic of Gončarova's work. The exaggerated forms and striking colour harmonies of these works do "sing" and create a dream-like impression.

In the next stanza Gumilev refers to India and Byzantium. Gončarova was particularly attracted by the art of both these cultures, which she had studied and had written about in her manifestos. Both, she believed, had contributed to the development of

Russian culture, particularly in the field of icon painting.(10) Furthermore, the strength of both cultures, she felt, had emerged in their attempt to express their different religious faiths, Eastern Orthodox Christianity and Buddhism. In the pantum, Russia is seen as the heir to these two traditions but Russia (stanza four) is dozing, unaware of the cultural and spiritual riches she has inherited. Gumilev is referring to Gončarova when he talks of "the one who dreams of Christ and Buddha" (stanzas five and six). Those who, like Gončarova, rediscover their cultural and spiritual roots, Gumilev says, have "set forth on fabulous paths in sweet Persian miniatures". Gumilev suggests that Gončarova has been a precursor in this respect, having begun to explore a wealth of creative possibilities which previously lay hidden.

The reference to "sweet Persian miniatures" (stanza seven) indicates another Eastern art form which was close to Gončarova's heart and which she had once written about in the introduction to an exhibition catalogue,(11) declaring that Eastern art forms such as these had a freedom and power of expression as well as a decorative quality of colour which not only created great pictorial beauty but also perfectly expressed the life, tastes and aspirations of those who conceived them. Gončarova's interest in Indian, Byzantine and Persian art forms was shared by Gumilev. In *The Pillar of Fire* (*Ognennyj stolp*), for example, there is a poem called "The Persian Miniature" ("Persidskaja miniatjura") and we also have an account of how Gumilev's short story "The Black General" ("Černyj general") originated: it began with Gončarova's admiration for an Indian miniature which she and Gumilev happened to come across one day in Paris in July 1917. The miniature portrayed a black general and Gumilev, we are told, make her a present of it and dedicated to her his short story inspired by the miniature.(12) It is also interesting to note that Gumilev's tragedy *The Poisoned Tunic* (*Otravlennaja tunika*), which deals with a Byzantine subject, was begun in Paris at this time. So Gumilev's choice of images and words in this first theme of the pantum relates very specifically to interests shared with Gončarova and to her aesthetic ideology.

The second theme occurs in the second couplet of each stanza and refers to the paintings of Larionov. In the first stanza Gumilev says that Larionov possesses "the grandeur of real life". This is a complex reference which can be read on two levels. Firstly, Larionov was a painter of low life, who loved to depict bakers, soldiers, and prostitutes, for instance. He always empathised with such people, enjoyed their company and in his canvases gave expression to what he saw as their heroic qualities. Executed in a popular and crude style, often emulating the old "lubki" prints or grafitti drawings, these works evoke an excitement and passion for "real life", life as it was for the majority of the population. Like the painters Millet and Courbet before him, Larionov elevates the humble artisan or peasant woman and invests them with a grandeur previously reserved in painting for the aristocracy and the Church.

However, the references to Larionov and his art which follow suggest there is a spiritual or philosophical dimension to the phrase "the grandeur of real life". "The spinning of ferrous fire" (stanzas two and three) and "the wailing of the subdued element" (stanzas three and four) suggest something almost alchemical. Larionov was in fact interested in metaphysical concepts. In particular he seems to have accepted a view of the world in which all physical manifestations are spiritually related, and which postulated a higher existence in the spiritual realm.(13) The idea that behind the world as we perceive and experience it there lies a world which is more "real" occurs in many of Larionov's writings and it represents an important part of the theory and practice of his abstract style of Rayist painting.

When Larionov first initiated Rayism in 1912 it was a style of painting based upon the way light rays are reflected from objects arranged in a still-life composition. One of the first Rayist paintings, entitled "Glass" (Guggenheim Museum, New York), depicts a collection of glasses and bottles that reflect clusters of light rays which shatter and fragment the picture space, as in contemporary French Cubist and Italian Futurist painting. However, during the next two years Larionov began to omit the object from the composition altogether, concentrating on the vibrant and dynamic effects of the intersecting rays, and thus distinguished himself as Russia's first non-objective artist. However, these were not simply formal experiments, for as a result of his interest in contemporary science and in mysticism, the ray-line acquired a different and far greater significance for Larionov. In the Rayist manifestos of 1913 and 1914 Larionov refers to his ray-lines as "constituting the unity of all things". He even suggested that his Rayist works were a form of spiritual or mystical painting, going beyond time and space and related to the fourth dimension of space, what Larionov called "that superreal order that man must always seek...", and so the paintings "bear man's multiple soul to the upper reaches of reality".(14)

We find similar metaphysical ideas in Gumilev's work, especially in the book *Pillar of Fire*. In the poem "The Tramcar Gone Astray" ("Zabludivšijsja tramvaj"), for example, Gumilev journeys through time and space. A similar voyage is referred to in the poem "Stockholm" ("Stokgol'm"). In "The Drunken Dervish" ("P'janyj derviš") there is an intriguing reference, in view of Larionov's Rayism, to these ideas, when in the last line of each stanza Gumilev declares: "The world is but a ray from my beloved's countenance, all else is its shadow." There are specific metaphysical and alchemical references in the poem "Soul and Body" ("Duša i telo"). And in the poem "The Sixth Sense" ("Šestoe čuvstvo") the development of "an organ for the sixth sense" suggests, as does Larionov's Rayism, an appreciation of a higher reality.

"Sea Beach with Bather" (Ludwig Museum, Cologne) of 1913 is an interesting example of Larionov's Rayism in which some of his metaphysical ideas are given painterly form. This is one of a series of works by Larionov and Gončarova in which the spiritual integration of the human being and the environment he inhabits is indicated by a physical integration achieved by means of the ray-lines. In fact Larionov referred to these paintings as an attempt to recreate in painterly form "the whole world in its spiritual and concrete totality".(15) Gončarova attempted something similar in her "Green and Yellow Forest" which also dates from 1913, where the almost unidentifiable figure of a woman is integrated both physically and spiritually into her context by the ray-lines which "constitute the unity of all things".

Gumilev refers to these "sheaves of rays" (stanza five), which Larionov and Gončarova employ, as "the element renewed". Like air, earth, fire and water, Larionov's rays are elemental, but Larionov, like the alchemist, has discovered and mastered the element: it has been subdued and wails loudly (stanza four). The reference to "piles of stones" (stanza five) seems to be an allusion to the fractured, faceted and fragmented appearance of the artists' Rayist paintings.

Larionov was always keen to foster an esoteric explanation of Rayism, and early commentators remarked on this. Walter Propert, for example, discussed the world of the Rayist painter as being "... a new world where the mysterious fourth dimension crops up" and continued: "It is a stimulating thought that a new world awaits us if we but train our eyes to see it; though possibly a rayist like a medium is born and not made ... We must be grateful to these two visionaries [Larionov and Gončarova] for the many things of beauty (on the lower plane) that they have set before our untrained eyes, and wait patiently and cheerfully for the day when we too shall be counted among the illuminati."(16) However, the miners in stanza seven are not illuminati: their eyes have not been trained to perceive this new world which Larionov has revealed and so, when they come face to face with his paintings and his aesthetic, they scoff and roar with laughter. The reference to the miners is thus an allusion to materialists and critics of avant-garde art who are incapable of understanding the spiritual renewal discovered by artistic innovators such as Larionov and Gončarova in the field of painting and Gumilev himself in the field of poetry. The materialists are everywhere "in the fields and gloomy pits".

In the final stanza Gumilev masterfully draws his two themes together in a powerful conclusion. The spiritual grandeur of life which Larionov possesses can be found, Gumilev says, in the sweet Persian miniatures which are so dear to Gončarova's heart. And throughout the world, if you have eyes to see, there exists the beauty of "the tender and splendid East".

The pantum is a remarkable and unusual *hommage* to Gumilev's two friends and testifies to a much deeper relationship with them than a mere surface acquaintance. In fact, the two artists directly supported and collaborated with Gumilev in various ways. Larionov, who had been acting as the commissioning adviser for Diaghilev's "Ballets Russes" at this time, suggested that Gumilev provide the libretti for two ballets to be produced by Diaghilev with designs by himself and Gončarova. Gumilev proposed the text of *Gondla* as the basis for one ballet and wrote a piece called "Theodora", which was a first draft of *The Poisoned Tunic*, for the second, and the two artists frequently met with the poet to discuss and work on the projects. For *Gondla* Larionov wanted to engage the services of the British composer Lord Berners, with whom he was collaborating at that time, and for "Theodora" the Italian composer Respighi, whom Larionov had recently met and worked with in Rome. Larionov remembered that *Gondla* was full of rich material; the main problem lay in translating the play into choreographic form. Whereas

Gondla had already been written (in 1916) and published,(17) "Theodora" was worked out in collaboration with the two painters. Gončarova's enthusiasm for Byzantine art undoubtedly played an important role in the development of the plans for "Theodora" and hence in the origins of *The Poisoned Tunic* itself. For Gončarova it represented a second chance at staging a Byzantine ballet: in 1915 she had been engaged by Diaghilev to make designs in the rich and gorgeous style of the Ravenna mosaics for a production called *Liturgie*. Unfortunately plans for both *Gondla* and "Theodora", like plans for *Liturgie* two years before, fell through, and the two ballets went unrehearsed and unperformed.

A further area of collaboration was the illustration and decoration of an album of manuscript poems which the poet wrote during his stay in Paris and which he left with the artist Boris Anrep in London in 1918 before returning to Russia. The album found its way into the hands of Gleb Struve and is now in the collection of the Hoover Institution. The title page is distinguished by Gončarova's magnificent floral ornamentation.

Apart from Larionov and Gončarova, the artist Dmitrij Stelletskij (1875-1947), who was also working in Paris at the time, designed two illustrations for the album. Stelletskij was an old friend of Gumilev's who from 1904 to 1914 had lived and worked in St.Petersburg where he was well known (an important article devoted to his work and been published in *Apollon*)(18) and subsequently the two frequently met in Paris. Stelletskij was also friendly with Larionov and Gončarova: in fact the three painters had recently collaborated on the illustration of a book entitled *The Soul of Russia* (London, 1916), before being invited to illustrate Gumilev's poetry. The two illustrations by Stelletskij accompany the poem "The Serpent" ("Zmej") and represent Vol'ga drawing his bow to slay the monster who has captured the beautiful swan maiden. The depiction of the serpent in particular is a remarkably bold and effective piece of illustration, with its coiling body almost obscuring the greater part of the poem, completely unifying word and image.

Gončarova's contribution to the album comprised mainly ornamentation - the beautiful and delicate floral decoration on the title page shows Gončarova at her best as a decorative artist, whilst her designs for other poems in the album are refreshingly innovative. For the poem "On The North Sea" ("Na Severnom more", but entitled "V Severnom more" in the album), Gončarova's beautiful blue and brown ornamentation evokes ripples and waves on the one hand, and a boat buffeted by huge breakers on the other. The decoration to the poem "Autumn" ("Osen'", but entitled "Kartinka" in the album and dedicated to Larionov), also designed by Gončarova, which evokes something of the dynamism of the poem, is in a more abstract style; nonetheless we can pick out a reference to what Gumilev calls the "blood-red cluster of rowan berries" blown by the wind. The ornamentation to the poem "Andrej Rublev" recalls the habit and draperies of the Virgin Mary as depicted in Rublev's icons,(19) and incorporates the bold ray-lines found in Gončarova's Rayist paintings.

Finally, Larionov contributed two drawings in a coarse and primitive style, both to the poem "Mužik". A wonderfully evocative poem by Gumilev, "Mužik" takes as its theme the conflict between the mysterious forces of the old, dark, pagan Russia, symbolised by the muzhik (who is actually based on Rasputin), and the principles of Western civilization and culture which the capital tries to force upon the country. The muzhik visits St.Petersburg to enchant the Tsarina and the whole city rises to defend itself against this representative of dark forces which lie buried deep in the heart of Russia not only geographically but psychologically, in its collective unconscious. The poem creates a frightening and threatening atmosphere, and although the city succeeds in destroying the muzhik, Gumilev warns in the last stanza: "In the wild and wretched land / There are many such muzhiks / And the joyful rumble of their footsteps / Is heard along your roads."

The first drawing by Larionov in its rough hewn and heavy outline is a little reminiscent of a *kamennaja baba*, a visual metaphor for the strange, mythical and mystical Russia which gives birth to a creature such as the muzhik. The muzhik (in the second drawing) is a crude, monstrous and somewhat frightening beast which stalks through the forest and undergrowth of ancient Russia. The two illustrations admirably capture the atmosphere of the sombre depths of pagan Russia which the poem evokes.

The album thus represents an impressive and unique response by these three major Russian artists to Gumilev's poetry of 1917.

Gumilev's visit to Paris was a period in which the two painters Larionov and Gončarova played a crucial role not only practically, by supporting Gumilev in various ways, extending their warm friendship and placing their wide range of social contacts at his service, but also in the encouragement and development of his literary interests. They offered not only a direct form of inspiration for poems such as the pantum, but indirectly, through their own cultural and artistic enthusiasms, they exerted an important influence upon the development of Gumilev's poetry and dramatic works at this time. The pantum to Larionov and Gončarova is a monument to the crucial role which the poet Gumilev felt the two artists played in his life in Paris during 1917.

NOTES

1. N.Gumilev, "Vystavka novogo russkogo iskusstva v Pariže", *Vesy*, 11 (1907), 87-88; "Dva salona", *Vesy*, 5 (1908), 103-105 and "Po povodu 'Salon' Makovskogo", *Žurnal teatra literaturno-xudožestvennogo obščestva* 6 (1909), 17. Reprinted in N.Gumilev, *Sobranie sočinenij* (Washington, 1966-1968), vol.IV, pp.423-425, 425-429 and 429-431. (This last work hereafter referred to as *Sob. soč.*)

2. N.Gumilev, "Sadok sudej II", in *Giperborej*, V (1913), 29. Reprinted in *Sob. soč.*, vol.IV, pp.318-319.

3. See "Archaeology and Ethnography in Larionov's Neo-Primitive Work" in A.Parton, *Mikhail Fedorovich Larionov 1881-1964: A Study of the Chronology and Sources of His Art*, unpublished Ph.D. Thesis, University of Newcastle on Tyne, 1985.

4. I am grateful to Ben Hellman for drawing my attention to this.

5. See "Pis'ma M.Larionova o N.S.Gumileve", in *Mosty* 15 (1971), 403-410.

6. Larionov's portrait is reproduced as the frontispiece to *Sob. soč.*, vol.III, and also in T.Loguine, *Gontcharova et Larionov: 50 Ans à Saint-Germain des Prés* (Paris, 1971), p.70.
A portrait by Gončarova is reproduced as the frontispiece to *Sob. soč.*, vol.IV, and in *Art et Poésie Russes 1900-1930. Textes Choisis* (Paris, 1979), p.47. Her "Portrait of Gumilev with St.George Cross" is reproduced in L.Salmina-Haskell, *Catalogue of Russian Drawings in the Victoria & Albert Museum* (London, 1972), plate xxi.

7. "Gončarova i Larionov. Pantum" was written in July 1917 and was first published in *Spoloxi* 4 (1922).

8. I am grateful to Raoul Eshelman for this suggestion.

9. N.Gončarova, preface to the catalogue of her one-woman retrospective exhibition, *Vystavka kartin Natalii Sergeevny Gončarovoj 1900-1913*, (M., 1913).

10. "Suffice it to consider Arabian and Indian depictions to establish the genesis of our icons ..." in the preface to her catalogue, op. cit.

11. N.Gončarova, "Indusskij i persidskij lubok", *Vystavka kartin No.4* (M., 1914), 11-12.

12. See "Neizdannye proizvedenija N.S.Gumileva", *Volja Rossii* 1-2 (1931), 53-58. Cited in *Sob. soč.*, vol.IV, p.591.

13. See A.Parton, "Russian Rayism, the Work and Theory of Mikhail Larionov and Nataliya Goncharova 1912-1914: Ouspensky's Four Dimensional Super Race?", *Leonardo* 16/4 (1983), 298-305.

14. See the two manifestos: M.Larionov, "Le Rayonnisme Pictural", in *Montjoie!* 4-6 (1914), 15 and M.Larionov and Il'ja Zdanevič: "Počemu my raskrašivaemsja", in *Argus*, (Christmas, 1913), 114-118.

15. See M.Larionov: "Lučisty i Buduščniki: Manifest", and "Lučistskaja Živopis'", *Oslinyj xvost i mišen'* (M., 1913), pp.9-48 and 83-124 respectively.

16. Walter Propert: *The Russian Ballet in Western Europe 1909-1920* (London, 1921), pp.43-45.

17. In *Russkaja mysl'*, 1 (1917), 66-97.

18. See A.Benois: "Iskusstvo Stelletskogo", *Apollon*, 4 (1911), 5-16.

19. I am grateful to Earl Sampson for this observation.

THE "TWO ADAMS": GUMILEV'S CREATIVE PERSONALITY

ELAINE RUSINKO

"For man, poetry is one of the means of expressing his personality, and manifests itself through the word." With this declaration, Gumilev begins his article "Čitatel'", which was intended as part of a larger study on the theory of poetry.(1) Unfortunately, we have only two brief articles and a sketchy outline to indicate the thrust of Gumilev's projected book. Nonetheless, from the surviving articles and reviews, certain theoretical principles emerge as important to Gumilev. One of the central ideas of his theory is that which is expressed in the introduction to "Čitatel'" - the role of the poet and the expression of his personality, as mediated through the work of art.

The relationship between the poet and his work has ever been an elusive and precarious topic, frequently leading commentators to extremes of reductionism on the one hand, and complete avoidance of biography on the other. In the history of Gumilev criticism, the temptation has been for obvious reasons toward reductionism. Over the sixty-five years since his death, scholarship has tried to come to grips with his romantic biography and complex personality. From Ajxenval'd's notorious description of him as "the last of the conquistadors, poet-warrior, poet-cuirassier, with the soul of a viking",(2) to a more modern, though equally biased diagnosis of "a disordered personality, whose private hurts, revealed ruthlessly by his poetry, are our own and those of our age",(3) psychological speculation abounds, but in the end we are no closer to an understanding of the nature of the personality or its relation to the poetry than when we started, and we are left feeling the futility of the psychological approach to literary criticism. This paper represents an attempt, with the help of Jan Mukařovský's structuralism, to "depsychologize" the topic of Gumilev's creative personality.

A cursory survey of his writing demonstrates the importance of the topic for Gumilev. Most likely reflecting the influence of his "teacher" Valerij Brjusov, Gumilev accepts the idea, albeit with some uncertainty, that "the ardently creative feat of his life *is* the poet" (IV, 266). One of his most personally revealing poems begins, "*Ja, čto mog byt' lučšej iz poem ...*" (I, who might have been the best of poems, II, 169), and he achieves his dream of "inspiring admiration in all", at least in fantasy, by being transformed into an art object, a Persian miniature (II, 45). Life and art, the poet and the poem, are one. If the poet's personality is reflected in his work, his life also reflects and epitomizes his poetry. Odoevceva quotes Gumilev: "The poet's life is no less important than his work. The poet needs an intense, diversified life, full of struggle, joys and sorrows, flights and falls, and of course, love."(4) The idea, of course, is a cliché of popular "romanticism" and not universally true, but the extent to which Gumilev carried that prescription into his own life can only be considered extraordinary.

A self-conscious "poetic" personality is manifested in the many poems from the middle and later periods dedicated to self-analysis, to which I will return later in this paper. And the role of the poet is a recurring and significant motif throughout his work. It appears in his stories "Skripka Stradivariusa" and "Poslednij pridvornyj poet", in many of the lyrics, particularly in the love poems of the cycle "K sinej zvezde"(5) and in all of his dramas. His theoretical articles are often built around the role of the poet: "The peasant plows, the stone-mason builds, the priest prays, and judges judge. But what does the poet do?" ("Žizn' stixa", IV, 157). According to his plan, the introduction to the "Theory of Integral Poetics" was to begin with a a section dedicated to the questions "*Čto takoe poezija i čto takoe poet*" (What is poetry, and what is the poet) (IV, 557). Part three, dedicated to the composition of the lyric, begins: "In addition to the two [aforementioned] factors, [presumably phonetics and stylistics], a third is indispensable - the personality of the poet" (IV, 558). And he supplemented his plan with elaborate lists and diagrams which categorize poets according to certain types.(6) Even in his criticism, as Denis Mickiewicz notes, Gumilev seems to look for poets rather than poetics.(7) Clearly the poet's personality occupies a prominent place in Gumilev's personal poetic theory.

However indispensable, the poet's personality is but one element of Gumilev's poetics. It is important to note that the emphasis on expression of personality in the quotation with which we began is the introduction to an article devoted not to the poet, but to the *reader* of poetry. The article, "Čitatel'", is intended as an introduction to a "manual for readers". It examines the relationship between the poet and his reader and considers the communicative act that transpires between them. "Expressing himself through the word, the poet always addresses someone, some listener" (IV, 179). To be sure, Gumilev's terminology is romantic, ("Poetic creation is the impregnation of one soul by another through the word" [IV, 181]), but the emphasis of the article is primarily on poetry as communication, rather than self-expression.

Gumilev asserted the communicative role of poetry as early as his first theoretical article, "Žizn' stixa", from 1910, where he is already conscious of the importance of "the word" for communication of the poet's personality:

> By gesture (*žest*) in a poem I mean such an arrangement of words, the choice of vowel and consonant sounds, acceleration and deceleration of rhythm, that the reader automatically strikes the pose of its hero, copies his facial expresssions and movements, and thanks to the suggestion of his own body experiences

> what the poet himself did, so that the spoken word is no longer a lie but becomes the truth (IV, 162).

And in a later article, "O stixotvornyx perevodax", he repeats the thought: "A poet worthy of the name makes express use of form as the single means to express his spirit" (IV, 190).

In spite of his repeated emphasis on the expression of personality, it is not surprising that Gumilev the Acmeist would place communicative checks on the free expression of subjective emotion. The Symbolist period had intertwined life and art until "the poet's biography [turned] now into a Passion play, now into the testing ground for the poem".(8) In *The Double Image*, Victor Erlich contrasts Valerij Brjusov's extreme "life for art's sake" philosophy with Blok's view of poetry as "an act of total listening to elemental rhythms surging below".(9) In the former, art became a kind of subjective record of the poet's "omnivorous" (the term is Mandel'štam's) and amoral experiences. In the latter, poetry became self-sacrifice and confession, as poets readily surrendered themselves to forces beyond their control. In both cases, extreme individualism and subjective expression ruled the day. External reality was seen either as a separate order from which the poet was detached and independent, or as raw material to be manipulated in art, but lacking any value in itself.

In both cases, the poet could feel himself to be the creator of his own universe, and the expression of his personal vision through poetry was frequently accomplished to the total neglect of his reader, as Mandel'štam noted in "O sobesednike".(10) For the Symbolists, personality itself seems to be not only the main goal of artistic creation, but also the most effective means of poetic communication. In Blok's "Letters on Poetry" (1908), he writes:

> Only that which was the writer's confession, only that literary creation in which the author burned himself to

ashes can achieve greatness. If the soul immolated thus is enormous, it will move more than one generation, one people, one country. But even if the soul is not great, sooner or later it will move at last the poet's contemporaries, *not by his craft or originality* but by the sincerity of his self-sacrifice. (My italics. Quoted in Erlich, p.101.)

Compare this attitude to Gumilev's emphasis on *žest*, form, and the word, influenced undoubtedly by Brjusov's emphasis on art as craft. It is not surprising to find Gumilev closer to Brjusov's brand of Symbolism than to Blok's, on this question of creative personality as in so many other areas. But even Gumilev's acceptance of the romantic "cult of experience" did not blind him to the danger in the excesses advocated by Brjusov and others. Gumilev the Acmeist faulted Brjusov and others for neglecting "the laws of existence of objects" in favor of "the caprice and mistakes of his consciousness", and consequently for failing to say a "firm, manly yes or no" (IV, 320-321). Though owing much to Brjusov's Parnassian *ars poetica*, Gumilev's Acmeism pretended to correct precisely that part of it which gave overweening valuation to the poet's personality. "Acmeism," he writes in his manifesto, "demands a more precise knowledge of the relationship between subject and object than existed in Symbolism" (IV, 171).

As a reaction to this excessive emphasis on subjectivism and creative spontaneity, Acmeism proposed an objectivist aesthetics that "demoted" the poet (at least by Symbolist standards) from seer to craftsman and made a fetish of his raw material, that is, his word. And in his emphasis on the reader of poetry and the communicative act that passes between the poet and the perceiver, Gumilev anticipated the theoretical advances of the twenties that put forth the semiotic view of art. And thus, in our efforts to come to grips with the problem of personality in Gumilev's work, it may be useful to refer to structuralist studies of the creative personality.

"The poetic work is always a *sign* with respect to the poet's life."(11) This statement by the Czech structuralist Jan Mukařovský is a more scientific formulation of Gumilev's romantically phrased introduction to "Čitatel'" and an analysis of the structuralist position reveals further parallels, albeit in different terminology. Mukařovský begins his study of the creative personality by focusing his interest on the originator of the work of art, but only to ask the question, "Why did the originator create a work of art?" And his answer, of course, is that "art is made for others - for listeners and spectators, in brief, for perceivers".

> An utterance can pass between a speaker and a listener because it is a *sign* which both parties understand. In making his utterance, the speaker takes into account in advance how the listener will understand him; he formulates it with regard for the listener. It is exactly the same with the work of art. Its task is likewise that the perceiver will understand it in the same way as the author. In his creation the author heeds the perceiver, takes him into account; the perceiver, on the other hand, understands the work as the author's utterance and perceives the author behind it. Therefore theories which seek to reduce the work of art to a mere expression of the author's feelings and emotions are fallacious. Suddenly our view of artistic personality is completely different from the conventional view. We no longer see before us the author bound inseparably to a work and the spectator as a mere accidentality without any essential relation to the work. Instead we recognize that the author's attitude toward the work is not fundamentally

> different from the spectator's. They are
> simply two parties between whom the work
> mediates; and on account of this ability
> to mediate, the work is a *sign*, not an
> expression. (12)

Thus, concludes Mukařovský, the connection between the artist and his work is polysemous and indirect, rather than spontaneous, and "the time has come to devote our attention once again to the *activity*, whether conscious or subconscious, which brought about the work" ("Personality", p.165).

Compare with this Gumilev's statement from "Anatomija stixotvorenija": "Since in every address there is some volitional source, the poet (in order that his words be effective) must clearly see the relation between speaker and listener and sense the conditions under which a connection between them is really possible" (IV, 186). And recall his description of the ideal reader, the "reader-friend":

> [The reader-friend] thinks only of what
> the poet says to him, becomes as if he
> had written the given poem, repeats it
> through his intonations and movements.
> He experiences the moment of creation in
> all its complexity and poignancy, he
> knows very well how all the poet's
> achievements are connected through
> technique and how only its perfections
> are a sign that the poet is marked by
> God's favour. ... A beautiful poem enters
> his consciousness as an immutable fact,
> changes him, determines his feelings and
> actions. Only on condition of his
> existence does poetry fulfill its
> conciliatory purpose of ennobling the
> human race (IV, 182).

Thus, their emphasis on the reader has implications for the Acmeists' interpretation of the role of the poet and the moral power of poetry. Mandel'štam insisted that "the poet's precious consciousness of being right" is dependent on an awareness of the addressee, that without such an awareness poems are merely "tokens of an experience which has passed" and not "events" of intrinsic value ("O sobesednike", p.240). And the fulfilment of the "conciliatory purpose" of poetry, as Gumilev puts it, depends precisely on the effective communication between poet and reader. Thus, the obvious didacticism of much of Gumilev's poetry, a further indication of his respect for his reader, is the expression of *his* "precious consciousness of being right" and part of the moral imperative of Acmeism.

It is clear that the Acmeists intuitively recognized, as early as 1913, what was to become Prague school doctrine in the 1940's, even if it is not always phrased explicitly. Couched in arch-romantic terms and framed by ill disguised barbs directed at Symbolists and Futurists, the theoretical value of ideas expressed by Gumilev are not always appreciated. There is little information available concerning the Acmeists', and specifically Gumilev's, reaction to the contemporary Russian Formalist movement. The Acmeists may well have sympathized with the Opojaz reevaluation of poetic language and other correctives to the excesses of Symbolism, but they could hardly have accepted their belief in total immanence and their "mechanical" emphasis on device. (The second category of reader described by Gumilev in "Čitatel'", the "snob", found "exclusively among critics of the new school", bears a marked similarity to the Formalists, in his emphasis on device [IV, 181].) Moreover, the Formalists' rejection of tradition and their disregard for content and for the artist conflict with the "organic" (Mandel'štam's term) or "integral" (Gumilev's term) poetics proposed by Acmeism. Anticipating structuralism, Gumilev concludes "Čitatel'" by calling for a study of the "laws of life of the poem", "the interaction of its parts" (IV, 184). Still, Gumilev may have profited from the Formalists' linguistic approach to the study of literature that was so much in the Petersburg air at the time. He reveals an acquaintance with Potebnja in "Anatomija stixotvorenija", where he cites the latter's definition of poetry as a linguistic phenomenon. And according to extracts from university records, in 1909-1910 Gumilev studied linguistics under Jan Baudouin de Courteney, an influential linguist whose aesthetic and linguistic theories anticipated the structuralist orientation of the Prague school.(13)

I propose to explore further, then, the parallels between Acmeism and Prague structuralism that may be useful in interpreting Gumilev's creative personality.

Having established that poetry is a sign mediating between poet and reader and not direct self-expression, Mukařovský enumerates the multitude of factors which come between the artist and his work – external influences, extra-artistic motives (such as economic and social considerations) and the "living artistic tradition". The last, especially important for the Acmeists, is construed as follows: "By the very fact that the author intends to create a work of art he enters into contact with the previous conception of the work of art and art in general and the previous artistic devices. ... Insofar as the artist's mental state enters the work at all, it has already been objectified by the previous situation in art, been severed from its source and been transformed into a sign" ("Personality", p.166). And as the Soviet structuralist Jurij Lotman noted, Acmeism was distinguished from contemporary modernist Russian poetic movements by its orientation toward the literary tradition.(14)

This aspect of Acmeism has been explored in great detail in Soviet structuralist studies of the last two decades, which developed the methodology of intertextual analysis to elaborate the semantic and metacultural nature of Acmeist poetry. Their analytical method is a process of identifying poetic elements which owe their semantic value to "context" or to "subtext", and it emphasizes the creative freedom of both writer and reader.(15) The text itself, in its cultural orientation, prompts the reader to this approach, and it requires from him a special competence. However, to my knowledge, neither the Soviet structuralists, nor Mukařovský before them, provide any operational devices for the reader's perception of the poetic sign. Various Western structuralists have addressed themselves to the question of literary competence,(16) and their conclusions may be of use in analyzing Acmeist poetry, but that is the topic for another study. However, to demonstrate his "pre-pre-structuralist" theoretical sophistication, it is worth repeating that it was Gumilev's purpose in "Čitatel'" and in his unwritten poetics to "illumine the corners of the reader's dark soul with the lamp of knowledge" (IV, 180).

Given this orientation toward the reader on the one hand and toward the cultural tradition on the other, the reader of Acmeist poetry is doubly challenged. Eliminating notions of the poem as "expression", the reader is moved to participate actively in the production of meaning, and, specific to our discussion, in the recuperation of the artist's personality, that which, according to Gumilev, is communicated through the poetic form to the reader.

To bring some of this protracted theorizing to bear on Gumilev's poetry, let us address Gumilev's "creative personality" as expressed in some characteristic imagery.(17) In "Čitatel'" Gumilev follows up his important statement that "the poet always addresses himself to someone, to some listener", by saying that "often that listener is he himself, and here we are dealing with a natural split of personality" (IV, 179). Occasionally that split is itself the subject of a poem, and such a poem is "Dva Adama" (II, 168-169). Dated by Struve as 1917, "Dva Adama" was not published during Gumilev's lifetime.

The poem is a dramatic description of man's struggle with his conscience, representing the dual nature of man and the adversary relationship between the two sides of his personality. The "outer Adam" is a poet and lover, charming women by his manner and words. The "inner Adam" is a critic and judge, the "enemy", "tormented by gloomy spite". The conscience reminds the outer Adam of his love of freedom on the one hand, and of his responsibility on the other. He reproaches the outer Adam not only on a purely ethical basis, but in his own interest as well, for the woman abandoned by the rake is the only hope of reconciliation, integration, of the two personalities. Only the inner Adam speaks in the poem, and the impression created, especially by the colloquial exclamation and the final scene, is that his admonitions are ineffective and the struggle will continue.

The structural principle of the poem is the divided self, and the abstract notion of conflicting natures is embodied in the figures of the two Adams, and, in the concluding stanza, in the images of Pierrot and Harlequin. The symbolism is interesting. Adam is one of Gumilev's favorite characters – innocent, yet wise to the corruption of the world in "Son Adama" (I, 147), identified with the persona as a "youthful Adam in the youthful world" in "Ballada", a poem with strong personal relevance, presented to Axmatova on their wedding day. And in the primary variant of the conclusion to the blatantly autobiographical "Pjatistopnye jamby" (I, 301), the image of Adam resonates with its subsequent realization in the poem "Adam" (I, 272). The qualifying adjectives in both cases are "proud" [*nadmennyj*], "stubborn" [*uprjamyj*], and reference is made to Adam's grieving for the lost paradise. Also, in "Pjatistopnye jamby", as in "Dva Adama", the "decaying Adam" is a part of the persona, opposed to the one who is engaged in "devoutly raising the walls of a temple". Of course, Adam, as the "inventor of names", is a metaphor for the poet and figures prominently in Acmeist pronouncements, where the Acmeists appropriated the image for themselves with the alternate title "Adamism". The folk and traditional image of "the old Adam" as the primitive, elemental part of man's nature is here the "outer Adam". The "inner Adam" is a more spiritual entity, corresponding to the image of the "Adam" of the New Testament, Christ, come to redeem and reform the old Adam.(18) Thus, the reader's appeal to the context of

Gumilev's work indicates the significance and personal relevance of the Adam image.

The serious tone of the poem is lightened by the colloquial language of the final stanza and the image of Pierrot and Harlequin, the two eternal adversaries from the *Commedia dell'arte*. The external Adam in the poem is Harlequin, the jester and prankster, "credulous and diffident, a lazy-bones, but also a busybody, a mixture of cunning and ingenuousness, of awkwardness and grace".(19) He is also the singer among the Masks, performing a parody of the Italian *bel canto*. (Remember that it is the outer Adam who is the poet.) Pierrot, on the other hand, was traditionally of dreamy temperament. Blok's stage directions to *Balagančik* describe him as "dreamy, sad, pale, clean-shaven and browless, like all Pierrots", emphasizing the emblematic nature of the image. By the time Blok and Gumilev made use of the Pierrot figure, his personality was greatly colored by the modifications made in the traditional *Commedia dell'arte* character by the French Romantics and Symbolists. In sociological interpretations he was seen as representative of the downtrodden and misunderstood, and on a psychological level he was associated with the rejected lover. More importantly, he was generally identified as a symbol for the poet. It is not unlikely that the source for the Pierrot-Harlequin pair in Gumilev's poem is not the *Commedia dell'arte* directly, but Blok's *Balagančik*. The scene of the final stanza here recalls Pierrot's lament after Harlequin's abduction of his "cardboard fiancée", Columbine. Certainly the tone of Gumilev's poem is similar to the self-directed irony of Blok's play.(20)

Unexpected in the context of the poem, the two Masks are stock figures, frozen in their roles. The allusion to them here emphasizes the changelessness of the situation, while it objectifies the duality and grounds the text firmly in the poetic tradition. Appearing as the final image in the last line of the poem, it has the effect of subjecting a serious, potentially revealing situation to ironic humor and distancing it by means of the traditional cultural reference. This device places emphasis on the artifice of the poem, deflects the reader's attention from the expressive aspect, and cues the reader to the literary nature of the sign. Only the introductory stanza draws an explicit connection between the scenario and the poetic subject behind it. "Dva Adama" displays a stylistic technique that is basic to Gumilev's poetic orientation. Rather than presenting a formulated idea in lyrical style, he develops his point in a dramatic, dialectic manner. There is little, if any, subjective exposition, and the "two Adams" become the vehicle for the poet's personal expression.

The divided self motif, is, of course, a typical romantic device, popular also in the Symbolist period. With Gumilev, however, the motif becomes important only after his early Decadent period, and it continues as both a structural element and a conscious thematic principle throughout his work. The same theme appears in another poem, "Razgovor" (I, 219), with a more conventional symbolism. The split is between body and soul, and the philosophy expressed is similar to that of "Dva Adama", but on a higher metaphysical level and in a more serious tone. Again the theme is the dual nature of man – the spiritual, striving towards God, and the material, striving towards the earth. Although in this poem the spirit prevails, as in "Dva Adama" there is no resolution, and the conflict continues.

The dialogue in the poem is between the body and its sympathetic "Mother Earth", while the soul is silent. "Razgovor" may be seen as complementary to "Dva Adama", where only the admonishing conscience speaks. In contrast, "Razgovor" presents the case for the "outer Adam", the material side of man's nature. In both poems the presentation is dramatic and impersonal. In "Razgovor" there is no explicit lyrical persona behind the scene and dialogue, but the mention of the Neva and the Nile, two rivers significant for Gumilev personally, implies a subjective relevance.

This is a good example of Gumilev at his best, as a clear practitioner of the poetic conceit in a dialectic, or "rhetorical" style of poetry. Gumilev's personal style of Acmeism emphasized the dramatic or rhetorical mode even in his lyric poems, and this may be part of the reason for the seeming contradiction between Gumilev's theoretical emphasis on personal expression, and the reaction of the critics over the years, who have consistently reproached the poet for emotional coldness and lack of personal involvement. Brjusov noted this characteristic restraint as early as 1905 in his perceptive review of *Put' konkvistadorov*. Noting that Gumilev is reserved, that he avoids the first person and intimate confessions and prefers to hide behind the mask of one or another hero, he says, "Gumilev is more successful with the objective lyric, where the poet himself disappears behind the images he has drawn".(21) In the same sense, Gumilev's poetic theory complements and corresponds to his personal tendencies and his poetic practice; for him, restraint seems to be both a personal inclination and an aesthetic principle.

These poems demonstrate Gumilev's characteristic Acmeist style. Subjective as the persona may seem and "autobiographical" as the sentiments may appear, they are consciously sublimated and distanced by the stylistic techniques. The poet's personality is transformed by the dramatic structure, the complex narrative voice, colloquial dialogue, imagery, and the tendency to third-person objectivity. These techniques represent the process by which the poet expresses his personality and the means for the perceiver's reception of it. In this sense, both Gumilev's poetry, with its elaborate system of personae, and his Acmeist poetics, with its conscious restraint and objectivity, can be viewed as the expression of his personality.

All readers note a difference in atmosphere in the poems of the post-revolutionary period, and it is frequently attributed to the transformation of the poet's creative personality as a result of his war experience and the changes in his personal life. While the question of which influences have formed the poet's personality is a question for the biographer, it is the duty of the literary analyst to assess the creative personality as manifested through the poem by a study of thematic and structural technique. In this respect, the contrast between "Razgovor" and "Duša i telo" from *Ognennyj stolp* is revealing. Whereas the poetry of Gumilev's middle period was characterized by a sense of ambivalence, expressed thematically through the "two Adams" motif and stylistically through the dramatic use of fragmented personae, the poetry of the later period manifests a conscious effort to integrate the poetic personality and to synthesize the dissociated elements through the poetic theme and structure. As in "Razgovor", the theme is the conflict between soul and body and the presentation is dramatic and impersonal. However, unlike the earlier poem, in "Duša i telo" there is a definite, though ambiguous, persona behind the body and soul, a particular "*ja*", of whom the body and soul are distinct manifestations.

I will refrain from a detailed analysis of the poem here, but pause to consider the imagery of its resolution. The identity of the self, of which the body and soul are but reflections, is expressed in mythical terms, which evoke a universal earth spirit. Like the world-tree Yggdrasill of Nordic myth, it sustains the entire universe for all times and encompasses all of life. In previous poetic dissociations, there was no foundation, no controlling or directing force behind separate entities, as there was no thematic resolution to the dramatic situation. Now an immanent self controls the lesser manifestations or roles with which the persona confronts the world. The ambivalence of "Dva Adama" and "Razgovor" is resolved in the ambiguity of "Duša i telo" and in much of the mature poetry of *Ognennyj stolp*.

This search for integration is expressed in this period through traditional and archetypal symbols. As in "Duša i telo", the tree is a recurrent image and its significance is expressed explicitly in the opening poem of *Koster*, "Derev'ja": *"Ja znaju, čto derev'jam, a ne nam, / Dano velič'e soveršennoj žizni"* (I know that to trees, and not to us / Is given the grandeur of perfect life). The tree image is also central to a poem which is ostensibly about the art of the Russian icon painter Andrej Rublev (II, 4). The saint's face in the icon is equated with paradise, the state of perfection and completion, and then metaphorically described as a tree. Thus, the integration which is found in nature is equated with the wholeness of art, and together they contribute to the completeness of man. The poetic persona can achieve a sense of unity at least figuratively through an imaginary transformation, as in the "*slijanie s prirodoj*" of "Detstvo", or in the identification with art, as in "Persidskaja miniatjura". Interestingly, the poet sees the possibility of integration in art, not in the artist. In contrast to the ironic aspirations of the cycle "K sinej zvezde" to inspire love in "future Ligeas" through his prowess as a poet (II, 148), he now sees the fulfilment of his dream not in the creation of art, but in art itself. And it is the work of art, the sign, the "word", in Gumilev's terms, that communicates that sense of wholeness to the reader.

The interface between Gumilev's life and work is substantial, and his conscious theoretical design, stressing communication and the reader's perception, justifies the critical approach which seeks to judge the aesthetic and communicative value of the poet's personality as mediated by the text. The author's creative personality is not an extraneous causal factor in reference to the work of art, but is, in Mukařovský's terms, an "equilibrium of influences", a part of the total structure of the work, and it has meaning only in that context. That is, the poet consciously uses the poem, and not simply the persona, to communicate his personality to his readers. And the perceiver's role in the communication process is no less imporant. Mukařovský points out that the creator's personality is a projection of the perceiver's mental act of "grasping the work of art", experiencing the unity of its form:

> The perceiver, too, is active vis-à-vis the work. The semantic unification that he reaches during perception . . . has the nature of an effort by means of which the interrelations among the individual components of the perceived work are bound together. This effort is even creative in the sense that the incorporation of the components and parts of the work into complex and unified relations gives rise to a meaning not contained in any of them taken by itself or even resulting from their mere sum.(22)

The force which binds together the individual parts and components of a work into the unity that gives the work its meaning is "intentionality", a semantic energy which is shared by both creator and perceiver and is necessary for full communication ("Intentionality", pp.96-97).

Intentionality in art, says Mukařovský, is necessarily opposed in dialectical tension by unintentionality. Whereas intentionality is oriented toward what has semiotic validity in the work (that is, the tendency to view the work of art as a sign), unintentionality tends toward an immediate experiencing of the work as a thing, an "unintentional reality". There are many ways in which elements independent of the artist's conscious intention can penetrate the work of art. Mukařovský cites subconscious and semiconscious unintentionality. (Note Gumilev's comment: "Through style, God reveals himself in his creation. The poet gives himself away, but a secret self, unknown even to himself, and allows us to guess the colour of his eyes, the shape of his hands" ["Žizn' stixa", IV, 162].) But because the estimation of what is intentional and what is unintentional from the poet's position is extremely difficult and involves unverifiable speculation, Mukařovský emphasizes the reader's perception:

> Since a semantically unregulated thing
> (which the work is because of its
> unintentionality) acquires the capacity
> to attract to itself the most varied
> images and feelings, which need not have
> anything in common with its own semantic
> charge, the work thus becomes capable of
> being closely connected to the entirely
> personal experiences, images, and
> feelings of any perceiver - capable of
> affecting not only his conscious mental
> life but even of setting into motion
> forces which govern his subconscious. The
> perceiver's entire *personal* relation to
> reality, whether active or contemplative,
> will henceforth be changed to a greater
> of lesser degree by this influence.
> Hence, the work of art has such a
> powerful effect upon man, not because it
> gives him - as the common formula goes -
> an impression of the author's
> personality, his experiences, and so
> forth, but because it influences the
> *perceiver's personality, his experiences*,
> and so forth.
> ("Intentionality", pp.106-107)

In Gumilev's terms, this is the ideal, productive relationship which exists between the poet and his "reader-friend". And his implicit recognition of the semiotic nature of the poem creates the vehicle for the conciliatory role of poetry, the "moral force" of Acmeism.

Taking a more poetic and less technical approach, Robert Penn Warren speaks from his authority as poet and critic and comes to similar conclusions regarding the expression of personality in art.(23) Seeing "the dwindling of the self" in modern poetry, Warren notes that the poet must achieve a heroic coherence in his work to restore the fragmented self. In this sense, poetry is both diagnostic and therapeutic. While the poet himself may be less than organized and integrated, the poem, the "made thing", stands as a model of the organized self, the "regenerate self", as it were, of the disorganized man. This sense of wholeness is communicated to the reader through the form:

> The form of a work represents, not only a manipulation of the world, but an adventure in selfhood. It embodies the experience of a self vis-à-vis the world, not merely as a subject matter, but as translated into the experience of form. ... The "made thing", the "formed thing", stands as a perennial possibility of experience, available whenever we turn to it, it provides the freshness and immediacy of experience that returns us to ourselves and, as Nietzsche puts it, provides us with that "vision", that "enchantment", which is, for man, the "completion of his state" and an affirmation of his sense of life (p.72).

Thus, it is the "point of unification" (in Mukařovský's term), or the form and the "*klang* of being" it generates (in Warren's phrase [p.74]), that communicates the poet's personality, rather than any single component of the poem. And its perception depends on the active and creative participation of the reader, who feels and benefits from the creative process through the created product.

The terminology of the structuralists and other modern analysts might well repel Gumilev, but there is no doubt that he would agree with the spirit of their theoretical statements. Mukařovský's method of analysis is not an escape from the psychology that is undoubtedly a part of the poem.(24) He insists that "in all its objectivity - its non-psychologism - semantic analysis is capable of establishing a much more immediate connection with psychological study than an analysis of 'content' or 'form'" ("Intentionality", p.128). Certainly, inferences can be made relating to the psycho-physical person of the poet, and indeed, this is part of the reader's responsibility. The literary analyst, however, is on firmer ground with an approach that, like Mukařovský's structuralism, centers on the work of art, rather than the artist's expression. Gumilev's creative personality cannot be extracted from his work, but it informs his thematic and stylistic poetic practice, as well as his aesthetic theory, and is consciously transmitted to the reader through the poetic form.(25)

ДВА АДАМА

Мне странно сочетанье слов "Я сам",
Есть внешний, есть и внутренний Адам.

Стихи слагая о любви нездешней,
За женщиной ухаживает внешний.

А внутренний, как враг, следит за ним,
Унылой злобою всегда томим.

И если внешний хитрыми речами,
Улыбкой нежной, синими очами

Сумеет женщину приворожить,
То внутренний кричит, "Тому не быть!

"Не знаешь разве ты, как небо сине,
Как веселы широкие пустыни,

"И что другая, дивно полюбя,
На ангельских тропинках ждёт тебя?"

Не хочет ни стихов его, не глаз -
В безумьи внутренний: "Ведь в первый раз

"Мы повстречали ту, что нас обоих
В небесных успокоила б покоях.

"Ах ты, ворона!" Так среди равнин
Бредут, бранясь, Пьеро и Арлекин.

[1917?]

NOTES

1. N.Gumilev, *Sobranie sočinenij v četyrex tomax*, ed. G.P.Struve and B.A.Filippov (Washington, 1962-1968). Further references to this edition will be cited in the text by volume and page number.

2. Julij Ajxenval'd, *Siluety russkix pisatelej*, vol.3 (Berlin, 1923), p.265.

3. Dale L.Plank, Review of N.Gumilev, *Sobranie sočinenij v četyrex tomax*, vol.2, *Slavic and East European Journal*, 3 (1966), 340.

4. Irina Odoevceva, *Na beregax Nevy*, (Washington, 1968), p.174.

5. See Elaine Rusinko, "*K sinej zvezde*: Gumilev's Love Poems", *Russian Language Journal*, XXXI, No.109 (1977), 155-66.

6. *Neizdannyj Gumilev*, ed. G.P.Struve (New York, 1952), pp.234-37. Gumilev divides poets into four castes, "warrior," "clerk", "merchant", and "pariah", and classifies various poets according to these parameters; for example, Lermontov is a "warrior-clerk", Nekrasov is a "merchant-pariah", Blok is a "clerk-pariah".

7. "*Apollo* and Modernist Poetics", *Russian Literature Triquarterly*, 1 (1971), 236.

8. Victor Erlich, *The Double Image* (Baltimore, 1964), p.70.

9. Quoted in Erlich, p.101.

10. Osip Mandel'štam, *Sobranie sočinenij v trex tomax*, ed. G.P.Struve and B.A.Filippov (New York, 1971), II, pp.233-40.

11. Jan Mukařovský, "The Poet", in *The Word and Verbal Art*, trans. and ed. John Burbank and Peter Steiner (New Haven, 1977), p.143.

12. Jan Mukařovský, "Personality in Art", in *Structure, Sign and Function*, trans. and ed. John Burbank and Peter Steiner (New Haven, 1978), p.162. Interestingly, Mukařovský also uses the term "semantic gesture", in a sense not unlike Gumilev's "žest": "The semantic gesture is something completely different from form conceived as the external 'garment' of a work. It is a semantic fact, a semantic intention, though qualitatively undetermined. And precisely because of its semantic essence it makes possible the comprehension and determination of the external connections of a work with the poet's personality, society, and other spheres of culture." ("On Poetic Language", in *The Word and Verbal Art*, p.54)

13. Extracts from university records were given to me by Soviet "unofficial" scholars. Baudouin de Courteney, Polish-born linguist, held the chair of linguistics at Kazan 1875-1883, and was professor at the University of St.Petersburg 1901-1918. His work is available in English in *A Baudouin de Courteney Anthology*, trans. and ed. Edward Stankiewicz (Bloomington, 1972).

14. Ju.M.Lotman, "Stixotvorenija rannego Pasternaka i nekotorye voprosy strukturnogo izučenija teksta", *Trudy po znakovym sistemam*, 4 (1969), p.229.

15. See Elaine Rusinko, "Intertextuality: The Soviet Approach to Subtext", *Dispositio*, IV, 11-12, 213-35.

16. For a general survey of the subject, see Jonathan Culler, *Structuralist Poetics* (Ithaca, 1975).

17. In "O stixotvornyx perevodax" Gumilev writes, "The first thing that attracts the reader's attention and, in all probability, the most important, if often unconscious, basis for the creation of a poem is its idea or, more exactly, its image, since a poet thinks in images. The number of images is limited, prompted by life, and the poet is rarely their creator. Only in his relationship to them is his personality revealed" (IV, 191).

18. The contrast is developed by Paul in several of his epistles. "There is a natural body, and there is a spiritual body. The first man Adam was made a living soul; the last Adam was made a quickening spirit. ... The first man is of the earth, earthy; the second man is the Lord from heaven" (1 Cor. 15:44-47). And in his epistle to the Colossians, Paul exhorts the Christian to "strip off the old Adam and his deeds and put on the new Adam, so that he may be renewed unto perfect knowledge according to the image of his creator" (Col. 3:9-10). See also Rom. 5:12.

19. Giacomo Oreglia, *The Commedia dell'arte* (New York, 1961), pp.56-57.

20.
    И всю ночь по улицам снежным
    Мы брели — Арлекин и Пьеро ...
    Он шептал мне: "Брат мой, мы вместе,
    Неразлучны на много дней ...

    Aleksandr Blok, *Balagančik*, in *Teatr* (Biblioteka poeta, Bol'šaja serija) (Leningrad, 1981), pp.59, 66. Gumilev's poem also recalls his model Théophile Gautier's treatment of the Pierrot theme in his play *Pierrot posthume*, where Pierrot is uncharacteristically "a Hamlet in dialogue with himself". Pierrot has been convinced that he is dead, and is concerned with an underlying philosophical question: "Is there an *I* who *is*?" What restores his sense of self is a reunion with his wife Columbine, at which he invites Harlequin to share their ménage. Cited in Robert Storey, *Pierrots on the Stage of Desire* (Princeton, 1985), pp.123-25.

21. *Vesy*, 11 (1905); reprinted in *Dalekie i blizkie* (1929; rpt. Ann Arbor, 1964), p.144.

22. Jan Mukařovský, "Intentionality and Unintentionality in Art", in *Structure, Sign and Function*, p.98.

23. Robert Penn Warren, *Democracy and Poetry* (Cambridge, 1975).

24. In his London interview of 1917, Gumilev says of contemporary Russian poets: "They write ... poems of psychologic content in touch with present-day cultural and philosophical currents of thought, both Russian and foreign." (Elaine Rusinko, "Gumilev in London: An Unknown Interview", *Russian Literature Triquarterly*, 16 [1979], p.82.)

25. *This research was assisted by a grant from the American Council of Learned Societies under a program funded by the National Endowment for the Humanities.*

THE PROSE FICTION OF NIKOLAJ GUMILEV

EARL D. SAMPSON

Nikolaj Gumilev's literary output was quite varied, embracing lyric, narrative and dramatic poetry, prose fiction, autobiographical prose, criticism and literary theory. But he was above all a poet, of course, and his place in Russian literature depends on his poetry and on his critical/theoretical writings - most of which deal with poetry. His other prose - the fiction and the first-person sketches - is for the most part of relatively little intrinsic significance and has attracted virtually no scholarly attention.(1) Still, it is of interest, as part of the canon of a major literary figure, as a little-known facet of Gumilev's literary activity, one whose development parallels in certain ways that of his poetry. As Cleanth Brooks has written, "However limited, however perfunctory, the works of a man of genius are rarely completely unrewarding."(2)

The body of his prose fiction is quite small, occupying only some 130 pages in the Kamkin edition. It includes ten short stories, a fragment and one incomplete *povest'*. Several of the stories were published during Gumilev's lifetime, in various periodicals. Shortly after his death, in 1922, there appeared a volume entitled *Ten' ot pal'my*, containing nine stories and a travel sketch. The book carries no indication of editor or compiler, and it is not known if Gumilev himself participated in its preparation.

Gumilev's interest in prose fiction manifested itself at two different periods, separated by several years. His earliest extant piece of fiction is the fragment "Gibeli obrečennye", which appeared in the short-lived (two issues) literary-artistic magazine *Sirius*, which Gumilev published in Paris in 1907.

Between 1908 and 1911 he published six more stories in periodicals, then, apparently, turned his attention away from prose for several years. He published no more fiction during his lifetime, but there are three works extant that may be dated to about 1917-1919: "Putešestvie v stranu efira", published in *Ten' ot pal'my*,(3) "Černyj general", published posthumously,(4) and the incomplete *povest'* "Veselye brat'ja".

The earlier stories are quite varied in setting and plot, but are pretty much of a piece in terms of style, tone and thematics. They have close affinities with the poetry of *Romantičeskie cvety* (1908) and *Žemčuga* (1910), though they stand on a lower level of literary achievement. They present a still more concentrated essence of the exoticism and literary decadence characteristic of Gumilev's poetry in this period, and are even more derivative. There is a strong note of stylization in them, and they have the flavor of formal experiments, as if Gumilev were casting about in search of a prose style. It cannot be said that he discovered an individual style in these stories, and one assumes that he himself realized this, and abandoned the attempt in order to concentrate on poetry. The tentative return to prose in later years, including an attempt at a serious work of rather significant size and scope (the incomplete short novel), raises the possibility that had he lived longer he might have directed more of his literary energies into prose.

The exotic flavor of Gumilev's first attempts at prose fiction stems primarily (though not entirely) from their settings: Renaissance Italy, Africa, the Crusades; even the setting of "Black Dick", an English fishing village, is fairly exotic to the Russian reader. All of them are set in the more or less distant past, with the exception, again, of "Black Dick".

The two themes most central to this group of stories, and common to almost all of them, are religion, including pagan belief as well as Christian,

and love, treated in some cases as purely sensual
passion, in others more or less idealized. The two
themes are often intertwined, sometimes in a manner of
rather questionable taste, with a strong element of
decadent eroticism, bordering on perversion. For
example, in "Princessa Zara", when the heroine
wantonly offers her body to the hero, who believes her
to be the new incarnation of his tribal goddess, he
commits suicide on the spot, unable to bear this
profanation of his holy of holies. Only then is it
revealed that her words were a capricious lie:

> Гордая своей красотой, она хотела только
> испытать, останется ли ее прелесть
> необоримой и в унижении... И в ее душе
> уже шевелилось сожаление, зачем,
> подчинясь опасному девичьему капризу, она
> солгала и обманула пришельца... (IV, 19).

The eroticism of this story is relatively mild, the
sensuality psychological rather than physical (the
female indulging in her fantasies of promiscuity and
in a test of her power over the male). What gives it
its decadent flavor, of course, is the combination of
the sexual motif with the motifs of religious belief
and of death: the "maiden's whim" leads to a fatal
outcome because of the strength of the Arab's piety.

Two other stories of this period, "Lesnoj d'javol"
and "Černyj Dik", also combine the same three motifs,
but go somewhat further in the direction of the
perverse; in both, the sexual motif takes the form of
violent assault.

In "Lesnoj d'javol" a baboon, maddened by a snake
bite, encounters a caravan of the court of Hanno of
Carthage, and attacks a horse carrying one of the
court maidens. The horse bolts into the forest, where
the baboon kills it, and then becomes sexually aroused
by the sight of the girl. But while he is tearing at
her garments the venom takes effect and he dies. The
girl is found unconscious and half-nude by the
baboon's corpse; the priests decide that she has been

ravished by the Forest Devil in the shape of a baboon and that she is tainted and must die. But Hanno's practised eye perceives that she is still a virgin, and he agrees with her belief that the goddess Ishtar had answered her prayers for help, killing the beast before it could violate her; to prove his faith in her purity, he announces that he will take her for a wife. The wedding is celebrated, and that night, on the way to Hanno's tent to consummate it, she notices the baboon's severed head, stuck on a stake for all to contemn. She is suddenly seized by pity for this creature that, as she believes, died because of her, and implants a kiss on its dead lips, and,

> когда наконец она отшатнулась, она была совсем другая ... Ее щеки больше не пылали, и не вздрагивало сердце, когда она думала о Ганноне. Первый девственный порыв ее души достался умершему из-за нее лесному дьяволу (IV, 59).

Thus ends the story. The sexual motif obviously is given a more perverse form here than in "Princessa Zara", yet in a sense it is again more psychological than physical. The girl was not violated, but psychologically she is no longer a virgin after the kiss.

The theme of bestiality is also intertwined with that of religious belief in "Černyj Dik", in a still more fantastic manner. The plot-spring of the story is the conflict between the village pastor and the title character, the ne'er-do-well Black Dick. In response to one of the pastor's tirades, Dick proposes to his companions as a gesture of defiance a sacrilegious joke. On a nearby island a twelve-year-old mute lives with her demented mother; no one knows who her father is, but village rumor has it that she is the devil's offspring. Dick suggests that it is their Christian duty to bring this demon's seed to the village and "baptise" her with spirits. The others take up his suggestion as an amusing diversion, but as they return to the village with their prey it is becoming obvious that Dick now has other "sport" in mind. He heads for his house with her, but she slips out of his grasp, runs towards the shore, and plunges headlong over a sheer cliff; Dick, in pursuit, leaps after her. The rest scramble down the cliff and find the girl dead from the fall, and some great hairy beast with its claws sunk in her flesh. In horror, they attack the beast with their boathooks, and only when it falls dead under their blows do they recognize, from scraps of clothing, that the monster was Black Dick.

The air of decadence that hangs about these three stories is hardly diminished by the fact that the perverse act does not take place, but is only attempted (in the case of "Princessa Zara" only imagined), especially since in each story sexual union, in two instances violent, is prevented only by the death of one of the protagonists. While decadent motifs are not uncommon in the poetry that Gumilev was writing at about the same time as these stories, nothing in it goes as far in the direction of the perverse as "Lesnoj d'javol" and "Černyj Dik". "Princessa Zara", with its milder eroticism, is rather closer to the early poetry; in particular, there is a fairly close parallel between it and the poem "Varvary", from *Žemčuga* (1910).

The juxtaposition of the themes of love and religion is handled in a far more delicate and less perverse fashion in "Dočeri Kaina". The hero, a Crusader lost in the mountains of Lebanon, comes across seven beautiful maidens surrounding an open marble coffin where an old man lies. In answer to his questions, one of the maidens casts him into a dream, in which he learns that Cain had conceived a passion for his youngest daughter; to prevent the sin that Cain harbored, God instructed his daughters to place him in the coffin, where he would lie, alive but unable to move - as long as his daughters stood guard - until Judgement Day. The knight appeals to the daughters to leave their melancholy vigil, return to the world of man, and becomes the wives of him and his fellow Crusaders. The appeal is in vain, but as he turns to leave the youngest daughter casts on him a gaze full of hopeless love, and his heart, "vzdrognuv, okamenelo, čtoby ne razorvat'sja ot toski" (IV, 49). He returns to the Crusades and eventually to England, but his heart remains petrified and never knows again the joys of either love or battle.

The subtle tension between earthly love and divinely-inspired feminine purity that informs "Dočeri Kaina" recurs in a wide variety of forms and contexts in Gumilev's poetry; in fact, one of the primary springs of his lyric poetry is the conflict between sensuality and spirituality. Gumilev carried with him through life a Romantic image of the ideal, ideally pure woman, of the ideal spiritualized love, but his devotion to that image often came into conflict with the more sensual side of his nature; and a good deal of his poetry is either an expression of that conflict or an attempt to resolve it.

That tension is lacking, however, in the story "Radosti zemnoj ljubvi". The introductory paragraph seems to be setting up a contrast between earthly and heavenly love:

> Одновременно с благородной страстью, которая запылала в сердце Данте Алигиери к ... Беатриче, Флоренция видела другую любовь, радости и печали которой проходили не среди холодных небесных пространств, а здесь, на цветущей итальянской земле (IV, 5).

But the love that the story relates is actually quite Dantesque, spiritualized and idealized, without a trace of sensuality, and in fact the final episode does take place, in spite of the title and the introduction, in Heaven. The story, dedicated to Anna Andreevna Gorenko (Axmatova), has the sub-title "Tri novelly", but, rather than three separate stories, it consists of three episodes in the courtly love of the poet Cavalcanti for the maiden Primavera.

Three of the early stories, "Gibeli obrečennye", "Zolotoj rycar'" and "Skripka Stradivariusa", lack the theme of love altogether, but the latter two are linked with the rest by the theme of religion.

In "Zolotoj rycar'" seven English Crusaders lose their way in the desert regions of Lebanon, and die of thirst. But as a reward for their courage, faith, and piety Jesus Christ himself appears to them in the guise of a knight in golden armor, and after defeating each of them in turn in jousting, leads them up a marble stairway to Heaven. This story, in its tone of unsullied religious exaltation, presents a sharp contrast to such a story as "Černyj Dik", with the latter's emphasis on the darker side of religiosity (the narrow fanaticism of the pastor and the blasphemy of Dick and his cohorts; the considerable power of the demonic).

If religious faith is the central, indeed the sole theme of "Zolotoj rycar'", the more complex story "Skripka Stradivariusa" intertwines the theme of religion with that of art: the problematics of the story have to do with the moral status of art, its relation to good and evil.

The violin of the title, Stradivarius's masterpiece, was given by the master himself to the story's protagonist, the composer and virtuoso Paolo Bellicini. The Devil, who had tried unsuccessfully to enlist the pious Stradivarius to his purposes, finds in Paolo a more tractable (though unwitting) tool, and achieves through him the destruction of the violin.

The story's imagery is a bit vague and somewhat contradictory, but the import of the contrast between Stradivarius and Bellicini seems to be that art is morally equivocal: it can be turned to good or evil, depending on by whom and in whose name it is created. Thus the Devil fears the work of the religiously-minded artist and, having failed to ensnare Stradivarius, his goal becomes the destruction of his best work:

> ... я ... предложил ему свою помощь. Но упрямый старик и слушать не хотел ни о каких договорах и по целым часам молился Распятому ... Я предвидел страшные возможности. Люди могли достичь высшей гармонии ... но не во имя мое, а во имя Его (IV, 65).

In his article "Žizn' stixa",(5) published about a year after "Skripka Stradivariusa", Gumilev expressed the opinion that art must serve something beyond itself, not from *a priori* intent, to be sure, but by its inherent nature, by virtue of what the artist puts of himself into it. This implies that the artist must have something within himself to put into his work, some spiritual content, some suprapersonal ideal, else he will be a mere manipulator of form:

> Поэт должен возложить на себя вериги трудных форм ... но только во славу своего Бога, которого он обязан иметь. Иначе он будет простым гимнастом (IV, 159).

Paolo is such a gymnast, a flawed artist despite his great technical virtuosity and theoretical knowledge, because he lacks the patience, humility, and spiritual commitment and depth necessary to the true artist.

In the posthumously published article "Čitatel'"(6) Gumilev made explicit his view on the relationship between poetry and religion:

> Поэзия и религия - две стороны одной и той же монеты.... Руководство ... в перерождении человека в высший тип принадлежит религии и поэзии (IV, 177-78).

In "Skripka Stradivariusa" he ascribes a similar role to music, but music is probably intended here as a metonym for artistic creativity in general, or as a metaphor for poetry, which Gumilev considered the highest of the arts.

When the Devil expressed his apprehensions about the divine potential of Stradivarius's achievement, in the passage already quoted, he continued: "Ešče odno tysjačeletie takoj že naprjažennoj raboty, i ja naveki pogružus' v pečal'nye sumerki nebytija" (IV, 65). And when Paolo awakes from his dream, the narrator, anticipating the destruction of the violin, exclaims: "I opjat' na mnogo vekov otdalitsja svjaščennyj mig pobedy čeloveka nad materiej" (IV, 66). Thus the process of the artist gaining ever more complete mastery over the material medium of his art is treated as one element in man's transcendence of matter in general; the triumph of art is equated with the defeat of the Devil (that is, of the physical, earthbound aspect of man's dual nature), with the "pereroždenie čeloveka v vysšij tip".

"Skripka Stradivariusa", then, reflects ideas about art that Gumilev held throughout his adult life, and is the most serious of the early stories in intent, as well as one of the most successful in execution.

The theme of art is also implicitly present in Gumilev's earliest published prose fiction, the unfinished story "Gibeli obrečennye". The extant fragment portrays the first man's first day on earth. Having recovered, toward evening, from the wounds he had received in a victorious encounter with a wildcat, this first man

> чувствовал себя внезапно созревшим. Он знал борьбу, знал страдание и видел смерть. Но тем глубже, тем прекраснее показался ему мир. Опьяненный самим собой, своей красотой и мощью, он начал пляску, первую божественную пляску, естественное выражение чувтсва жизни (IV, 85).

Dancing, he dislodges a stone, which falls to the bottom of an abyss. In the echo of its fall, he perceives a word, "tremograst",(7) and repeats it, first in a whisper to himself, then in a joyful shout, which is answered again by the echo. The last paragraph of the fragment begins: "On byl v vostorge, najdja sebe imja takoe zvučnoe i napominajuščee paden'e kamnja" (IV, 86). This formulation, as well as the association of this first spoken "word" with an art form (the dance), would seem to indicate that the event portrayed is intended as the origin not only of speech, but of the artistic word. There is no way of knowing whether Gumilev intended a further development of this theme in the story, but the concept of speech is given notable emphasis in the short extant fragment: besides the passage just described, we find two passages near the beginning that refer to the "word":

> Жадным и любопытным взором смотрел он на новый доставшийся ему мир, а в голове его еще бродили смутные воспоминания, знакомые, но полузабытые слова.... Но он уже чувствовал, как законы нового бытия заставляют трепетать каждый фибр его тела безумной жаждой движения и слова (IV, 83).

It is tempting and perhaps not too unreasonable to see an anticipation here of Acmeist ideas: the role of the first man as giver of names to all the objects of the physical world, as a metaphor for the role of the post-Symbolist poet in reasserting the concrete and literal denotative function of the artistic word, and reestablishing the here-and-now physical world as a legitimate subject of poetry. It should be remembered, however, that Gumilev himself did not lay particular emphasis on this aspect of Acmeism, and preferred "Acmeism" to "Adamism" as a label for the new school.

The early stories are all quite short, ranging from around a thousand to around 2500 words. For the most part, the style is quite similar from story to story, with a certain degree of variation associated with the differing settings and subjects. This style is closely related to that of the poetry of this period: it strives toward and often overdoes the colorful and the gorgeous; it is saturated with recherché, decorative epithets and images. Hardly a noun is left without an adjective, hardly a verb without an adverb; hardly a paragraph passes without at least one more or less extravagant simile. Perhaps even more so than in the poetry of this time, the nature of epithets and images in in the first place decorative and "atmospheric"; their function is not to provide greater visual or sensory precision, but to evoke a mood, to contribute to the atmosphere, and not seldom, one feels, to display the author's ingenuity and inventiveness. Some examples:

> ... сердце Кавальканти томилось безосновательной, но жгучей ревностью, подобно тому, как благородная сталь военного меча разъедается ржавчиной в холодной сырости старых подвалов ("Радости земной любви", IV, 9).
> Звезды наклонялись близко-близко и бывали лживы и уверенны, как очи девушки, которая согрешила и хочет скрыть свой позор ("Принцесса Зара", IV, 14).
> ...огненный дракон жажды перестал терзать их горло и грудь, сделался совсем маленьким и с беспокойным свистом уполз в темную расщелину скал, где таились его братья скорпионы и мохнатые тарантулы ("Золотой рыцарь", IV, 22).
> Ночь, словно сумрачное оратория старинных мастеров, росла в саду, где звезды раскидались, как красные, синие и белые лепестки гиацинтов ("Скрипка Страдивариуса", IV, 62).
> "Хорошенькая вещица!" сказал, засмеявшись, его спутник. "Но упряма и

> капризна, как византийская принцесса с опаловыми глазами и дорогими перстнями на руках" ("Скрипка Страдивариуса", IV, 65).

The style is "poetic" prose by virtue not only of the imagery, but also of the sentence structure and the cadences. There is a clear effort to make the prose rhythmical (cf. "Zolotoj pobeditel' sidel s nimi i el i pil, i smejalsja" ["Zolotoj rycar'", IV, 23]); and the use of such devices as word-order inversion and polysyndeton is suggestive of poetic syntax:

> Тяжко зазвучали на мраморе копыта земных коней, и легкий касался к ним конь золотистый ("Золотой рыцарь", IV, 24); Молчали девы *и*, казалось, не слыхали ничего.... *И* снова таинственный сон подкрался к рыцарю *и*, как великан, схватил его в свои мягкие бесшумные объятья. *И* снова открылось его очам прошедшее ("Золотой рыцарь", IV, 47).

Among the early stories only "Černyj Dik" departs significantly from the stylistic principles just outlined. The only first-person narration among the early stories, it ostensibly is related many years after the fact by a participant, one of Black Dick's boon companions. The style, accordingly, is relatively simple and down-to-earth, and colored with a fair amount of colloquial vocabulary and phraseology, especially at the beginning:

> Бог знает, что это был за человек! Высокий, красивый, сильный, как бык, он легко побивал всех парней в округе, а драться не любил. Наши девушки были от него без ума и ходили за ним, как побитые собаки.... Ну конечно, он и пользовался этим, а мы, другие, ничего не смели сказать, потому что за обиду он разбивал головы, как пустые тыквы, да и товарищ он

> был веселый. Божился лучше королевского солдата, пил как шкипер, побывавший в Америке...(IV, 30).

Especially striking here is the contrast between the sort of similes quoted above from the other stories, and the similes in this passage, with their simple and homely vehicles (*sil'nyj, kak byk; xodili ... kak pobitye sobaki; razbival golovy, kak pustye tykvy; pil, kak škiper, pobyvavšij v Amerike*).

The colloquial tone is more pronounced at the beginning, then gradually gives way to a more neutral literary style: "literary" primarily in the sense of being cast in the standard literary language, as opposed to the colloquial, although there are also occasional passages of literary style in the sense of "fine writing", writing with an obvious eye to stylistic effect, using linguistic and artistic resources beyond the reach of the putative narrator, a poor uneducated English fisherman. For example:

> Но огненно-строгие слова пастора еще звенели в ушах, и джин был отравлен томительным неясным страхом (IV, 36).

Occasionally the narration even manifests the fanciful and decorative style typical of the other early stories:

> Мы ... знали, что это постройки древних мохнатых жителей страны, которые никогда не слышали об Иисусе Христе, но зато ездили на белоснежных морских конях и дружили с демонами морскими, равнинными и горными. Эти древние серые мхи наверно видели их и в лунные ночи часто вспоминают зарево их костров (IV, 36).

This stylistic shift may be the unintended result of the writer's insufficient control, but is more likely a deliberate device: the author establishes the illusion of oral narration at the beginning, but then surreptitiously takes over from the narrator.

The story "Poslednij pridvornyj poet" is difficult to date. There is no external evidence as to when it was written (its first and only publication - other than the 1968 Kamkin edition - was in *Ten' ot pal'my*), and it does not fit in with the early stories either stylistically or thematically. Thus it would appear to have been written later,(8) although the example of "Černyj Dik" shows that even in his earlier period Gumilev was capable of writing in a prose style more neutral than that of most of the early stories. The exoticism, the extravagant imagery, the poetic epithets and cadences of those works are virtually absent from "Poslednij pridvornyj poet", as are the erotic and religious motifs. It is a rather slight satirical piece in a contemporary setting (witness the first sentence: "On byl leniv, etot korol' našego veka, IV, 25). The poet of the title, under the sting of a courtier's insult, finds in himself the strength and courage to abandon the easy clichés of official panegyrics and in his old age become a true poet, learning from his younger and more independent contemporaries. He is even audacious enough to fly in the face of court etiquette by reading genuine, serious poetry at a court function. Of course he is removed from his post, but this loss has no meaning for him in the face of his inner triumph. The satirical element in this story would seem to link it with the later stories, one of which is a humorous-satirical trifle, while the other two contain at least hints of parody.

In any case, whether "Poslednij pridvornyj poet" is a late story, a stylistic anomaly among the early stories, or a step in between, Gumilev's prose style had definitely changed in his later fiction, which completely eschews the "romantic" and poeticized style of the early works.

Gumilev published no prose fiction after 1911, and apparently wrote none between that date and 1917. However, he did write and publish in this period some non-fiction, namely a travel sketch, "Afrikanskaja oxota",(9) and a series of front-line reports under the title "Zapiski kavalerista".(10) Both of these pieces of journalism *cum* autobiography are written in a restrained, lucid, objective yet expressive style. As Professor Struve puts it in reference to the African sketch: "Xorošij obrazčik suxoj i točnoj prozy Gumileva, bez romantičeskix 'prikras'" (IV, 595). They would seem, then - not to detract from their intrinsic interest and worth - to have served as the stylistic laboratory in which he relinquished the artificially decorative style of his earlier stories and worked out the prose style for his later fiction.

The shortest and slightest of the late prose pieces, "Černyj general" has no intrinsic significance; it is a purely personal and occasional piece, a humorous "explanation" of the origin of an Indian miniature that Gumilev gave to his friend Natalija Gončarova in Paris in 1917 (see IV, 591). He certainly never intended it for publication.

"Putešestvie v stranu efira is more seriously intended and executed, although it too is apparently an occasional piece, in that it seems to have been inspired by an experiment that Gumilev himself made in sniffing ether, an incident that the artist Jurij Annenkov relates in his memoirs.(11) The story tells of an ether-sniffing experiment by a decadent ménage-à-trois consisting of the narrator, Grant, a man named Mezencov(12) and a girl called Inna. Nearly half of the text of over 3000 words is devoted to the narrator's description of his ether-induced visions, which include making love to Inna.

The prominent strain of decadent eroticism in the story gives it a certain affinity with Gumilev's early fiction:

> Нагая Инна стояла предо мной на широком белом камне. Руки, ноги, плечи и волосы ее были покрыты тяжелыми драгоценностями, расположенными с такой строгой симметрией, что чудилось, они держатся

> только связанные дикой и страшной Иннтой
> красотой (IV, 74); Знаю только, что ни в
> одном из сералей Востока, ни в одном из
> чайных домиков Японии не было столько
> дразнящих и восхитительных ласк (IV, 75).

However, the overall atmosphere of this story, with its contemporary Russian setting and relatively restrained style, is quite different from that of the early erotic stories, with their exotic settings and decorative style. The description of the drug-induced dream is, as one would expect, somewhat more fanciful in style than the surrounding narrative, but even here there is a perceptible difference from the style of the early prose. Take for example the following simile:

> ...как жаворонок, сложив крылья, падает
> на землю, так золотая точка сознания
> падает вглубь и вглубы и нет падению
> конца, и конец невозможен (IV, 73).

This is not, to be sure one of the simple and homely similes of "Černyj Dik", but it is also qualitatively different from the "atmospheric" similes characteristic of the other early prose: whereas in those similes the link between tenor and vehicle is little more than a pretext for one more extravagant stylistic incrustation, here the simile serves its proper metaphysical function, that is, the vehicle serves to make more vivid the concept represented by the tenor.

Gumilev's narrator, Grant, seems to take himself and his companions and life-style quite seriously, but there appears to be at least a trace of irony in the author's attitude toward his characters. Compare the narrator's reaction to a doctor's suggestion to experiment with ether:

> Я ... думаю, что нам придется прибегнуть к чему-нибудь такому, если мы не хотлм, чтобы наша милая тройка распалась. Бодлера мы выучили наизусть, от надушенных папирос нас тошнит, и даже самый легкий флирт никак не может наладиться (IV, 70).

Judging by Annenkov's report, Gumilev's attitude toward the whole enterprise of "a journey into ether-land" may well have been ironic, even though he tried it himself:

> Гумилев лежал с закрытыми глазами, но через несколько минут прошептал, *иронически* улыбаясь: "Начинаю грезить ... Вдыхаю эфир ...". Вскоре он, действительно, стал впадать в бред и произносить какие-то непонятные слова, или, вернее, сочетание букв (Annenkov, op.cit., p.104; emphasis mine; ellipsis author's).

Unfortunately, Annenkov, who did not participate, did not wait for the ether-sniffers to revive and relate their visions, so we do not know if Grant's ether-dream is pure invention, or based in any way on Gumilev's own experiences under ether.

The incomplete *povest'* "Veselye brat'ja", even in its unfinished state, is easily Gumilev's most interesting venture in prose fiction. It is known only from a partial manuscript that Gumilev left in London when he returned to Russia in 1918.(13) Thus we know that he was working on the story in 1918, but there is no evidence presently available as to when he started it, nor as to whether he continued or completed it after returning to Russia. The manuscript includes two chapters and the beginning of a third, and is about ten thousand words in length. It relates the discovery by the Petersburg *intelligent* Mezencov of a secret international society — the "Joyful Brotherhood" of the title — "postavivšee sebe cel'ju skomprometirovat' vsju evropejskuju nauku, posledovatel'no vvodja v nee nevernye dannye" (IV, 133). For example, one of the Russian members of the society, a mathematician-autodidact named Miša, had been assigned the task of disproving the law of conservation of matter and, when he has accomplished that, to "prove" that the sun revolves around the earth.

The story's setting is east-central Russia, and although the brotherhood is international the only members actually met with are Russians, uneducated or self-educated peasants (some report of the society's activities elsewhere is given by two brothers who have just returned from France). Thus what was apparently intended to be the central theme — insofar as we can judge from the extant portion — is one that was not uncommon in Russian literature, especially in the early part of this century: the revolt of the ancient native traditions and instinctive faith, held to mainly by the peasants, against the European secular and scientific culture of the upper classes. The "brethren" aim at discrediting European science because they perceive it as being at odds with Christian belief, and its adherents as followers of Satan.

It is difficult, though, to judge what sort of development and treatment of the theme Gumilev intended: objective or partisan, serious or humorous. There is a good deal of ambiguity in the work as it stands — ambiguity of tone, and ambiguity of characterization — which might or might not have been cleared up as the story proceeded. Professor Struve alludes to the ambiguity of tone:

> Местами кажется, будто Гумилев кого-то и что-то хочет пародировать (приходит на ум, например, "Серебряный голубь" Андрея Белого), но рядом с этой пародийностью чувствуется и наличие серьезного замысла (IV, 592-93).

In 1916 Gumilev had used the Rasputin affair as the basis for a poetic treatment of this theme of the native tradition versus the imposed alien tradition, in the well-known poem "Mužik". This treatment emphasizes the sense of dread in the face of the dark, irrational forces of forest Russia.(14) While there are hints of this aspect of the theme in "Veselye brat'ja", it would appear that overall the story was conceived in quite a different key from the nightmarish atmosphere of the poem.

There is a good deal of humor, especially in the portrayal of the brothers Evmenid and Filostrat Sladkopevcevy (reminiscent, as Professor Struve comments, of Leskov: see IV, 593), who derive a childish amusement from the hoaxes and forgeries that members of the Brotherhood have passed off on scholars.(15) Even aside from these comic - and apparently episodic - figures, the Brotherhood is not cast in a particularly portentous light, as the title itself indicates. The leader, whom Mezencov does not meet in the extant portion, but apparently would have further on, is described by Miša as follows:

> Повели меня к старшине, старичок такой там есть, худенький да белый. Как увидел я его, так и обомлел. Потому каждый человек когда опечалится, когда разгневается. А этот, сразу видно, не печаловался и не гневался за всю евоную жизнь. Смотрю, как это он весело да как это он ласково... (IV, 111).

On the other hand, there are ominous notes as well. The passage just quoted continues: "... i muraški po spine tak i begajut. I čego bojus', sam ne znaju." The Brotherhood is not just a "joyful" band of practical jokers; it has a serious purpose that it pursues seriously, the comic figures and the old man's serene manner notwithstanding. Miša, at least, who does not agree with their aims and was recruited against his will, is convinced that they are capable of violence:

"A ne rabotat' nel'zja. Zakoljut (IV, 113)." And above all there is the dark figure of Mitja, a recruiter and "enforcer", who inspires fear in the other members.

Thus the elements present in the extant portion would seem to allow for various possibilities in the continuation, without pointing very clearly toward any particular one: a tragic outcome, for example, or a harmonious resolution to a serious dramatic conflict, or even possibly (though not likely) a thoroughly comic treatment.

The ambiguities of characterization, on the other hand, are probably not the result of the unfinished state of the work, bur rather a reflection of the author's intent. That is, the two main protagonists, Mezencov and Mitja, are not conceived in black and white terms, but as amalgams of positive and negative traits.

Mezencov is the "hero", the central character, from whose point of view the story is narrated,(16) and thus in a sense a stand-in for the author, with whom he shares a generally similar background (member of the gentry and of the urban intelligentsia). But Gumilev does not seem to identify especially closely with his hero, and injected a definite note of irony into his characterization. For example:

> Он лег, потому что по привычке многих горожан лучше всего думал лежа (IV, 101);
> Он понял, что все произошло оттого, что он так позорно заснул ... (IV, 102);
> Через полчаса, с небольшим свертком в руках (зубная щетка, сотня папирос и томик Ницше), Мезенцов вышел из деревни гимнастическим шагом, который по теории не должен был утомлять. Однако уже после трех верст он остановился и, окликнув возницу проезжавшей телеги, попросил подвезти его (IV, 103).

The irony, however, is rather mild, and would seem to be aimed more at the social group Mezencov represents than at the individual. As an individual, Mezencov has his good qualities; moreover it would appear that he was intended to undergo a positive evolution that would ameliorate his socially-determined negative traits. Just as in the course of his wanderings with the peasants Mitja and Vanja he sheds the attributes of urban culture that he set out with - "Davno Mezencov dokuril vse svoi papirosy, poterjal vkonec istrepavšegosja Nicše i slomal zubnuju ščetku" (IV, 123-24) - perhaps he was to shed his gentry prejudices and gain a clearer understanding of the peasantry. As Mitja tells him when he joins them:

> ... я обещаю показать вам что-то, о чем вы, горожане, и не подозреваете. Мужики только с виду простые. Попробуйте увидать их такими, какие они есть, и вовек уж не забудете (IV, 105).

Mitja, Mezencov's main antagonist, is the story's darkest figure. Though he works for the Brotherhood, and thus ostensibly for the "true" faith, for God and against Satan, he is anything but pious and virtuous. He is above all a rake who apparently seduces girls in every village he passes through, and leaves them behind without the least concern; and the impression is created that he has other sins, perhaps crimes, on his soul. There are a number of indications that he is to play the role of villain as the plot unfolds (for example, Miša's words: "Beregites' ego, barin milyj, balovnoj on, i nož u nego čto britva" [IV, 112]); yet he is not without a certain charm - the charm of a clever rogue whom we admire against our will - and it is not at all clear how negative a role the author had in store for him.

About all that one can presume about the further development of the plot is that Mezencov was to be taken to the Brotherhood's headquarters, a secret city hidden in the Urals, and meet their leader, the "belyj staričok". We can only guess as to what would have happened thereafter, as the story is not moved far enough along to provide any clear indications as to how Mezencov's attitude toward and relationship with the brethren were to develop. But it is a highly intriguing beginning, promising an original and adroit treatment of a fairly widespread theme, and one both regrets that the work stands incomplete, and nurses the hope that, after all, a continuation lies buried somewhere in an archive and may yet be discovered.

"Veselye brat'ja" also makes one wish that Gumilev had been granted more time, not only to finish that particular work, but also to pursue further his new-found interest in prose fiction (if, indeed, that is what "Veselye brat'ja" represents). Gumilev's early death was of course a loss to Russian poetry above all. He was still developing as a poet when he was executed, and, it would appear, moving in a new direction, and there is little doubt that he could have surpassed his already considerable achievement, and come to rank still higher in the pantheon of Russian poets. His unfulfilled potential as a prose-writer is more uncertain. If we had only his early stories, there would be no cause for regret on this score. But "Veselye brat'ja" changes the picture. A single unfinished work is admittedly a meager basis for speculation, but it raises at least the possibility that Gumilev could have made a not insignificant contribution to Russian prose fiction. (If Puškin had died in 1828, we could not, after all, have said much more than this on the basis of *Arap Petra Velikogo*.) At the very least it proves that Gumilev had transcended the mannered prose and dated fictional world of his early stories, and was capable of applying the stylistic principles of Acmeism to prose as well as to poetry.

NOTES

1. Valuable information on the prose works may be found in the commentary to vol.IV of *N.Gumilev. Sobranie sočinenij*, ed. G.P.Struve and B.A.Filippov (Washington, D.C., 1968), pp.585-95. Further references to this edition will be given in the text, using Roman numerals for volume and Arabic numerals for pages.

2. Cleanth Brooks, *Toward Yoknapatawpha and Beyond* (New Haven, Connecticut, 1978), p.101.

3. Besides "Putešestvie v stranu efira" and the travel sketch "Afrikanskaja oxota", *Ten' ot pal'my* includes the six stories published in 1908-11 ("Radosti zemnoj ljubvi", "Princessa Zara", "Zolotoj rycar'", "Černyj Dik", "Lesnoj d'javol" and "Skripka Stradivariusa") and two stories, like "Putešestvie..." apparently not published earlier: "Dočeri Kaina" and "Poslednij pridvornyj poet". The former, by its style and subject-matter, is almost certainly contemporaneous with the previously published stories; the latter was very possibly written later.

4. In the Berlin journal *Spoloxi*, 1922, No.10.

5. "Žizn' stixa", *Apollon*, 1910, No.7, 5-14; reprinted in IV, 157-70.

6. "Čitatel'", *Almanax Cexa Poetov* II-III (Berlin, 1923), pp.98-107; reprinted in IV, 177-84. The time of writing of the article is now known, but it undoubtedly belongs to Gumilev's last years: see IV, 601.

7. The word of course is made up, of sounds chosen for onomatopoetic value, but perhaps it was suggested to Gumilev, possibly unconsciously, by the word "termokarst" (thermokarst).

8. Although *Ten' ot pal'my* consists mainly of Gumilev's early stories, it does include one definitely written in his last years, "Putešestvie v stranu efira".

9. Published in 1916, in a supplement to the journal *Niva*, and reprinted in *Ten' ot pal'my*. See IV, 595.

10. Published in the newspaper *Birževye vedomosti* at irregular intervals from February 1915 to January 1916. See IV, 624-30.

11. Ju.Annenkov, *Dnevnik moix vstreč: Cikl tragedij* (New York, 1968), I, pp.103-104. See also N.Gumilev, *Sobranie sočinenij*, IV, 588.

12. Gumilev had used the name Grant as a pseudonym – his first published fiction, the fragment "Gibeli obrečennye", was signed "Anatolij Grant" – and the central character of "Veselye brat'ja" (written before "Putešestvie...") was also named Mezencov.

13. The manuscript, a rough draft, was part of a file of personal papers and literary MSS that Gumilev left with a friend, B.V.Anrep. Most of this material was first published, with careful commentary, in *Niezdannyj Gumilev*, ed. G.P.Struve (New York, 1952). Along with the Russian MS of "Veselye brat'ja" there was a typed English translation, entitled "The Joyful Brotherhood". See IV, 591-92.

14. See my *Nikolay Gumilev* (Boston, 1978), pp.123-24.

15. Including the 18th-century forgery of the *Slovo o polku Igoreve* – an interesting anticipation of Mazon and Zimin (see IV, 133 and 595).

16. The narrative is grammatically third-person, but structurally it is camouflaged first-person; that is, nothing is presented that Mezencov himself did not see, hear, or think.

КОЛЧАН

"ЧЕТВЕРТАЯ КНИГА" СТИХОТВОРЕНИЙ Н.ГУМИЛЕВА(1)

(квазиповествовательный текст: система и организация)

С.ШВАРЦБАНД

> Взаимосцепление стихов, их разворот, единая лирическая мысль и единство мироощущения делают книгу особой формой, обладающей собственным сюжетом и своими закономерностями.
>
> Н.Я.Мандельштам(2)

I

Несомненно, книга как "особая" форма "взаимосцепления стихов" волновала разных поэтов от Пушкина до Блока. Тем не менее, думается, что акмеизму принадлежит заслуга в создании нового типа поэтической книги. Если предшественники (и современники) акмеистов рассматривали "сюжет" поэтической книги как развитие(3) лирического героя на определенном отрезке жизненного пути, то для Гумилева и Мандельштама "сюжетом" их книг стало "сцепление идей"(4) в поэтическом мышлении. Вот почему понятие "акмеистическая книга" включало в себя не *развивающуюся во времени* личность, а *сиюминутный срез бытия* поэта - не становление, а явление. Следствием этого оказалась "синхрония" образной системы, для которой ценность "вещей" человеческой культуры заключалась не в *истории* их возникновения, а в *свойстве* быть "высшей степенью чего-либо" (IУ, I7I). Вместо погружения личности в "диахронию" культуры, акмеизм предложил погружение культуры в саму личность.

В конце 1915 г. вышел из печати *Колчан* Н.Гумилева.(5) И если "акмеизм [...] всего полнее и отчетливее выразился в [...] сборнике *Чужое небо*"(6) (1912), то *Колчан* по праву следует считать первой *акмеистической книгой*. Собственно говоря, попытки критиков(7) и последующих исследователей творчества поэта(8) осознать исторический вклад Гумилева в развитие русской литературы во многом были неудовлетворительны именно потому, что отдельные стихотворения, взятые "в розницу", не позволяли определить новаторство и своеобразие поэта, "четвертая книга" которого не разложима ни на русские или итальянские "ноты", ни на темы "войны и мира", ни на "конквистадорские" или "религиозные" мотивы. Вовсе не случайно, писавшие о *Колчане* так или иначе "циклизировали" *расциклизированные* Гумилевым произведения.(9) Видимо, "дисциплина ума" исследователя должна определить единственно правомерный, по Гумилеву, *системный* подход к "особой форме" поэтического творчества - книге. Напомним, что в своей рецензии на *Вторую книгу отражений* И.Ф.Анненского Гумилев с удовлетворением отметил: "Как систематик, разбирает он сцепление идей [...], снабжает свою статью чертежом" (IУ, 412).

В статье "Анатомия стихотворения" Гумилев писал: "Композиция имеет дело с единицами идейного порядка и изучает интенсивность и смену мыслей, чувств и образов, вложенных в стихотворение" (IУ, 187). Не трудно заметить, что при этом композиция опирается на *линейную последовательность* "смены мыслей, чувств и образов". Вместе с тем Гумилев достаточно хорошо понимал ограниченность композиционного знания, предполагая, что только эйдология (не понятая Блоком)(10) "подводит итог темам поэзии и возможным отношениям к этим темам поэта" (IУ, 187). Другими словами, "эйдология" Гумилева должна была иметь дело не с линейными последовательностями, а с иерархическими явлениями. Вот почему, если композиция трехтомного *Собрания стихотворений* Блока ("трилогия вочеловечения") определяла "путь лирического героя" в линейной последовательности "от изначальной гармонии [...] - через "болотистый лес" [...] к "рождению человека",(11) то "линейная последовательность" стихотворений Гумилева в книге *Колчан* (тождественная "оглавлению") ничего, кроме частностей, определить не могла. "Эйдологический" (системный) подход оказался необходим.

Подчеркнем, что *иерархия* подразумевает подчинение и соподчинение элементов системы на разных уровнях ее функционирования. Вот почему композиция книги Гумилева *Колчан* (т.е. "линейная последовательность" стихотворений) дает исходный материал для системной интерпретации.

2

Прежде всего о названии книги Гумилева. Первые рецензенты - Б.М.Эйхенбаум и В.М.Жирмунский - обратили внимание на "воинственную" номинацию книги, однако сочли, что она порождена только "военными стихами".(12) Как нам кажется, дело обстояло иначе. Публикуя в седьмом номере за 1912 г. *Русской мысли* три произведения ("Рим", "Пиза" и "Генуя"), Гумилев объединил их под названием "Итальянские стихи" и пометил: "Италия, 1912". Несомненно, что подобная публикация главы только что сформировавшегося направления в русской поэзии (акмеизм) преследовала вполне определенные полемические цели. Напомним, что в 1911 г. вышел сборник А.Блока *Ночные часы*, а в 1912 г. - третий том *Собрания стихотворений*: в обеих книгах Блока имелся цикл стихотворений - "Итальянские стихи" (в *Ночных часах* из девяти, а в третьем томе - из двенадцати пьес). Спустя два года в *Русской мысли* (№ 5 за 1914 г.) Блок напечатал еще десять стихотворений, посвященных "итальянским впечатлениям". Блок, приглашенный в свое время в "синдики" образовавшегося "Цеха поэтов", вероятно обратил внимание на публикацию Гумилева. По крайней мере, концовки стихотворений "Пиза" и "Падуанский собор" не могли не вызвать сопротивления у Блока. Действительно, гимн католицизму в "Падуанском соборе" вряд ли был по душе Блоку:

> Скорей! Одно последнее усилье!
> Но вдруг слабеешь, выходя на двор, -
> Готические башни, словно крылья,
> Католицизм в лазури распростер.   (I, 237)

Не мог он принять и "былое... бремя", продолжающее "жить в настоящем":

> Сатана в нестерпимом блеске,
> Оторвавшись от старой фрески,
> Наклонился с тоской всегдашней
> Над кривою пизанской башней.   (I, 226)

Стоит ли удивляться тому, что стихотворение "Сиена" Блока фактически стало ответом Гумилеву ("О, янтарный мрамор Сиены..."):

> О, лукавая Сиена,
> Вся - колчан упругих стрел!
> Вероломство и измена -
> Твой воинственный удел!
>
> От соседних лоз и пашен
> Оградясь со всех сторон,
> Острия церквей и башен
> Ты вонзила в небосклон.(13)

В блоковском черновике (1914 г.) после третьей строфы - еще одна:

> И, неся грозу долинам,
> Как военная стрела,
> Ты, на зависть гибеллинам,
> Ту, последнюю, взнесла!(14)

Упоминание гибеллинов в черновике Блока, возможно, возникло также при знакомстве со стихотворением Гумилева "Пиза":

> Ах, и мукам счет и усладам
> Не веками ведут - годами!
> Гибеллины и гвельфы рядом
> Задремали в гробах с гербами. (I, 225)

При публикации стихотворения Блока в *Русской мысли* у "Сиены" была еще одна - заключительная строфа:

> Иль, сама о том не зная,
> С безрассудством красоты,
> Строгой готикой играя,
> В сердце Бога метишь ты?(15)

Реминисценции - показательны: "Готические башни..." (Гумилев) - "Строгой готикой..." (Блок), "Сатана... Наклонился... Над..." (Гумилев) - "В сердце Бога метишь..." (Блок). Вместе с тем, в пятом номере за 1914 г. *Аполлона*, вышедшем в одно время со стихами Блока, имелась рецензия Гумилева на книгу А.Ахматовой *Четки*, незадолго до этого подаренной автором Блоку. Поэтому, вероятно, знакомство обоих поэтов с публикациями в *Русской мысли* и *Аполлоне* обоснованно. Думается, что, даря Блоку 8 февраля 1916 г. *Колчан* с многозначительной надписью: "Моему любимому поэту Александру Блоку с искренней дружественностью",(16) Гумилев самим названием книги напоминал о полемике в "итальянаской теме"(17) и отказывался от ее продолжения. Сознательная расциклизация одиннадцати (включая "Леонард", "Средневековье" и "Ода д'Аннунцио")(18) стихотворений, посвященных Италии, определила "акмеистический" подход к составлению книги.

3

В рецензии, опубликованной в *Аполлоне* (№ 5 за 1914 г.), на книгу С.Городецкого *Цветущий посох*, Гумилев писал: "Цветущий посох" всецело состоит из восьмистиший ... Сборник таких "восьмерок" дает впечатление очень непринужденного дневника ... Правда, было бы возможно иное отношение к своей задаче: у многих идей есть антиподы, настолько им противоположные, что даже не угадываешь возможность синтеза" (IУ, 334). Гумилев тоже воспользовался формой, "впервые разработанной во Франции Мореасом" (IУ, 334), - стихотворение "Счастье" состояло из пяти восьмистиший. Следом за "Счастьем" шло стихотворение с "формальным" названием: "Восьмистишие". Однако Гумилев вместо книги, в которой каждое стихотворение содержало восемь строк, создал иную поэтическую систему: восемь стихотворений, идущих в "линейной последовательности", составили *восьмерки* в качестве основных элементов *Колчана*. При этом каждая такая "восьмерка" имела свои композиционные и стилистико-образные основания.

Обозначим в композиционной последовательности книги Гумилева каждое стихотворение порядковым номером. Стихотворения "Война" (№ 2), "Венеция" (№ 3), "Старые усадьбы" (№ 4), "Фра Беато Анджелико" (№ 5), "Разговор" (№ 6), "Рим" (№ 7), "Пятистопные ямбы" (№ 8), "Пиза" (№ 9) - составили первую "восьмерку". Во-первых, "итальянские стихи" в "восьмерке" строго чередуются, занимая нечетные номера. Во-вторых, чередование стихотворений построено не только формально, но и содержательно: каждое стихотворение о действительности "порождает" стихотворение "культурологическое" ("Война" - "Венеция", "Старые усадьбы" - "Фра Беато Анджелико", "Разговор" - "Рим", "Пятистопные ямбы" - "Пиза"). В-третьих, строго чередуются "лирические" и "эпические" повествования. Однако при этом происходит перегруппировка стихотворений в отношениях: 3 ("Война", "Венеция", "Старые усадьбы") - 3 ("Фра Беато Анджелико", "Разговор", "Рим") - 2 ("Пятистопные ямбы" и "Пиза"). Не трудно заметить, что в первой группе "эпическое" повествование помещено между двух "лирических": молитва воина ("Ныне, Господи, благослови...") - событие ("Он, оборвавшись, упал...") - авторская сентенция ("И не расстаться с амулетами..."). Во второй группе - "лирическое" помещено между двух "эпических": констатация ("Есть Бог, есть мир...") - действие ("И тело...") - констатация ("Волчица, твой город тот же ... Покуда..."). В заключительной группе "лирическое" впервые в "восьмерке" выступает в форме авторского "я": "Я помню... Я плыл... Я их жалел..." и т.д. Антиподом повествованию от личного "я" становится повествование обобщенно-безличное:

> Солнце жжет высокие стены...
> . . . .
> Все спокойно под небом ясным...
> . . . .
> Все проходит, как тень, но время
> Остается, как прежде, мстящим... (I, 225-226)

В следующей "восьмерке" соотношения повествовательных типов ("эпическое" - "лирическое") меняется: вслед за "эпическим" стихотворением следуют два "лирических". И если первая "восьмерка" завершалась "эпическим", то вторая завершится "лирическим". Действительно, за "Юдифью" ("Какой мудрейшею из мудрых пифий Поведан будет...") следуют "Стансы" ("...Я взял и слушал... Я побежден...") и "Возвращение" ("Я из дому вышел..."). Затем в новой группе первым явится "Леонард" ("...И народ сказал Леонарду..."), а за ним - "Птица" ("Я не смею больше молиться...") и "Канцоны" (1. "... Угадали ль вы, дорогая...", 2. "... Но мне, увы, неведомы слова..."). Наконец, вслед за "Персеем", имеющим "объектный" подзаголовок "Скульптура Кановы", следует "Солнце духа" ("Как могли мы... Чувствую, что скоро осень будет...").

В третьей "восьмерке", задав бинарную коллизию "лирического" и "эпического" в "Средневековье" ("...Но мы спокойны... Ты помнишь... Мы попросили...") и в "Падуанском соборе" ("Да, этот храм и дивен, и печален..."), Гумилев определит доминирующее значение "лирического" типа повествования: "Отъезжающему" ("Нет, я не в том тебе завидую..."), "Снова море" ("Я сегодня опять услышал..."), "Африканская ночь" ("...Завтра мы встретимся и узнаем... Вновь обхожу я бугры и ямы..."), "Наступление" ("... Мы четвертый день наступаем... Надо мною рвутся шрапнели..."), "Смерть" ("...Веришь... знаешь... Но и здесь на земле не хуже..."), "Видение" ("Лежал истомленный... и встал истомленный...").

Собственно говоря, первые три "восьмерки" составляют определенное целое в избранном поэтом "сцеплении идей": коллизия первой "восьмерки" (настоящее - прошедшее, событийное - вечное, реальное - искусство) приводит к итоговому противопоставлению "Бог - Сатана" ("Пиза"); коллизия второй объединяет культуры (ветхозаветную с новозаветной - "Юдифь", новозаветную с языческой - "Стансы", христианскую с буддистской - "Возвращение") и уравнивает культуру с религией ("Солнце духа"); коллизия третьей утверждает бессмертие духа над смертным телом ("Видение"). Вот почему, поместив вначале стихотворение "Памяти Анненского" - № 1 (смерть поэта и осиротевшая муза), Гумилев в трех "восьмерках" обосновал *рождение* нового поэта, точнее, *человека*, излечивающегося от болезни (борьбы души с собственным телом) во имя борьбы за души других людей:

> - "От битв отрекаясь, ты жаждал спасенья,
> Но сильного слезы пред Богом не правы,
> И Бог не слыхал твоего отреченья,
> Ты встанешь заутра, и встанешь для славы."
>
> (I, 242)

Так определяется смысл всей "подсистемы" - с первого стихотворения по двадцать пятое в "линейной последовательности" книги. При этом ни "военные стихи", ни "итальянские", ни "автобиографические", ни "антологические" связаны между собой не были. В то же время переплетение разных по тематике, материалу и образной стилистике стихотворений ("линейная последовательность" = композиция) возникло в результате синтеза сложных "антиномий сознания" (IУ, 334), образовав "эйдологическое" (системное) единство. Вот почему, начав со смерти поэта (№ 1 - "Памяти Анненского"), Гумилев завершил свой квазиповествовательный текст стихотворением "Смерть" (№ 24):

> Есть так много жизней достойных,
> Но одна лишь достойна смерть,
> Лишь под пулями в рвах спокойных
> Веришь в знамя Господне, твердь. (I, 241)

А между двумя точками (стихотворениями) начала и конца *кругового* движения мысли поместил единственно правомерное разрешение противоборства "духа" и "плоти" - "Видение" (№25):

> Вот солнце сверкнуло, и встал истомленный
> С надменной улыбкой, с весельем во взорах
> И с сердцем, открытым для жизни бездонной.
> (I, 243)

Блоковская метафора "колчан упругих стрел" (образованная как "стакан воды") была воспринята Гумилевым грамматически точно: колчан с упругими стрелами. Название, избранное Гумилевым для книги, обозначало только "футляр для стрел". Сама же книга содержала и "колчан" и "стрелы". Видимо, сложное переплетение двадцати пяти стихотворений с учетом "кольцевой композиции" (от смерти к смерти) должно было ассоциироваться в сознании поэта с "боевой сумкой", которую еще предстояло наполнить "стрелами" (стихотворениями).(19)

4

Считая, что акмеист "изображает не прекрасное, а свое ощущение от него", Гумилев писал: "В том-то и ошибка эстетов, что они ищут оснований для радостного любования в объекте, а не в субъекте" (IУ, 335). Вот почему "стрелами" в гумилевском "колчане" стали субъективные ощущения жизни:

> Я вежлив с жизнью современною,
> Но между нами есть преграда.

> Все что смешит ее, надменную,
> Моя единая отрада.   (I, 243)

Восемнадцать стихотворений ("линейная последовательность"), как и предыдущие двадцать пять, образовали квазиповествовательное единство. "Эйдологически" же это единство составили две "восьмерки" и два отдельных стихотворения, по-разному соотносящиеся с ними.

Не трудно заметить, что четыре стихотворения с ярко выраженными "лирическими" элементами (№№ 26,27,28,29) уравновешиваются "эпическими" повествованиями (№№30,31,32,33). Вместе с тем "дремучий сон бытия" в первой группе и "косный сон стихий" во второй (сон личности и сон окружающего) могли быть преодолены только "высоким косноязычьем" поэта. Напомним, что преграда между лирическим героем и жизнью возникла на пути "от иррационального к рациональному": "По Гумилеву - рационально все (и любовь, и влюбленность в том числе), иррациональное лежит только в языке, в его корнях, невыразимое".(20) Поэтому коллизия (преграда) определялась изначально:

> Победа, слава, подвиг - бледные
> Слова, затерянные ныне,
> Гремят в душе, как громы медные,
> Как голос Господа в пустыне.   (I, 243)

Достаточно сопоставить образно-стилистический поиск в "восьмерке" ("Где даме с *грудью выдающейся*/ Пастух играет *на свирели*" - "*Золотоглазой* ночью... *Сереброкудрой* зимою... Ведь есть же мир лучезарней,/ Что недоступен обидам/ *Краснощеких* афинских парней,/ *Хохотавших* над Эврипидом" - "Я не прожил, я протомился... Как-нибудь я жизнь дотяну..." - "И я *принцессе* на горошине... Хочешь, *горбун*, поменяться... У муки столько струн на лютне... Не святотатец, не вор... В тот день Христова Воскресенья..." - "Как некий благостный завет..." - "Мир мне кажется *рябым*... зелень стала чуть *зловещей...* Капли в лужах... бормочут свой *псалом...*" - "С надтреснутою *дыней* схож закат... кому доверены судьбы / *Вселенского* движения... Расковывая...*"), чтобы понять результат:

> В Генуе, в палаццо дожей
> Есть старинные картины,
> На которых странно схожи
> С лебедями бригантины.
>
> Возле них, сойдясь гурьбою,
> Моряки и арматоры
> Все ведут между собою
> Вековые разговоры.
> . . . .
> Миг один и будет чудо...
> . . . .
> "Если будете в Брабанте,
> Там мой брат торгует летом,
> Отвезите бочку кьянти
> От меня ему с приветом". (I, 249-250)

Бытие субъекта и ощущение субъектом бытия оказались противоположными: "громы медные", звучащие в душе, не нашли отклика среди людей, занятых "вековыми разговорами". Разнонаправленность рядом стоящих стихотворений (композиционная), как и разнонаправленность "субъективного" и "объективного", определивших "преграду" и "чудо" (системная), подсказывает: "стрелы" (стихотворения) укладывались в "колчан", а не выпускались по цели. Об этом свидетельствуют "бездеятельные" концовки: *воспоминания* "идола" (№26), *мечта* о мире, "недоступном обидам" (№27), *просьба* - "о будущей Ты подумай" (№27), "примнившееся" *искупление* (№29). Столь же очевидны и констатации: "Высокое косноязычье ... даруется..." (№30), "И душе ... Так и легче и вольней" (№31), "А те ... Слагают окрыленные стихи..." (№32).

"Географический хаос" ("Китайская девушка", "Ислам", "Болонья", "река Елизабет", "Неаполь", "парижский полусвет", Россия) второй "восьмерки" при наличии только одного "лирического" повествования ("Рай") *от имени* субъекта книги с предоставлением *права на говорение* китайской девушке (№34), "седеющему эффенди" (№36), "старой деве" (№40), "почтовому чиновнику" (№41) - все было определено системой, а не "линейной последовательностью". Собственно говоря, отказ от своей жизни (результат взаимодействия стихотворений в первой "восьмерке") в стихотворении "Рай" (№35) становится волеизъявлением:

> Апостол Петр, бери свои ключи,
> Достойный рая в дверь твою стучит.
> . . . .
> Мне часто снились райские сады...
> . . . .
> Внемировой природы чудеса.
> И знаешь ты, что утренние сны
> Как предзнаменованья нам даны.   (I, 251-252)

Если *имманентный* смысл стихотворения в обосновании "заслуженного рая" ("я в догматах был прям", "в дни войны сражался я с врагом", "душа моя чиста", "любовь растопит адский лед", "адский огнь слеза моя зальет"), то системный смысл иной: конкретные голоса других людей и эпически-безличные повествования в "Болонье", "Сказке" и "Неаполе" - объективируют голос *субъекта книги*.

Вот почему "истомленный" борьбой "души и тела" и субъективно обретший "два яркие света" в первой подсистеме (№2 - №25), лирический герой во второй подсистеме (№26 - №42), преодолев "преграду" между ним и "жизнью современною" (№34 - №41), вновь оказывается на "ложе болезни":

> В моем бреду одно меня томит
> Каких-то острых линий бесконечность...
> . . . .
> О, хоть бы сон постиг меня скорей!
> Уйти бы, как на праздник примиренья,
> На желтые пески седых морей
> Считать большие, бурые каменья.   (I, 261)

"Дремучий сон бытия" и "косный сон стихий", Господь, явившийся "мечтой", и требование рая, лирическое "я" и "личины" людей - такова явь современности, в которой "глас вопиющего в пустыне" - "бледные Слова, затерянные ныне". Но и "бред" колоколов Вечности не лучше:

> Мне кажется, что после смерти так
> С мучительной надеждой воскресенья
> Глаза впеpяются в окрестный мрак,
> Ища давно знакомые виденья.
>
> Но в океане первозданной мглы
> Нет голосов, и нет травы зеленой... (I, 261)

Вот поэтому без них "бред" о Вечности оборачивается "злыми, нескончаемыми волнами". И для "антиномий сознания" Гумилева (явь - бред) единственным разрешением становится сон *примиренья* разных стихий: воды ("седых морей") и камня ("каменья").

"Колчан" поэта был наполнен "стрелами" и "цели" для них были определены. Только теперь действие ("стрельба") стало закономерным для взаимодействия обеих подсистем книги, ибо судьбы мира в судьбе "торжественных поэтов". В "Оде д'Аннунцио" Гумилев синтезировал все "подлежащие" сорока двух стихотворений в "логически музыкальном, непрерывном ... развитии образа-идеи" (IУ, 309-310), представленном как "сказуемое" книги *Колчан*:

> Слова: "Встает великий Рим,
> Берите ружья, дети горя ..."
> - Грозней громов ...   (I, 263)

Синтез "антиномий сознания" позволил Гумилеву снять все противоречия и противоборства "образов-идей" отдельных стихотворений в "примиряющем" слове: море ("как мощь и слава"), горы (где "зреют молнии в лесах"), конь ("встающий на дыбы"), народ (поверивший в "правду света") -

"страшные судьбы", врученные "рукам изнеженным поэта". Вот почему:

> И все поют, поют стихи
> О том, что вольные народы
> Живут, как образы стихий,
> Ветра, и пламени, и воды.   (I, 263)

И если в "малом круге" стихотворений (№1 - №25) смерть поэта ("Памяти Анненского") соседствовала со "смертью" лирического героя ("Смерть"), возрожденного к жизни "Видением" (во имя "жизни бездонной"), то в "большом круге" обеих подсистем (№1 - №43) смерть поэта ("Памяти Анненского"), будучи исходной точкой развития, логически завершалась "одой" *живому поэту*.(21) "Стрела" ("Ода д'Аннунцио") настигла цель! Думается, что, даря 15 декабря 1915 г. "Колчан" М.Л.Лозинскому, Гумилев справедливо оценил свою книгу:

> От "Романтических цветов"
> И до "Колчана" я все тот же,
> Как Рим от хижин до шатров,
> До белых портиков и лоджий.
> Но верь, изобличитель мой
> В измене вечному, что грянет
> Заветный час, и Рим иной,
> Рим звонов и лучей настанет.   (II, 141)

В *Колчане* "звонов и лучей" не было: книга только подготавливала "стрельбу", но ею (за исключением "Оды д'Аннунцио") не была.

5

Если согласиться с предложенной интерпретацией "четвертой книги" Гумилева, то роль поэта в русской литературе предстает не только в тематическом, образно-стилистическом или жанрово-повествовательном новаторстве, но - и прежде всего - в новаторстве *организации* квазиповествовательного текста *книги* стихотворений.(22) Более того, это новаторство вскоре стало повсеместным явлением. Достаточно перечитать *Камни* О.Э.Мандельштама, *Белую стаю* А.Ахматовой, книги имажинистов и конструктивистов, чтобы увидеть - "сюжетом" этих разных поэтов был не "путь лирического героя", не его "жизнь" (вспомните, книги А.Блока и А.Белого), а "сцепление идей", представленных как "антиномия сознания" автора. Именно в этом видится историческая заслуга Гумилева и акмеизма.

ПРИМЕЧАНИЯ

1. По всей видимости, обозначая *Колчан* четвертой книгой, Гумилев считал, что *Путь конквитсадоров*, в большей части своей вошедших в *Жемчуга*, таковой не являлась. Следовательно, нумерация книг мыслилась в такой последовательности: первая - *Романтические цветы*, вторая - *Жемчуга*, третья - *Чужое небо*.

2. Н.М.Мандельштам. *Вторая книга*. Париж, 1972, с.435.

3. См.: З.Г.Минц. "Блок и русский символизм." В кн. А.Блок. *Новые материалы и исследования*. Кн. I. М., 1980, с.143-151.

4. Н.С.Гумилев. *Собрание сочинений в 4-х томах*. Вашингтон, 1962-1968, т. IV, с.412. В дальнейшем все ссылки на литературное наследие Гумилева приводятся по этому изданию. Том указывается римскими цифрами, страница - арабскими.

5. Судя по надписи на экземпляре *Колчана* М.Л.Лозинскому, уже в декабре 1915 г. Гумилев получил сигнальные экземпляры книги.

6. Г.Струве. "Н.С.Гумилев. Жизнь и личность." (I, xix).

7. См.: Б.М.Эйхенбаум. "Новые стихи Н.Гумилева." *Русская мысль*, 1916, №2; В.М.Жирмунский. "Преодолевшие символизм." *Русская мысль*, 1916, №12; М.Тумповская. "*Колчан* Н.Гумилева." *Аполлон*, 1917, №6-7.

8. См.: Г.Струве. "Н.С.Гумилев. Жизнь и личность." (I, xxiii-xxiv); Г.Струве. "Творческий путь Гумилева." (II, xxi-xxviii); L.Strakhovsky. *Craftsmen of The Word. Three poets of Modern Russia*. Connecticut, 1969, pp.34-38; E.D.Sampson. *Nikolay Gumilev*. Boston, 1979, pp.91-107.

9. См. например: E.D.Sampson, *ibid*, pp.100-101.

10. "Далее говорится, что каждое стихотворение следует подвергать рассмотрению с точки зрения фонетики, стилистики, композиции и "эйдологии". Последнее слово для меня непонятно, как название четвертого кушанья для Труффальдино..." - А.Блок. *Собрание сочинений в 8-и томах*. М., 1960-1963. Дополнительный том(9) без обозначения нумерации - *Записные книжки*. М., 1965; т.7, с.182-183. В дальнейшем при ссылке на *Собр. соч.* А.Блока указываем только том и страницу по данному изданию.

11. З.Г.Минц, *ibid*, с.145.

12. См.: Г.Струве, *ibid*, II, xxiix-xxvii.

13. А.Блок, *ibid*, т.3, с.113.

14. А.Блок, *ibid*, т.3, с.536.

15. А.Блок, *ibid*, т.3, с.535.

16. *Библиотека А.А.Блока. Описание*. Кн.I. Л., 1984, с.253.

17. Несомненно, что реминисценциями из Блока ("Венеция", II) Гумилев напитал свою "Венецию":

   У Блока:

   Холодный ветер от лагуны
   Гондол безмолвные гроба...

   У Гумилева:

   Верно скрывают колдуний
   Завесы черных гондол
   Там, где огни на лагуне...

   Простерт у львиного столба
   Лев на колонне, и ярко
   Львиные очи горят...

   На башне, с песнею чугунной,
   Гиганты бьют полночный час
   Поздно. Гиганты на башне
   Гулко ударили три.

   Марк утопил................
   Узорный свой иконостас
   Держит Евангелье Марка...

   Все спит.................
   Лишь призрака скользящий шаг...
   Может быть, это лишь шутка
   Скал и воды колдовство,
   Марево? Путнику жутко,
   Вдруг — никого, ничего?

18. L.Strakhovsky, *ibid*, p.34. Автор говорит о стихах не книги, а вообще посвященных Италии.

19. См. у В.М.Жирмунского (*ibid*, с.51): "стрелами" он назвал "военные стихи": "Эти стрелы в *Колчане* самые острые" (II, xxiii.)

20. А.Блок, *ibid*, т.7, с.371.

21. "Два отрывка. Из абиссинской поэмы", возможно, представляли такую же "вставку" в системе книги, как и стихотворение "Видение" в первой подсистеме. Но, включенные в поэму "Мик", они требуют иного осмысления.

22. Думается, что сопоставление книг акмеистов как особых квазиповествовательных текстов позволит обнаружить не только теоретическое, но и практическое единство, определяющее *школу*.

N.S. GUMILEV AND THE RUSSIAN IDEOLOGY

EWA M. THOMPSON

The popularity of the word "ideology" today testifies to the conceptual need which this word meets. "Ideology" may be a trendy word, but it is also a useful one. It is used by people of different philosophical persuasions and, depending on who uses it, its meaning changes slightly or substantially.(1) But its multiple meanings do not cancel out its semantic core. I would like to suggest that "ideology" is a generic word, somehow like "tree" or "animal". The core of the word has to do with a body of beliefs and a set of perceptions about human affairs that have not been examined empirically or rationally. Thus ideology differs from religion which deals with the world transcending human affairs. But it shares with religion an ability to generate commitment, something that a social or political theory cannot do. The reason is that, unlike the social or political theories which are abstractions created by intellectuals, ideologies are rooted in life itself: the life of a family, a nation, a male or female part of the population. This element of "life lived" makes them command loyalty, which abstract theories cannot do.

Thus I do not accept the classical Marxist definition of ideology as ultimately economically determined. Nor do I accept the profoundly misanthropic definition of Karl Mannheim who refines the Marxist concept but whose notion of the utopia is so arbitrary as to become itself ideological. But Mannheim does offer one insight into ideology that is worth noting. It is this: ideology is a system of beliefs whose acceptance implies a loss of control over one's intellectual life. The beliefs possess an ideologically-minded individual rather than the other way round. Unlike Mannheim, I think that we are talking here of short-term possession. Men can, and do, have long-term control over their ideologies. They are not slaves to them but rather consent to them. Still, temporary helplessness vis-à-vis one's ideology is a key element in being "ideologized".

But why invoke all this in regard to Gumilev? Because in many of his works, Gumilev displayed a variety of attitudes to a common Russian self-perception and its aftermath which together seem to form the Russian ideology, and he did so in ways that are artistically interesting. While some Soviet scholars see Gumilev as a spokesman for Russian imperialism, I perceive in his poetry a struggle to get beyond the received ideas and knee-jerk emotions of Russian culture, and to distance himself from them. While in some poems Gumilev's speaker seems not to notice the contradiction between the Russian self-perception and Russian history, in others he is very much aware of it.

The self-perception is that of a humble and gentle "Holy Russia", the Russia of Platon Karataevs and Prince Myshkins, the Russia of bast shoes and of the Byzantine saints. We all know this Russia from the books written by the enormously talented Russian writers of the nineteenth century. A Soviet rendition of this self-perception can be found in the works of Valentin Rasputin. But, paradoxically, as one looks at Russian history, one notices that this self-perception has generated a recipe for external action which can be summarized as: push, push and push again.

The Russian ideology seems to consist in an acceptance of this contradiction. It involves a self-perception of Russians as the underdogs combined with an aggressive posture vis-à-vis their neighbors. This acceptance has promoted Russia's spectular territorial expansion over the centuries. Russian governments have never accepted stable borders, and

Russian writers surrendered to this actuality of their history without questioning it, while at the same time presenting their nation as one which has suffered terribly from foreign invasions. Thus the Russian ideology involves turning a blind eye to Russia's aggression, but seeing historical and contemporary Russia as primarily a victim rather than an executioner. It involves a curious paradox: a combination of aggression and humility which are perceived as somehow reconcilable in the Russian context. In *Dnevnik pisatelja*, Dostoevskij spoke of the "removal of contradictions" in Russian culture. The historian James H.Billington entitled his interpretative history of Russia *The Icon and the Axe*. The icon symbolizes the self-perception of Russians as the gentle Slavs who formed their first state not by conquest but by peaceful agreement. The axe symbolizes the external actions of Russians and their role as inheritors of the Mongol drive to conquer and to establish a world empire.

Among the most striking examples of the hypertrophy of both humility and aggressiveness in the Russian literary imagination are Fedor Tjutčev's poems. Tjutčev saw Russia as a country of "poor villages" (*bednye selen'ja*) and "humble landscape" (*skudnaja priroda*), and Russians as meek, mistreated and misunderstood by the "haughty foreigners" (*gordyj vzor inoplemennyj*.) At the same time Tjutčev took it for granted that the Russians should lord it over the other Slavs, and in one of his poems, he called Poland a "Judas" for resisting Russian rule. Significantly, Tjutčev's imagery was created at the time when Russia was experiencing her best years and when she asserted herself with spectacular success in the military, political and cultural spheres of European life. This perceiving of oneself as a lowly and abused underdog while in fact transforming others into underdogs has been unique to Russia. Ideologies of the successful nations generally do not include this kind of self-image. For instance, the ideology of the two other successful European nations, England

and Germany, is virtually free of the idea of being downtrodden. While there is much less self-pity in Gumilev than in Tjutčev, both poets invoke in their poetry the "removal of contradictions" of which Dostoevskij spoke. Gumilev does so mainly in his early verse, whereas Tjutčev remains committed to this attitude throughout his artistic career.

Let us now look at the reflection of these ideas in Gumilev's poetry.

In 1907, Gumilev wrote the poem "Turkestanskie generaly" (I,182).(2) It refers to the Russian generals M.D.Skobelev, K.P.von Kaufman, M.G.Chernjaev and N.P.Lomakin who conquered Turkestan in the 1860s and 1870s. The generals are painted in extremely flattering colors. The poem begins with a description of the life of the Russian upper class: balls and receptions held in wealthy private homes. Ever since the time of Puškin, such balls and receptions have evoked the sarcasm of Russian writers. This "deadening swirl of life in high society" (*mertvjaščee upoen'e sveta*) is invoked in Gumilev's poem as a backdrop against which are displayed "the strange figures" of the old generals. They are tall and upright, their eyes are bright and their manner kind. They are surrounded by the "sweet-smelling legend" (*blagouxajuščaja legenda*) of their mysterious exploits. What is suggested here is not the warrior-like qualities of the generals but rather their similarity to the Russian saints who, as everybody knows, excelled in humility. Later in the poem, the loss of a Russian army unit is mourned: here again Russians are presented as those to whom harm was done rather than as those who inflicted harm on others. Finally, the conquered cities are named: Ust'-Kuduk, Kinderli, and "the white city of Khiva and the Russian flag above it" (*russkij flag nad beloj Xivoj*). As presented by the speaker, these victorious generals are cultivated and refined, modest and gentle; one might get the impression that they were engaged in preaching Christian love and humility to the tribesmen of Turkestan rather than in an aggressive war.

History offers the following information on the generals' activities: in the years 1853-85 the Russians invaded Uzbek territory on numerous occasions and eventually annexed the ancient centers of Turkic culture, the cities of Turkestan (conquered in 1864), Tashkent (1865) and Khiva (1873).(3)

Russian designs on Turkestan first became apparent in 1858 when Tsar Alexander II sent Count N.P.Ignat'ev as envoy to the khanate of Khiva. Ignat'ev was supposed to negotiate a trade agreement but his real goal was intelligence gathering. His visit ended on an amicable note, Ignat'ev assuring the Khan that Russia had peaceful intentions, but in 1864, largely on the basis of the information he and his successors had procured, Alexander II started his campaign against the Turkomen. It was so successful that in 1867 General von Kaufman was appointed the first Governor-General of the province of Turkestan. In 1873 the attack on Khiva began. While it was in progress, Alexander dispatched Count Petr Shuvalov to London to assure the British government that he did not intend to occupy or annex the khanate. But he did not keep his word. In the same year, the Russians attacked and took the city of Khiva, and then declared it to be a protectorate. In 1875, a rebellion broke out in Turkestan and General Skobelev was dispatched to quell it, which he did at some expense to the people of Turkestan. After that pacification, there was no more talk of the protectorate. In 1876 the Khiva and Kokand khanates were simply annexed by Russia.

So it appears that in his conquest of Central Asia Alexander II used tactics similar to those which had once been used against the Kievan principality by the Mongols: having gathered enough intelligence, he attacked his neighbors without declaring war, annexed their territory and forced the hapless Turkomen to pay a large indemnity to the Petersburg treasury.

However, the perception of Russians as aggressors is entirely absent from Gumilev's poem. We witness here the poet's inability to leave the confines of the national ideology even when dealing with past events. In this poem, the Russian generals are presented in the way in which Russian saints used to be presented on Muscovite icons: radiant and virtuous and ready to sacrifice themselves for a just cause. In Russian literature, one observes a tendency to ascribe virtue rather than strength to military leaders and suggest that they won because of their gentleness and modesty rather than because of their military talent.(4) In "Turkestanskie generaly" Gumilev surrenders to this tendency rather than try to develop a perspective on it.

The title of the poem is in itself an exercise in ideological rigidity: the Turkestan generals. We are obviously talking here of the Russian generals and not of the Turkic ones. The implications of Gumilev's usage can be gauged by imagining a successful conquest of the Soviet Union by Hitler, and future German poets' reference to such generals as Heinz Guderian and Friedrich von Paulus as "the Russian generals". Indeed, ideology plays strange tricks on people, it possesses them to the point of making them blind to the elementary rules of logic and experience. Predictably, "Turkestanskie generaly" is not one of Gumilev's best poems.

In the poem "Sestre miloserdija" (II,136), a similar surrender to ideology is evident. The speaker exhorts a military nurse not to waste her time on the care and feeding of those who have been weakened and incapacitated by war, but instead to trust in the "health of the [Russian] spirit" which will "make [Russians] soar from Vilno to Vienna with the speed of lightning" (*ver'te... v zdorov'e duxa/V moln'enosnyj ego polet../ On ot Vil'ny do samoj Veny/ Neuklonno nas dovedet*). The metaphors of soaring and lightning appear here, and elsewhere in Gumilev, to connote aggression. The familar tendency to attribute victory to virtue rather than strength is also in evidence: it is the spirit and not military might that will lead Russians all the way into Western Europe.

In "Otvet sestry miloserdija" (II,138) the self-perception of Russians as the underdogs is again invoked, while their military victories are taken for granted. The nurse acknowledges that the Russians will return victorious from the foreign lands, but she also invokes "Plač Jaroslavny" (Jaroslavna's Lament) from *Slovo o polku Igoreve* which mourns a twelfth-century Russian defeat. It is on such remote defeats as the one described in *The Igor Tale* that Gumilev's nurse feeds her self-perception as a humble and misunderstood victim of other people's aggression. The invocation of Jaroslavna in the epigraph to the poem and then again in the last stanza makes the nurse's lament tribal rather than universal. In other words, the Russian state's external agression (marching from Vilno to Vienna, neither of which are Russian cities) does not destroy the Russians' self-perception as a downtrodden nation suffering from the injustices of history. We witness here a surrender to the clichés of Russian self-perception rather than a poetic interpretation of them, a rhymed restatement of the Russian ideology rather than a discovery of new poetic ideas.

In his book *The Russian Idea* Nikolaj Berdjaev has suggested that Hegelian dialectic found so many adherents in Russia because it seemed to agree with the Russian mode of being, the Russian love of paradoxes and contempt for the truth of reason and reflection. Indeed, no poet of note has given the Russian literary language the dimension of rationality which in English was arrived at through the writings of such poets as Alexander Pope. Thus, even though Gumilev was a member, indeed a leader, of a school of poetry which functioned under the banner of Apollonian clarity and harmony, his poetry abounds in metaphors of untamed aggression, Romantic rebellion and disorder. His "conquerors of the new lands", his captains and explorers, hunters and archers and travelers to Africa are all variations on the theme of the Romantic rebel. Gumilev longs for neoclassical clarity and for the peacefulness of the *gorodki* and *starye usad'by* of old Russia, but his poetic temperament leads him into the chaos and brutality of military raids and hunting expeditions. In the cycle "Poemy" (I,13) the speaker is a rebel who declares that he and his companions "will take away the truth from God by the force of their flaming swords" (*Pravdu my voz'mem u Boga/ Siloj ognennyx mečej*). In "Molitva" (I,133) the speaker exhorts the sun to destroy and burn the present in the name of the future (*Solntse, sožgi nastojaščee/ Vo imja grjaduščego*). The present is worth destroying for the sake of the future. Such an attitude is a common element of any nationalistic ideology, and we have become accustomed to seeing it in Russia ever since the time of Peter the Great.

In the title of his first volume of poetry, Gumilev invoked the Spanish *conquistadores*. These explorers are among the least admirable "travelers to the new lands". They are reputed to have gone to America to get rich and to plunder the continent rather than contribute to it. The conquistador came to symbolize the exploitative attitude. He brought misery rather than happiness to the new land. Unintentionally, Gumilev here created an allegory expressing the attitude of Russians vis-à-vis their territorial acquisitions both in the East and in the West. Suffice it to mention the connotations of the word "Siberia" ever since the Tsars conquered it.

It is interesting to note that the image of Europe as conquered by the Russians appears repeatedly in Russian literature. In Gumilev's poetry, this dream is expressed by means of allusions ("from Vilno to

Vienna"), but in his prose one encounters startling directness. In "Zapiski kavalerista" Gumilev, who volunteered for the army in 1914, describes his entry into what today is Eastern Poland in the following way: "All these little houses made of stone, with their red tile roofs... filled me with the sweet desire to push forward. The dreams of Ermak, Perovskij and other representatives of conquering and triumphant Russia became my dreams. And... this is the way to Berlin... which one should enter not as a respectful student but on horseback and with a rifle over one's shoulder" (IV,445). This is a direct expression of the aggressive part of the Russian ideology. There is no beating about the bush here and no humble posturing. There is only an elegantly expressed surrender to a political goal.

Emphasis on the obverse side of the medal, i.e., that aspect of the Russian ideology which involves seeing oneself as humble and powerless, is very much in evidence in such poems as "Gorodok" (II,7) or "Starye usad'by" (I,215). Here the innocent Russia and her internal passivity and docility dominate the picture. Here soldiers are not *soldaty* but *soldatiki* (in "Gorodok"), and the conquering captains' vessels (*korabli* of the "Kapitany" cycle) become *lodočki*. Instead of invading Turkestan, the young men are being kissed and caressed by the young girls. In the country houses, shelves are stocked with "Baron Brambeus i Russo", two non-militaristic suppliers of patriotic and utopian imagery. However, the instruments of violence are not altogether absent: the two authors reside on the shelf "narjadu s pistoletami" (alongside the pistols).

Thus Gumilev's speaker yearns for the humble and holy Russia of his dreams and of his self-perception. This Russia sometimes appears to him in the form of old country houses, sleepy little towns or impoverished pilgrims. Sometimes it assumes the names of countries and lands symbolizing peace and spirituality, such as India and the Buddhist Far East. Gumilev's speaker wants to sit by the stream like a simple Hindu, gaze at the world yet be indifferent to it, somewhat like the inhabitants of "the old country houses" and "the little Russian towns". He wants to travel to the "India of the spirit" (*Indija duxa*) or to return to Buddhist passivity (in "Vozvraščenie", I,228). A desire for *stranničestvo*, for wandering and poverty, for humiliation and humility, is repeatedly expressed, especially in the later period. In "Uniženie" (II,148) the speaker exclaims: "Ax, bežat' by, skryt'sja by..." (I would like to run away, to hide). In "Priglašenie v putešestvie" (II,174), the same feeling is present: "Uedem, brosim kraj dokučnyj" - in order to live like a wanderer and seek spiritual wisdom.

It is in these poems about humility and spirituality that a new attitude toward ideology begins to take shape. These poems lack the political overtones of "Turkestanskie generaly" or of the other "aggressive" poems. Their peaceful imagery is dotted with warlike allusions, but the speaker does not try to convince us of the moral superiority of the aggressive attitude. Melancholy, spiritual awareness and remembrance of a struggle with which the speaker does not identify predominate in such poems and create an impression of poetic detachment. The end result is artistically more satisfying than the rhymed rhetoric of the "aggressive" poems.

"Mužik" (II,12) is a fine example of such poetic detachment. The poem is based on the life of Grigorij Rasputin, but it does not lapse into the political sermonizing which the Rasputin affair often triggers off in Russian ideologues. The poem moves forward not by expressing political views or invoking a series of political events but by the startling connotations of its imagery. Gumilev's peasant wears a cross on his chest, his smile is childlike, he carries with him his meagre belongings: he is an archetypal Russian wanderer, a Vlas, a saintly *strannik*. But his words are "mischievous, oh so mischievous":

>   Взглядом, улыбкою детской,
>   Речью такой озорной,
>   И на груди молодецкой
>   Крест просиял золотой...
>
>   Песней протяжной, негромкой,
>   Но озорной, озорной...
>
>   В диком краю и убогом
>   Много таких мужиков,
>   Слышен по нашим дорогам
>   Радостный гул их шагов.

These lines allude in an original way to the paradox of the icon and the axe in Russian history. Walking together are the *strannik* Vlas and the greedy conquistador, and they are one and the same person. The reader is likely to remember that the Turkestan battles were fought by such peasants under the command of the "Turkestan generals". The Russian ideology which Gumilev eulogized in "Turkestan generals" is looked upon sceptically in this poem, and the scepticism is not distinct from but identical with the structure of the poem. Here meaning lies in structure and cannot be separated from it.

On a different scale, a reconsideration of the paradoxes of Russian ideology is apparent in the play *Gondla*. Even though the play deals with remote times and obscure conflicts, its thematic similarity to the ideology-bound works of Gumilev is striking. The theme of *Gondla* is a confrontation between aggressiveness and brutality on the one hand, and passivity, humility and gentleness on the other. Ostensibly, *Gondla* has nothing to do with the history of Russia but dramatizes two opposing principles in the early medieval history of Europe: the gentleness of the Celts who embraced Christ and were poets and singers (they are presented through the metaphor of the swans), and the brutality of the Germanic tribes who knew no gentleness or forgiveness and no art or culture, but who worshipped strength and power and acquired a good measure of both; they are presented through the metaphor of the wolves. These two images, the swans and the wolves, alternate in the play, which deals with an imaginary Irish Prince Gondla who by a quirk of fate is sent off to Iceland to be educated there, with a view to uniting the two kingdoms through marriage. Gondla turns out to be a foundling, the real prince having perished in a storm in his babyhood. Also, Gondla is a hunchback and a weakling. But just as he is about to be defeated by the victorious Icelanders, a troop of Irishmen arrives, rescues him and proclaims him king. But Gondla commits suicide to persuade the Icelanders to convert to Christianity, which they promptly do.

The plot is schematic to the point of being unconvincing. But the play is significant in that it tries to present a reconciliation of "the icon and the axe" without restating the clichés of Russian self-perception or appealing to the stock emotions which usually accompany these clichés. The two opposite elements in Russian culture, the homeless pilgrims and the Turkestan generals, are allegorized here into the gentleness of the swan and the brutality of the beast of prey, and then "reconciled" through the action of a single heroic individual. While this reconciliation is not entirely convincing either historically or artistically, the play is not a mere celebration of the Russian ideology but an attempt to explore the ways out of and beyond it. By leaving the Russian turf, Gumilev proved himself capable of separating historical events from their prescribed interpretations, a feat which he did not manage to accomplish in his early poetry.

But the most brilliant invocation of the two contradictory aspects of the Russian ideology can be found in "Zabludivšijsja tramvaj" (II,48). Here the poetic speaker ceases to depend on the voice imposed on him by tribal culture and instead creates an original work out of a web of allusions to the contradictory elements of this culture. For "Zabludivšijsja tramvaj" is less a dream in search of a Freudian interpreter than the work of a man who was intimately familiar with Russian history and its reflections in Russian literature.

"Zabludivšijsja tramvaj" makes very little sense unless it is viewed as a palimpsest, or an inscription of a new text on several older texts, in particular, on Gogol's *Mertvye duši* and Puškin's *Mednyj vsadnik* and *Kapitanskaja dočka*. It contains a critique of the aggressive political behavior of Russians and references to many events of Russian history. In a poetic way, the poem annuls the message of "Turkestanskie generaly" and "Zapiski kavalerista".

How does Gogol enter the landscape of Gumilev's poem? In the last two paragraphs of *Dead Souls* an aggressive image of the *trojka* is invoked. A carriage drawn by three wild horses rushes forward so swiftly that it seems to "fly in the air". Other nations and countries step aside to let the mad carriage pass by. Gogol's troika echoes the horses of the Apocalypse and the horses of the Mongols who once dominated Russia. The Khans' empire of the thirteenth-fifteenth centuries was made possible largely because the Mongols knew how to breed the extremely swift and light horses who beat all records in crossing the vast Siberian plains and getting as far as Kievan Rus'. The association with the Mongols is reinforced by Gogol through the image of the lightning (*molnija*) which is the traditional Slavic metaphor for divine punishment. Just as the Mongols were seen by the Slavs as the scourge of God, so is the Russian troika a scourge for "other nations and countries". "Rus', kuda neseššja ty?... Daj otvet. Ne daet otveta": Russia cannot explain her frenzied surge beyond her own borders. Her violent actions leave other nations either "trampled down" or "moving aside". Gogol's troika is a case of the brakes giving in and the vehicle rushing forward with great speed not to glory but to its death, and the death of those who are in the way.

"Zabludivšijsja tramvaj" likewise expresses a mad and purposeless drive forward. Unlike the *trojka* which was an image appropriate for the nineteenth century, *tramvaj* is a vehicle which appears in cities at the beginning of the industrialization process (which Gumilev witnessed in his Russia), and it is associated with the shabby side of city life. A streetcar does not provide the comforts of a personal carriage but it can carry a lot of people to work.

The poem echoes the key metaphors of Gogol's brilliant piece. The horses flying in the air, the lightning, the bridge; unanswered questions are invoked in both works and they create an impression of a frantic and violent stampede. Russia rushes forward, but it is also lost; it is ahead of others but it is unable to control its own behavior. Here are some examples of Gumilev's borrowing from Gogol. (Gogol is quoted in roman, Gumilev in italic):

... [кони] летящие по воздуху ...
... *летел трамвай* ...

... гремят мосты ...
... *Мы прогремели по трем мостам* ...

Куда несешься ты? Дай ответ. Не дает ответа.
Где я? Так томно и так тревожно /Сердце мое стучит в ответ ...

... что значит это наводящее ужас движение — и что за неведомая сила заключена в сих неведомых светом конях?
Он заблудился в бездне времен ... /... *И два копыта его коня* ...

This last phrase looks back not only to Gogol but also to Puškin's presentation of Catherine's monument to Peter the Great (in *The Bronze Horseman*): "A za mostom letit na menja /Vsadnika dlan' v železnoj perčatke/ I dva kopyta ego konja."

The allusions to Puškin appear mainly in the speaker's words addressed to a certain Mašen'ka. She has been hurt by the speaker's desire to advance himself in the world and the ensuing neglect of her own needs. Mašen'ka echoes both her namesake in *The Captain's Daughter* and Evgenij's fiancée Paraša in *The Bronze Horseman*. She cries when the speaker "goes to introduce himself to the Empress": a hint at the empire-building activities of Catherine the Great and of the other tsars and tsarinas, in which the men of Russia participated to the detriment of their women. The bitter irony of this passage is augmented by the fact that in *The Captain's Daughter* it is Mašen'ka who goes to see the Empress, and she does so to ask forgiveness for her beloved rather than to seek success in the world. The empire-building activities in which Gumilev's hero wants to participate include a cultivation of the same wordliness which was dreaded by Puškin, who described it as "mertvjaščee upoen'e sveta". Notwithstanding this warning, Gumilev's hero rushes to the Empress in his "powdered wig". And like Puškin's Paraša, Gumilev's Mašen'ka perishes.

The Mašen'kas of Russia and what they represented (the desire to live private lives, to manufacture household items rather than history books) have been destroyed by the momentum of Gogol's *trojka* and Gumilev's *tramvaj*. Russia's political triumphs, the Turkestan generals and the Empresses and Emperors of Petersburg brought death to the Mašen'kas and sadness (*grust'*) to the poem's speaker whose understanding of events grows with the poem and who seems to represent an average Russian.

As the poem progresses, the streetcar leaves behind the old Russia. Its trajectory takes it to France, to Africa and other tropical regions of the world ("My proskočili skvoz' rošču pal'm,/ Čerez Nevu, čerez Nil i Senu..."). The poem is a daring summary of Russian history from the time of Puškin and Gogol to Gumilev's own day, and it contains a prediction that Russia's territorial appetite will extend far beyond the areas mentioned in "Turkestanskie generaly" and in

"Zapiski kavalerista". The deranged push forward continues; the streetcar, or the modernized though shabby Russia, still rushes forward, the brakes are gone, the goal is unclear. The gods, who were present in Gogol, are absent in Gumilev: the streetcar leaves behind St.Isaac's Cathedral, "the bulwark of Orthodoxy" (*tverdynja pravoslavija*). It is sheer madness now. One can only rely on the streetcar's conductor but he is either unable or unwilling to take charge of the vehicle. The formerly agricultural and peaceful landscape changes into a murderous country: "Vyveska... Bukvy glasjat - Zelennaja...[no] tut... mertvye golovy prodajut" (the sign says Greengrocer - [but] they sell dead heads there). Human heads lie in a box, the speaker's head among them, at the very bottom of the box: an uncanny presentiment of the author's own death. These heads conjure up the image of the guillotine in the French Revolution, and they remind us of the destruction of life in the Russian Revolution. They symbolize the enormous amount of suffering which Russia has caused to itself and to its neighbors by its insatiable craving to expand. The result? - "Naveki serdce ugrjumo, i trudno dyšat', i bolno žit'". The speaker loves Russia, but he is terribly sad for it. "The Lost Streetcar" expresses the victory of the aggressive and brutal Russia over the gentle and Holy *Rus'*, and it differentiates between the Russia of reality and the Russia of legend, between national practice and the national myth. It does so through its imagery and structure rather than by invoking the received ideas of the national ideology. "The Lost Streetcar" creates its own perceptions and point of view. There is no surrender to ideology here, but rather a creative use of it. Here Gumilev accomplished what his contemporary Viktor Shklovskij wanted all art to accomplish: he made the reader *see* rather than merely *recognize* the national ideology, and reflect on it instead of indulging in a knee-jerk reaction to it.

To sum up, there developed in Russia a self-perception which saw the country as Holy Russia, humble and peaceful, sweet and gentle and passive, the Russia of thinkers and peasants, the Russia of the victims of Napoleon and Batu-Khan. Yet another and complementary part of the Russian ideology saw nothing wrong with the many centuries of Russian aggression. Russian artists and poets have seldom pondered the incongruity between the passive and gentle *Rus'* and the Russia whom a foreign writer once described as "the prison of nations". In poems such as "Zabludivšijsja tramvaj" and "Mužik", Gumilev broke away from the ideological rigidity of Russian literature, but in "Turkestanskie generaly", "Sestre miloserdija" and "Otvet sestry miloserdija" he surrendered to it. He struggled with it in many other works, with greater or lesser success. And it is ironic but not unprecedented that the combination of passivity and aggressiveness which characterizes the Russian ideology eventually boomeranged and hit Gumilev himself (as it did many other Russian writers). He was killed with the same secret brutality with which Russia has handled those who had the misfortune to get under the hoofs of her *trojka*. Russian historians keep silent about the victims of those Turkestan generals whom Gumilev, Dostoevskij and Tjutčev painted in such warm colors in their literary and non-literary works. Likewise, we do not know much about the circumstances of Gumilev's execution. He was accused of threatening the security of the Russian state. In the nineteenth century, the politically insignificant Turkestan tribesmen were accused of threatening the Russian Empire, and on that pretext they were destroyed. Thus, while Gumilev's deep religiosity has probably saved his soul, his body was a victim of the same Russian ideology which he repeatedly and ambivalently invoked in his literary works.

NOTES

1. Karl Marx, "The German Ideology", Part I, in *The Marx-Engels Reader*, ed. R.C.Tucker (New York, 1972), pp.146-202; Karl Mannheim, *Ideology and Utopia* (London, 1948); Kenneth Minogue, *Alien Powers: The Pure Theory of Ideology* (London, 1985); Nicholas Rzhevsky's *Russian Literature and Ideology* (Urbana, 1983) perpetuates the clichés of the Russian ideology without critically assessing them. Fedor Dostoevskij's *Dnevnik pisatelja* (1873-1880) and the writings of the Russian Slavophiles abound in expressions of the self-perception which forms the basis of the Russian ideology: F.M.Dostoevskij, *Dnevnik pisatelja*, 3 vols. (Paris, n.d.). See also I.S.Kireevskij, *Polnoe sobranie sočinenij* (M., 1911).

2. All quotations from Gumilev's works come from N.Gumilev, *Sobranie sočinenij v četyrex tomax*, ed. G.P.Struve and B.Filippov (Washington, D.C., 1962-8).

3. Sources are scarce concerning Russian policies in Central Asia and virtually all English-language books are based on Russian or Soviet accounts. See Richard A.Pierce, *Russian Central Asia 1867-1917* (Berkeley and Los Angeles, 1960), and Hugh Seton-Watson, *The Russian Empire 1801-1917* (Oxford, 1967), pp.441-5.

4. Alexander Nevsky is an example of this tendency. He was canonized by the Russian Orthodox Church but, as recent research has shown, he was abjectly servile to the Mongols and betrayed his own relatives to them, while his fight against the Swedes bordered on the trivial. His popularity with the chroniclers seems to have rested on his unrelenting hostility to the Catholic Swedes. See

John Fennell, *The Crisis of Medieval Russia 1200-1304* (London-New York, 1983), pp.101-21.

NOTES ON CONTRIBUTORS

Dr Louis Allain holds the Chair of Russian at the University of Lille. His interest is in Russian literature from Puškin to Blok, but he is best known for his work on Dostoevskij; he is the author of *Dostoïevski et Dieu: la morsure du divin* (Lille, 1981) and *Dostoïevski et l'Autre* (Lille and Paris, 1984).

Michael Basker is a lecturer in Russian at the University of Bristol; he is currently completing a doctoral thesis on Gumilev and Acmeism. He has published articles on Gumilev and was co-editor of N.Gumilev: *Neizdannoe i nesobrannoe* (Paris, 1986).

Professor Jean Bonamour teaches Russian at the Sorbonne. Apart from many articles on nineteenth-century Russian literature, he is the author of *A.S.Griboedov et la vie littéraire de son temps* (Paris, 1965) and *Le roman russe* (Paris, 1978).

Dr Inna Chechelnitsky is Assistant Professor of Russian in the Department of Slavic Languages at Brown University. She completed her doctoral dissertation on Axmatova's *Poem without a Hero* in 1982 at Brown.

Raoul Eshelman recently completed his doctoral thesis on Gumilev under the supervision of Professor Igor Smirnov at the University of Konstanz; he published an article on Gumilev, "Gumilevskoe 'Slovo' i misticizm", in *Russkaja Mysl'*, 29 August 1986.

Ben Hellman teaches at the University of Helsinki. He is working on a dissertation on "The First World War in Russian Literature 1914-1918". Among his published articles there is one on Gumilev: "A Houri in Paradise: Nikolaj Gumilev and the War", *Studia Slavica Finlandensia*, I, 1984.

Denis Mickiewicz is Professor of Russian and Comparative Literature at Emory University; among his many articles on Russian literature there are several on Acmeism and the Silver Age, including "*Apollo* and Modernist Poetics" in *The Silver Age of Russian Literature*, ed. C. and E.Proffer, Ann Arbor, 1975, and "The Acmeist Conception of the Poetic Word" in *Towards a Definition of Acmeism* (Supplementary Issue), *Russian Language Journal*, 1975. He has a special interest in the semiotics of poetry and music.

Dr Eulalia Papla lectures in Russian literature at the Jagiellonian University in Cracow. She is particularly interested in modern Russian poetry and is working at present on Innokentij Annenskij. She has published a book entitled *Akmeizm. Geneza i program* (Wroclaw, 1980) as well as articles on Annenskij, Axmatova and Gumilev.

Dr Anthony Parton is an art historian; he lectures on the history of Russian art at St Andrews University. His book on Larionov, *Mikhail Larionov and the Russian Avant-garde*, will be published by Yale University Press later this year (1987). He is also co-author with John Bowlt of *Mikhail Larionov* (Stockholm, 1987). He is the British Branch Secretary of "L'Association des Amis de Gontcharova et de Larionov".

Dr Elaine Rusinko, Assistant Professor at the University of Maryland, Baltimore County, is one of the foremost authorities on Gumilev among Western Slavists, having published several articles on Acmeism and Gumilev in leading academic journals, including "*K sinej zvezde*. Gumilev's Love Poems", *Russian Language Journal*, 109, 1979, "The Theme of War in the Works of Gumilev", *Slavic and East European Journal*, 2, 1977, "Gumilev in London: An Unknown Interview", *Russian Literature Triquarterly*, 16, 1979, "Acmeism, Post-symbolism and Henri Bergson", *Slavic Review*, Fall, 1982.

Earl D. Sampson, Professor of Slavic Languages and Literatures at the University of Colorado at Boulder, is well known as a Gumilev scholar; he has published several articles on the poet and is the author of *Nikolay Gumilev* (Boston, 1979).

Dr S. Schwarzband, who is a research associate in Russian literature at the Hebrew University of Jerusalem, is the author of many articles on nineteenth- and twentieth-century Russian literature which have appeared in journals in the Soviet Union and the West. He has recently completed a monograph entitled *Logika xudožestvennogo poiska. A.S.Puškin 1831-1833 gg.*, which will be published in Jerusalem in 1987.

Ewa M. Thompson is Professor of Slavic Studies and Chairman of the Department of German and Slavic Studies at Rice University. Her most recent book is *Understanding Russia: the Holy Fool in Russian Culture* (Lanham - New York - London, 1987).

Sheelagh Graham teaches Russian at the University of Strathclyde. She has published several articles on Gumilev and was co-editor with Michael Basker of N. Gumilev: *Neizdannoe i nesobrannoe* (Paris, 1986).

ISBN 0-933884-60-5 (pbk.) $16.00

NIKOLAJ GUMILEV
1886–1986

A collection of thirteen studies by scholars of the Russian poet Nikolaj Gumilev (1886–1921), principal founder of the Poet's Guild and the Acmeist movement. Gumilev was executed by the Bolsheviks in 1921 and his works have long been in official disfavor in his homeland — but, as Sheelagh Graham points out in the introduction, in the prevailing spirit of *glasnost'*, he now appears to be destined for at least partial rehabilitation.

Berkeley Slavic Specialties   P.O. Box 3034   Oakland, CA 94609